DIRECTIONS:
A Guide to Libraries in Manitoba

DIRECTIONS:
A Guide to Libraries in Manitoba

Edited by Donna G. Strike

©1998, Manitoba Library Association

All rights reserved. No part of this book may be reproduced, stored in a retrieval system or transmitted in any form or by any means without written permission from Watson & Dwyer Publishing, an imprint of J. Gordon Shillingford Publishing Inc., except for brief excerpts used in critical reviews.

Cover design by Terry Gallagher/Doowah Design Inc.
Cover photographs: (Top) William Avenue Carnegie Library by Valentine & Sons
(Middle) Jake Epp Library by Wes Keating
(Bottom) RPG Partnership, Report on the Millennium Library Square Project, October 1997
Printed and bound in Canada

Published with the assistance of the Manitoba Arts Council, The Canada Council for the Arts, The Thomas Sill Foundation and The Winnipeg Foundation.

Dividends: The Value of Public Libraries in Canada, ©1997, by Leslie Fitch and Jody Warner, is protected by copyright and pages iii–iv are reproduced with the permission of the Book and Periodical Council of Canada which owns the copyright.

Donald Hamilton, the Association for Teacher-Librarianship in Canada, the Canadian School Library Association and the Association pour l'avancement des sciences et des techniques de la documentation for permission to reproduce the *Summary Statement of the National Symposium on Information, Literacy and the School Library in Canada*, ©1997.

Carolyn Ledwell for permission to reproduce pages 1–3 from *Building Better Learners: A Parent's Guide to Preparing Students for the Information Age Using the School Library Program*, ©1998.

Thomas Quigley and the Canadian Library Association for permission to reproduce pages 9–10 from *Public Libraries and Literacy: Toward a Front Line Strategy*, ©1995.

Canadian Cataloguing in Publication Data

Directions: a guide to libraries in Manitoba

Co-published by the Manitoba Library Association.
Includes index.
ISBN 1-896239-35-8

    1. Libraries—Manitoba—Directories. I. Strike, Donna G. II. Manitoba Library Association.
Z735.M3D49 1998   027'0025'7127   C98-901239-5

Table of Contents

Acknowledgements / 7
Preface / 9
Introduction / 11
Chapter One
  Public Libraries in Manitoba / 15
Chapter Two
  College and University Libraries in Manitoba / 32
Chapter Three
  School Libraries in Manitoba / 43
Chapter Four
  Special Libraries and Information Centres in Manitoba / 56
Chapter Five
  Government Libraries Serving the Citizens of Manitoba / 67
Chapter Six
  Collections of Significance in Manitoba's Libraries / 76
  Agriculture Collections / 77
  Services to the Business Sector / 80
  Canadiana and Canadiana-Manitoba Collections / 80
  Consumer Health Information / 83
  Fine Arts, Architecture and Urban Studies / 92
  First Nations Collections / 95
  French Language Collections / 99
  Multicultural Collections / 101
Chapter Seven
  Towards the Virtual Library: The Future and Manitoba's Libraries / 106
Chapter Eight
  The Library and Information Profession / 114
Chapter Nine
  The Library User / 119
Contributors / 128
Appendix 1: Professional Library Associations / 131
Appendix 2: Directory of Libraries in Manitoba / 135
Index by Type / 165
Index by Subject / 168
Index / 176

Photo Credits

The cover of *Directions: A Guide to Libraries in Manitoba* represents the theme of "Libraries in Manitoba: Past, Present and Future". The top photograph shows the William Avenue Carnegie Library, Winnipeg, built in 1905. It is now the City of Winnipeg Archives and Records Control Centre. The middle photograph shows the Jake Epp Library, Steinbach which was officially opened in 1997. The bottom drawing is an artist's conception of the proposed Millennium Library, Winnipeg.

Page 9	Viking Publishers, New York
Page 11	Provincial Archives of Manitoba
Page 11	Winnipeg Centennial Library
Page 15	Norman Beattie
Page 15	Norman Beattie
Page 20	Winnipeg Public Library and Cooper Rankin Architects
Page 24	Laurel Roberts, with permission of the *Interlake Spectator*
Page 30	Provincial Archives of Manitoba
Page 30	Manitoba. Historic Resources Branch
Page 31	South Interlake Regional Library, Stonewall, Manitoba
Page 31	Boissevain and Morton Regional Library, Boissevain, Manitoba
Page 31	The Pas Public Library
Page 33	Brandon University
Page 36	University of Manitoba Archives
Page 44	Collège universitaire de Saint-Boniface
Page 59	National Research Council of Canada Institute for Biodiagnostics
Page 65	Western Canada Pictorial Index
Page 78	Ed Ledohowski
Page 84	Manitoba Culture, Heritage and Citizenship Legislative Library
Page 89	The Children's Hospital Family Information Library
Page 92	Ernest Mayer, The Winnipeg Art Gallery
Page 95	Colleen Cutschall and Brandon University
Page 99	Collège universitaire de Saint-Boniface
Page 113	The Winnipeg Public Library and RPG Partnership
Page 125	Winnipeg Centennial Library

Acknowledgements

The Manitoba Library Association, founded in 1936, is a voluntary, non-profit organization which provides leadership in the promotion, development and support of library and information services in Manitoba for the benefit of Association members, the library community and the public.

Manitoba's libraries constitute a major cultural and educational resource for the citizens of Manitoba. *Directions* is a sourcebook designed to inform the public about the range of resources and services available in Manitoba's public, academic, school, and special libraries and information centres. It is the first publication of its kind to be published in Manitoba, combining directory information about libraries, with detailed profiles of the specific collections and services offered by individual libraries.

The Manitoba Library Association would like to acknowledge the funding support received for this project from The Winnipeg Foundation, The Thomas Sill Foundation, an anonymous donor, and from several past presidents and honorary life members of the Manitoba Library Association: Mrs. Grace D'Arcy, Miss Kathleen Gillespie, Miss Margaret MacKenzie, Mrs. Helen Robertson, Miss Nettie J. Siemens, and Mrs. Margaret C. White. Our thanks as well to the Manitoba Association of Library Technicians for their financial contribution to the project. The letter of endorsement for the project sent by the CASLIS Manitoba chapter in the early stages of the project was sincerely appreciated by members of the Editorial Committee.

The research and writing of this book has been a collaborative effort involving library staff throughout the province. We would like to thank everyone who took the time to complete the directory questionnaire, provided articles and background information, answered questions, and made thoughtful suggestions regarding the content and form of the book. The contributors section at the end of *Directions* gives the name and affiliation of everyone who contributed articles to the book.

The executive of the Manitoba Library Association would like to express its appreciation to the Editor and Project Coordinator, Donna Strike, and the members of the Editorial Committee whose members represent a cross-section of Manitoba's library community. Those Committee members are: Ruth Reedman, Canadian Wheat Board Library; Ganga Dakshinamurti, Management Library, University of Manitoba; Gerald R. Brown, Library and Information Services Consultant; Norma Godavari, Engineering Library, University of Manitoba; Bruno LeGal, Coordinator of French Language Services, Winnipeg Public Library; Louise Robbins, Public Library Services, Brandon.

Thanks as well to Louise Shah, formerly of Public Library Services, and Heather Graham, formerly of the Winnipeg Public Library, who both served on the Editorial Committee during the early stages of the project. Ganga Dakshinamurti was the Editorial Committee's chair until May 1998 when Ruth Reedman was able to take over that position. Catherine Taylor and Jill Warsaba worked as project assistants during the summer of 1998, and their skills and hard work expedited all aspects of the book. We thank them and Lucy Emond of the Canadian Wheat Board Library for their assistance with the project.

The Manitoba Library Association would like to thank Public Library Services for providing access to its database of library information that was used to create the 1993 Directory of Libraries in Manitoba. That database of information was used as the starting point for obtaining up-to-date directory information from Manitoba's libraries.

Thanks as well to Mr. Abe Anhang, co-chair of the Winnipeg Public Library Foundation, Inc. for providing office space and meeting space for the Editor and Editorial Committee during the first stage of the project.

Norman Beattie generously made available to the Editor his archives of bibliographic information and photographs relating to the history of libraries in Manitoba.

Manitobans are very proud of Winnipeg-based, award-winning novelist Carol Shields. We are grateful to her for the preface which she contributed to *Directions*.

Finally, the Manitoba Library Association would like to extend its appreciation to Gordon Shillingford who saw the value of the book and agreed to co-publish it with our association under his Watson & Dwyer imprint. His support and publishing experience have been invaluable at every stage of the project.

The Manitoba Library Association is pleased to present *Directions: A Guide to Libraries in Manitoba* to the citizens of this province.

Jo Ann Brewster
President
Manitoba Library Association
9 September 1998

Preface

I remember my childhood as one that comprised an established trinity: the school, the church, and the library. In our early years we children were asked to navigate these three points uncritically, but it was always the library where I felt most at home. This was the public library in the town where I grew up, a Carnegie building, cool and commodious, and staffed by middle-aged, unmarried librarians, who knew me by name and always asked to be remembered to my mother.

Compared to school and church, the library had fewer rules, as long as one remembered not to talk out loud or chew gum. Theoretically, we were not allowed to borrow books from the adult section until we were twelve, but I don't remember that anyone made much of a fuss over this issue.

Carol Shields

Libraries were safe places where parents could confidently send their child, and library time was unstructured time. One was expected to linger, even to loiter. You could pass the larger part of a summer afternoon at one of the polished oak tables, flipping through the *National Geographic* or turning over the pages of Betty Smith's *A Tree Grows in Brooklyn*, the first adult book I remember reading. Incredibly, all these privileges—time, space, safety, shelter, freedom—came without cost. Acceptance was part of the pact, too, for once inside the double glass doors we were treated with respect, welcomed to what I must have known even then was a fortunate gathering place. This was where we met like-minded friends, where we were persuaded that what we were doing—reading books—was of value.

I count as my good fortune the fact that no one ever said to me, "Get your nose out of that book and go get some fresh air." On the contrary, we zealous young library users were awarded gold stars for the number of books we could read in a month. Our library cards were the first official documents we were issued after our birth certificates, and we carried them proudly. They allowed us to experience other worlds without leaving home, to experiment without danger, to try on new selves without loss of our own.

It was many years later that I learned about the research component of libraries, or thought of them as repositories that conserved our culture. I had no idea that there were specialized libraries devoted to art or local history or wildlife or law, or that libraries would eventually expand beyond books into the realm of electronic information.

Libraries have changed in a dozen different directions, but what hasn't changed is the unspoken and unadvertised refuge they offer. Inside the library, opportunities multiply. More altogether seems possible. Under its embracing roof we are free to become more than we are.

This new directory will assist citizens across the province of Manitoba. We live in the age of knowledge, but we need to know where to find it and how to interpret our findings. The information resources of the province are rich. This valuable publication lists for us the various places where we can find answers and perhaps formulate new questions.

Carol Shields

Introduction

In 1977, in celebration of Manitoba's 100th birthday, the City of Winnipeg built a new central library: the Winnipeg Centennial Library, located at 251 Donald Street. The beginnings of library service in Manitoba, however, predate its entry into Confederation. The first libraries in Manitoba were started in the fur trading posts that the Hudson Bay Company established in Northern outposts like York Factory, the oldest permanent settlement in the province, founded in 1684.

A public library service in Winnipeg can trace its roots back to the arrival of the Selkirk Settlers. The Red River Library, with 2,000 volumes, was started in 1848 and was organized and paid for by local citizens. Included in that collection were 500 books bequeathed in 1822 to the Red River Colony by Peter Fidler, Chief Surveyor of the Hudson's Bay Company. What remains of the Red River Library can be seen today in the Rare Book Collection of the province's oldest library, the Manitoba Legislative Library, established in 1870.

Donald Gunn's house c1923 near Lockport, Manitoba where half of the Red River Library was located between 1862 and Gunn's death in 1878.

Winnipeg Centennial Library

Taken together, Manitoba's public, academic, school, government, and special libraries and information centres constitute a major cultural and educational resource for the citizens of this province. Manitoba's libraries are sophisticated participants in the Information Age, and are well-positioned to meet the challenges of service delivery in the twenty-first century. Staff in all types of libraries routinely access electronic sources of information to supplement their print and audiovisual resources. Librarians and information specialists have established their place in cyberspace by designing home pages to allow the public access to their online catalogues through the Internet, and to showcase their collections and services. Library staff are using the latest technologies to speed up the process by which libraries across Canada and the world share resources through a system of inter-library lending.

This book, the first of its kind to be published in Manitoba, is aimed at library users (and potential users) whether they are students and researchers, business or professional people, parents taking pre-schoolers to their first story time, or seniors finally able to pursue some long-postponed informal learning.

With the publication of *Directions: A Guide to Libraries in Manitaoba*, there is now an affordable and comprehensive listing of Manitoba's public, academic, government and special libraries and information centres. The directory section located at the end of this book provides a brief description of each type of library, including address and contact information (by telephone, fax, or electronic means). The subject areas and special collections of each library are noted.

Although academic and special libraries have as their primary clientele their students, instructors, employees or members, their resources may usually be used on-site or borrowed through a system of interlibrary loans. Manitoba's major college and university libraries do extend borrowing privileges to the public, although a fee for membership is sometimes levied. The policies of individual libraries in these areas are discussed at the end of each directory entry under the heading 'external users'.

In the first five chapters of *Directions*, we have provided a brief introduction to each type of library, and described the resources and services of selected libraries that we feel have special relevance for the wider community. All of Manitoba's major college and university libraries are described, together with a selection of public, special, government and school libraries.

In the chapter on public libraries, the Winnipeg Public Library highlights its newest branch—Sir William Stephenson—a library that was designed from the outset to meet the needs of the Information Age. The French language resources and services available to the Francophone community through Winnipeg Public Library's St. Boniface Library are discussed in detail. Pauline Johnson, aged 102 years and eight months. is possibly the oldest person still using public library services in Manitoba. The Pauline Johnson Library in Lundar, Manitoba was a 100th birthday gift from former pupil, Don Johnson. We describe the dedication and entrepreneurial skills of volunteers who have worked with consultants from the provincial agency, Public Library Services, to establish public library service in places like Lundar, Selkirk and Morris, Manitoba.

Although space limitations prevented us from listing all of the province's 975 school libraries in our directory section, we have devoted a chapter to discussing the critically important role of the school library program and have documented two exemplary library programs at Sun Valley School and Gordon Bell High School in Winnipeg. Both programs are under the direction of teacher-librarians who have won prestigious national awards for their professional work.

The profiles of special libraries that we have included range from a thoughtful account of the pioneering efforts to develop a 'virtual library' at the NRC's Information Centre to meet the needs of scientists and researchers working at the Institute for Biodiagnostics, to an overview of work being carried out by the Hudson's Bay Company Archives, the Manitoba Museum of Man and Nature, and the Western Canada Pictorial Index to preserve Manitoba's historical record. Two libraries specializing in issues relating to the environment and sustainable development are also profiled.

In Chapter Five we discuss four government libraries whose mandate is to serve the community: the Manitoba Legislative Library and Public Library Services of the Department of Culture, Heritage and Citizenship, and the Instructional Resources Unit and the Direction des ressources éducatives françaises (DREF) of the Department of Education and Training.

Chapter Six describes collections of significance in Manitoba's libraries. We have chosen to feature the following subject areas which are of special interest to the citizens of this province: agriculture, business, fine arts, architecture and urban studies, Canadiana and Canadiana-Manitoba collections, consumer health, French language collections and multicultural collections.

The next two chapters focus, respectively, on the skills and education of the members of the library and information profession, and on possible future developments in libraries in Manitoba. Winnipeg Public Library's Millennium Library Project is discussed in detail.

The final chapter consists of a series of questions and answers targeted at the library user. We have answered questions that library professionals are especially well-positioned to answer, such as: How do I set up a library or information centre? How can our town get its own public library? How can the library help me find my way through the maze of resources available on the Internet? Can you suggest ways in which I can encourage my children to read? And so on.

The directory listing of libraries in Manitoba, fully-indexed by type of library and subject, completes the book. The directory information will be up-dated regularly at the Manitoba Library Association's Web site: (www.mla.mb.ca).

CHAPTER ONE

Public Libraries in Manitoba

Introduction

The formal opening of Winnipeg's Carnegie Library at 380 William Avenue by Canada's Governor-General, The Earl Grey made the front page of *The Manitoba Free Press* for Thursday, October 12, 1905. The newspaper account described the separate men's, ladies' and children's reading rooms, a lecture hall, and newspaper room, all occupying spacious, well-lit and ventilated spaces. The new library, built at a cost of $75,000, was a significant improvement over its previous location, several rooms in Winnipeg's City Hall.

The William Avenue Library was funded by Andrew Carnegie's Foundation which gave over $56 million to finance more than 2,500 libraries across North America in the early twentieth century. In Canada, 124 Carnegie libraries were built between 1909 and 1923, although only 13 were located outside Ontario. Carnegie money also financed the St. John's (1914) and Cornish (1914) branch libraries in Winnipeg, and the Selkirk Carnegie Library (1909) (now demolished).

Andrew Carnegie, a self-made millionaire, took up the cause of public libraries because, in his own words, "They give

The Cornish Public Library, erected in 1914, where women's rights activist Nellie McClung gave lectures in the basement meeting room.

nothing for nothing. They only help those who help themselves." The motto over the entrance of the William Avenue Library is "Free to All". Cities that applied for a Carnegie grant, however, had to pledge themselves to maintain a free public library at an annual cost of one-tenth of the amount awarded for the erection of the building.

That public library of 1905 had a collection of books, magazines and newspapers. Today's public libraries offer lending services not only for books and magazines, but also for films and videocassettes, audiocassettes and compact discs, and talking books and large print books for the visually impaired. The card catalogue has been replaced by an online public access catalogue (OPAC). Public libraries have developed home pages to offer Internet access to their online catalogues and services.

Today's public library plays a vital role in the community by offering sophisticated information and reference services and creative programming and outreach services directed at young parents and preschoolers, schools and youth organizations, the elderly and housebound, ethnic minority groups and adult learners. Today's public libraries play many roles: as community activity centres; as community information centres serving as a clearinghouse of information on community organizations, issues and services; as a formal education support service; as an independent learning centre; and as a research centre and reference library. Today's public libraries sponsor lectures and provide space for meetings, recitals and exhibitions of art. Public libraries are a unique institution in the life of the community.

'The Library Action Committee of the Book and Periodical Council of Canada recently published a pamphlet entitled *Dividends: The Value of Public Libraries in Canada* in order to document the social and economic benefits that public libraries contribute to society. This chapter begins with an excerpt taken from the introduction to this timely publication.

One of the most important activities undertaken by public librarires relates to the promotion of literacy in the general population. Thomas Quigley, convenor of the Canadian Library Association's Action for Literacy Interest Group describes the public library's role in promoting literacy through its collection, its instructional programs and its support services.

In 1997, the Winnipeg Public Library opened its latest branch, the Sir William Stephenson Library, located in the Northwest corner of the city. This Library was designed from the outset to be a resource for the Information Age; its planning and development represent a successful collaboration among library staff, interested citizens, planners, architects and interior designers. The St. Boniface Library, offering resources and services to Winnipeg's Francophone community, is also profiled.

While urban dwellers very often take public library service for granted, such is not the case in rural Manitoba where many towns and municipalities still do not have their own public library. We present the stories of how three communities, Lundar, Morris, and Selkirk, struggled to get a public library established. These stories document what can be accomplished by hard-working, persistent and creative volunteers working with consultants from Public Library Services.

Although only one town in rural Manitoba received Carnegie funding to erect a new building, other communities have adapted historic buildings to a new use as a public library. Our photo essay documents the range of buildings that have been recycled in this fashion.

What is the Value of the Public Library?

When you ask Canadians what the public library means to them, you get an astonishing variety of answers. For some it is the place to find essential career or job search information; or the place that welcomes literacy learners and tutors; or the place to find information for homework assignments or about pressing legal, medical or financial needs; or the place for children to start their lifelong learning association with the library; or to connect to the Internet; or to find books to borrow and enjoy.

Frequently overlooked, however, in the consideration of the 'value' of a public library are the economic benefits it provides to its own community; to the businesses that supply services to the library; to the retailers, wholesalers and publishers who sell to libraries; and to the national economy by the active promotion and support given to literacy and literacy based programs, and indeed, to Canadian culture.

The acquisition and delivery of public library services contribute profound social and economic dividends. These dividends are not limited to library users; nor to the businesses, industries, trades and professions that supply libraries; nor are the benefits limited to the local economy, the national cultural industry sector, or to Canadian culture and our democratic society; nor to literacy, children, students and lifelong learners. Each of these community of interests is served by Canadian public libraries. In order to continue to do so, stable funding is required.

Canada and the Public Library

Public libraries play a vital role in the lives of Canadians and are extensively used from coast to coast. Research shows that people who make use of the library tend to do so regularly. For many Canadians the public library is part of the integral fabric of their everyday lives. With the increasing importance of information, the public library has an increasingly important role to play.

Public libraries and their Critical Financial Situation

Fiscal restraint, restructuring and identifying efficiencies of operations are hallmarks of the 1990s. Public libraries have been a part of this societal shift, and budget reductions are now being felt in a number of areas: reduced materials expenditure, reduced staffing levels and reduced service hours, at the same time that inflation and the costs of new technologies are pressuring existing budgets.

Public libraries are Cost-Effective Information Providers

Public libraries provide a wealth of information resources services in a timely and cost-effective manner, save businesses and people time and money, and help to contribute to better decision making, due to their highly trained staff and organized methods of information storage and retrieval.

The Value of Information

The increasing value of information is recognized world wide and information is vital to the success of organizations and businesses. Public libraries are well positioned to make information available and accessible in many formats to the broadest possible community in a timely fashion.

Public libraries Support the Local Economy

Public libraries bolster the economic prosperity of their communities: they contribute to the economic well-being of the businesses that surround them, they improve the market worth of their communities, they support their local economies, they benefit local business, and they offer Canadians highly skilled and often highly technical jobs in an automated environment.

Public Libraries Support the Cultural Industry Sector

Public libraries are a critical link in the book and periodical trade as they buy print materials to a level that ensures that the book trade in Canada remains healthy. Other cultural industries including producers and distributers of music, computer products and videos concur. Public libraries are a vital link in supporting the creation, production and dissemination of print, audio-visual and electronic materials in Canada.

Public Libraries Support Canadian Culture

Public libraries are an indispensable part of the cultural fabric. Libraries not only purchase material written, illustrated, designed, performed and sold by Canadians but also make this culture available to the broadest possible spectrum of Canadians. The existence of public libraries helps to ensure that Canadian culture continues to flourish and thrive.

Public Libraries Support a Democratic Society

A citizen's access to information is an essential component of a smooth democratic process. The access to information that public libraries offer to Canadians regardless of race, income, class, age or gender, assists in supporting and encouraging democracy.

Public Libraries Support and Promote Literacy

An informed and literate population is essential to Canada's economic strength and yet Canada's literacy rate is troubling. The cost to the Canadian economy of low-level literacy skills is more than 10 billion dollars annually. Public libraries play an active role in national efforts to increase the literacy skills of Canadians.

Public libraries Support Children and Students

The formal education system in Canada and the informal lifelong learning resources of public libraries work together to support children and students. Canadians believe that the public library's role in educating children and students should be a top priority. Investment in public libraries yields a high return to the educational health of students. Studies from around the world show that public library use is a positive factor in the attainment of high reading and comprehension levels. Well-educated students guarantee that Canada will be economically competitive into the next century.

Public libraries Support Lifelong Learning

Public libraries are a lifelong learning resource for all Canadians. People need to be informed, to make informed personal decisions, and to constantly upgrade their work and life skills. Canadians recognize and value the role of libraries in the lifelong learning process. Canadians must have the necessary job skills for Canada to remain competitive in the 21st century economy, and public libraries will help people gain these skills.

Public libraries and Emerging Technologies

The public library has a key role in ensuring the accessibility of the Information Highway to all Canadians by guaranteeing all users access to sophisticated computer technology, especially those without access to a computer or the Internet at home, school, or work. Canadians are sending clear signals to decision makers that they want the public library to be involved in providing electronic resources, including the Internet.

Leslie Fitch and Jodie Warner, The Book & Periodical Council

The Role of Public Libraries in Promoting Literacy

Thomas Quigley, the current convenor of the Canadian Library Association's Action for Literacy Interest Group, prepared this summary statement for the National Working Summit on Libraries and Literacy held in Calgary, June 14, 1995:

> Libraries and the literacy issue have a long involvement with each other. As an institution whose primary focus is reading, and whose mandate includes responding to community needs, libraries try to have the right material for the right person at the right time; that includes literacy learners, tutors and other providers. It is clear that literacy has an important role in libraries' workings. The public library is the "people's university", a resource for lifelong learning and information needs; literacy fits naturally into this picture. Libraries are often more accessible and less threatening than schools for learners.
>
> Literacy services in public libraries are normally grouped into three categories: literacy collections; literacy instructional programs; and literacy support services.

These categories can be defined in terms of what libraries actually do. For example, the "literacy collections" category includes the basic activities of providing print and audiovisual materials for adult learners, tutors and other literacy providers. Providing microcomputers and basic skills software is another related activity. Creating new material—such as books, audio recordings, video recordings, or microcomputer software—complements the collecting process of this category.

In the "literacy instructional programs" category, the primary activities include recruiting, training, and placing volunteer tutors, and recruiting and placing adult learner students. The Library in this role also may conduct these activities jointly with another literacy provider or in support of literacy projects in the community. Another feature of this role is raising staff awareness of the literacy issue in general, of the characteristics of people who have limited reading and writing skills, and of the general needs of adult learners.

In the "literacy support services" category, the activities incorporate many cooperative efforts, such as jointly publicizing area literacy services, participating in a literacy coalition, referring persons in need of literacy education to the appropriate providers, and advocating the literacy issue. This role also includes providing library facilities for tutoring, classes and tutor training sessions.

Given different community needs and community services, it is natural that library involvement in literacy will vary. It is not a simple case of a library either being involved or not. Instead, it is understood that libraries, based on their community's need, will emphasize different roles in their literacy services, and may select activities from any of the three categories that best fit their own situation.

Thomas Quigley

A Library Designed for the Information Age
The Building of the Sir William Stephenson Library

Set in a fully landscaped park-like setting, the newest branch of the Winnipeg Public Library is located in the Northwest corner of the city, at 765 Keewatin Street. The Library, which had its official opening on June 17, 1997, was named after Sir William Stephenson who was born in the Point Douglas area of Winnipeg in 1896. After a teaching career in mathematics and science at the University of Manitoba, Stephenson moved to England in the 1920s where he invented the first device for transmitting photographs by wireless (an early prototype of the fax machine). Prime Minister Winston Churchill appointed him Director of British Security Coordination in the Western Hemisphere during World War II. His wartime experiences are recounted in the book *A Man Called Intrepid*. He received the Order of Canada in 1980 and died in Bermuda in 1989. A sculpture of Sir William Stephenson, donated by the internationally-renowned artist Leo Mol, was unveiled at the library's official opening.

The Sir William Stephenson Library was designed from the outset to meet the needs of the Information Age. As such, it was chosen to be the pilot site for the introduction of several new services in the Winnipeg Public Library system. Although building a new library is never an easy task, the planning process for the Sir William Stephenson Library benefited from the involvement of the local community and represented a successful collaboration among library staff, several civic departments including the Planning Department, developers, architects, interior designers and technical experts.

The "Northwest Library", as it was initially called, began to take shape in 1990 as part of the Library Department's long-term development plan. Budgetary considerations halted the project from 1992 until late 1995. Under the direction of the City of Winnipeg Planning Department, representatives from the Library Department and various other city services chose a 2.5 acre location on city-owned property at the corner of Keewatin Street and Burrows Avenue. The location was selected not only to serve established neighbourhoods, but also to reach the newer communities of Garden Grove and Tyndall Park.

The development of a detailed Request for Proposal (RPF) was completed in early 1996. Following the tendering process, Shelter Canadian Properties Inc. was selected as the developer and Cooper Rankin Architects as the designer. The final design chosen for the Library was based on criteria that included accessibility, functionality, visibility and landscape design, combined with the need to meet the technical specifications of the RPF. It was a fascinating experience that involved hearing presentations from several developers and architects, evaluating proposals, and recommending a specific plan to City Council. Initially conceived as a lease arrangement, the decision was made in the end to lease the 13,500 sq. ft. facility for a one-year period, and then to purchase the building outright. The final price tag for the project was $1.66 million.

Construction began in early July 1996 and continued through February, 1997. Only the exterior landscaping had to be delayed until the spring of 1997. This was due, in large measure, to the early, severe winter and Manitoba's Flood of the Century in April 1997.

Library staff gained valuable experience working closely with the architects and interior designers. Decisions had to be made on a daily basis regarding the layout of rooms, the selection of carpeting, the location of fibre optic cabling, and the selection of color schemes for everything from baseboards to carpet to washroom fixtures. It was a hands-on experience that could never have been learned in library school. Those tasks, combined with the development of the collection, the purchase of furniture, and the selection of staff made for a hectic six-month period in the life of many Winnipeg Public Library staff members.

The Sir William Stephenson branch was built as a replacement for two older branches, the Brooklands and the McPhillips branch libraries. The last day of service for both libraries was February 15, 1997, but their closure was not accomplished without some opposition. However, with the support of local councillors, the Library Department was able to show the community the benefits and opportunities that a new, state-of-the-art library could provide. In an effort to deal with the local community's concerns about the new library, public service announcements were sent to the daily and community-based newspapers. A "name the branch" contest was held and displays were set up in the Garden City Mall. The local Library Advisory Committee helped to promote the new library.

As part of the transition process, Library staff decided to make a permanent donation of children's books to the Brooklands Junior High School and to the Robertson Elementary School. In addition, an outreach van service was set up at Andrew Mynarski School and the Brooklands Community Centre. Both initiatives were designed to lessen the impact of losing a library in the immediate community, and to provide a bridging mechanism for the public while they adjusted to the new library location.

The Sir William Stephenson Library was designed to be a state-of-the-art facility for the next century and a model branch where new services and operations could be pilot-tested and modified being introduced to the rest of the library system. The new Library was the first branch to offer a wide range of CD-ROM products for the public to use in-house. This technology brings in a wide range of users from across the city, ranging from the novice to the technologically sophisticated. A raceway installed in the library enables customers to bring in laptop computers and connect to their own local Internet provider or into the Library's online catalogue. As of August, 1998 Sir William Stephenson was the only branch in the Winnipeg Public Library system to offer full Internet access to the public.

The branch also offers a drive-up window—the first of its kind in Canada. At the drive-up window, clients can drop off materials or pick up items that have been placed on hold for them. Initially, the service was not popular because people wanted to see the interior of the new building. This innovative service has now caught on. Surprisingly library staff have to put up with very few "fries" jokes!

The Library opened for business in February 1997 with a collection of approximately 30,000 items, including books, magazines, paperbacks, music CDs, audio cassettes and videocassettes. The branch also houses a literacy collection, a Native Studies collection and a multilingual collection. Our diverse collections and services are designed to meet the needs of a diverse clientele. When the library first opened, books in four languages other than English were provided. In response to patrons' requests, the branch has increased the number of languages collected to 15, and is responding to requests for additional materials in all these languages.

The Library has a meeting room that seats up to 90 people. Groups such as cultural and professional organizations have made good use of this space. During the first year of operations, library staff gave tours and offered programming for local schools, the community college, literacy groups, home schoolers and Aboriginal groups. The library also provides a community art wall that can be booked by individuals or groups such as school classes.

Since opening its doors to the public the new Sir William Stephenson Library has surpassed expectations in terms of use and circulation. The popularity of the branch is reflected in the statistics. From mid-February to December 1997, 280,000 items were checked out, 168,200 users visited the branch, and 3,399 new patrons took out library cards. The high number of new registrations suggests that the new library is serving many clients from surrounding areas who were not being served by the now-closed McPhillips and Brooklands branch libraries.

The first year of operations was both challenging and unforgettable. We introduced many new services to the public. Aware that the success of the branch is closely linked to our customers, the staff at the new facility have been encouraging customers to provide feedback on services and on the collection. Many written customer comment forms—accolades as well as complaints and suggestions—have been received. A survey targeted at teens in 1997 generated 250 responses and led to the planning of some new teen programming that begins in the fall of 1998. A similar survey will target adult users to help determine where we are meeting their needs and where we need to make improvements. There is no better way to gauge how well the library responds to the pulse of the community than by asking the users themselves.

It took seven years for the Sir William Stephenson Library to become a reality. The knowledge and experience gained by Winnipeg Public Library staff during that time will be put to good use as planning gets under way to expand the current Centennial Library, built in 1977, into a state-of-the-art facility for the twenty-first century. The Millennium Library project is described in Chapter Nine of this book.

Theresa Yauk and Rick Walker

St. Boniface Library: Service to the Francophone Community

St. Boniface Library, located at the corner of Provencher and Taché, is Winnipeg Public Library's central resource for French language services and collections. St. Boniface Library provides information and reference services, adult and children's programs, and a reader's advisory service in both French and English, either in person or over the phone.

Adult Services provides access to a collection of over 50,000 books on many subjects. Among the highlights are historical novels, mysteries, science fiction, biographies as well as the latest titles from Manitoban, Canadian and European publishers. There is also an extensive collection of Canadian and European magazines and newspapers, a popular genealogical collection and government publications including the Manitoba and Canada Gazettes and Statistics Canada publications.

Children's Services provides picture books, non-fiction books, novels, magazines and even toys for readers of all ages. Children's programming takes place year-round with regular Story time for 3- to 5-year olds, special seasonal programs and a summer reading program for school age children.

St. Boniface Library also offers a collection of French videocassettes, including feature films, documentaries, how-to videos, travel videos and National Film Board productions. French music cassettes and compact discs, musical scores, language-learning tapes and books on cassette are also available. The Library features a popular video viewing area and listening centre.

Homebound services are available to people who are unable to leave their home. Arrangements can be made with Library staff who will choose books and library materials on a regular basis. Volunteers pick up and deliver the materials. St. Boniface Library also makes available French language materials to the print-handicapped.

The Library rents meeting rooms (12 to 60 people seating capacity) and equipment such as VCRs, film projectors and slide projectors.

Bruno LeGal

Public Libraries in Rural Manitoba: Some Recent Success Stories

Well Worth Waiting For: The Pauline Johnson Library, Lundar, Manitoba

The Pauline Johnson Library was officially opened by people of the Lundar area on July 12, 1998; as the ends of the blue ribbon fluttered from scissors to floor on that hot afternoon, they knew it marked the realization of more than a century of dreams. For the opening, nearly 200 people crowded into the 2400 square foot, brick-faced building planted firmly on Main Street in the heart of the West Interlake community's downtown. Some were seniors whose parents and grandparents had laid the foundation for the project that was being celebrated that day. Many others had been waiting years for their chance to help bring a library into being.

The most notable senior present, ribbon-cutter Pauline Johnson (102 years, eight months), had the honor of having the library named after her. That had come about when a former student of the retired teacher recognized Johnson's 100th birthday by giving

Pauline Johnson and Donald Johnson at the official opening of the Pauline Johnson Library, Lundar, Manitoba, July 12, 1998

the community $25,000 with which to start a public library in her name. The gift brought to an end a stalemate between some of the municipal council and library supporters which had put the library project on hold for years.

The history of libraries in Lundar goes back to the 1800s. The community was established by immigrants from Iceland, and when the farmer-fishers came to build a new life in Canada, the family books were among their most prized possessions. Every home had its own small and well-used library. Eventually, a collection of books for sharing was gathered. It was housed in a small building which was moved from home to home as responsibility for taking care of the books and lending them out was assumed by different people in the community. The largely Icelandic-language library service was discontinued in the early 1960s. Some of the books were preserved by individuals and are now on display at the Lundar Museum.

A number of efforts were made over the next 20 years to get a public library established in Lundar for the rural municipality of Coldwell. The concept of a shared school-community library was tried but without much success. In the mid-1980s, a group of volunteers tried again and this time managed to raise some start-up funds, enough to acquire a small building and move it onto Main Street. It was equipped with a starter collection of books and staffed by dedicated volunteers.

However, when the municipality was approached to assist with operation through a tax levy as required by provincial regulations, there was opposition from some of the councillors and later from some of their constituents. A library levy was approved in 1986 via municipal referendum, but with too narrow a margin to persuade the council. The library had to be closed and the building emptied and moved. The dream of a public library lay dormant for about 10 years. The establishment of a public library was identified as a top priority in a Community Round Table planning process in 1994–1995.

With November 1995 also came Pauline Johnson's 100th birthday. Many people from near and far gathered to honor the much loved and respected retired teacher. That afternoon Donald (Don) Johnson, 60, (no relation to Pauline), who by then had achieved the position of vice-president of Nesbitt Burns, a Toronto-based investment firm, announced his gift of seed money. Johnson said he wanted to do something for his boyhood home and, upon hearing of the dream of establishinig a public library, he decided this would also be a fitting tribute to the teacher who had inspired him as a child. His announcement left the crowd stunned and guardedly excited. They understood the implications of his gift and the problematic history of the project.

Very soon after, planning began anew. This time the municipal council approved establishment and support of the library, though by a slim majority. A board was formed, fundraising began, a provincial grant was awarded, the downtown site was selected and a building design finalized. All $120,000 needed was raised and construction started in the fall of 1997. The donation of land by CIBC significantly reduced expenses. Don Johnson made a second donation of $15,000, which was soon matched by additional donations. All work on the building was done by local workers, under the direction of the library board. Both Johnson families were able to participate in the grand opening.

"I'm so happy that Lundar will now have a library; it's very important for the community. I hope the children will enjoy it and keep on using it," said Pauline Johnson after she cut the ribbon to open the facility. "This is one of the greatest days of my life, but I still feel it's an undeserved honour." During the ceremony, Don Johnson and his family offered another $10,000 gift to help equip the library, on the condition that his contribution be matched by the municipal and provincial governments.

The Lundar district finally has its public library and people are using it. Many visitors, some of whom have been following the story for years through the local newspapers, family and friends, made a point of dropping by over the summer after the opening. They wanted to see it for themselves. On one occasion, visitors were thrilled to meet Pauline Johnson herself at the Library. She was busy checking out the Internet on the Library's computer. Those who know the lifelong educator well were not surprised.

Faye Goranson

From Rags to Riches: The Story of the Valley Regional Library, Morris, Manitoba

The drive to establish a public library in the Morris area began January 17, 1989 at a public meeting attended by about 20 people. The committee of volunteers identified through this meeting met throughout 1989 to lay the groundwork for a public library. In November 1989, the Valley Library Foundation was formed and the first fifteen-member Board was elected.

The purpose of the Foundation was to establish a public library in the Town of Morris to serve the town and surrounding municipalities, and to provide ongoing capital and acquisitions funding for it. Foundation members and an ad hoc committee worked for over three years before the town of Morris and the Rural Municipality of Morris agreed to pass the necessary bylaws to establish and fund a regional library. The name 'Valley Regional' came from the original plan for a library region stretching from Emerson to St. Norbert, possibly encompassing the R.M. of Macdonald and extending as far East as Niverville. Several branches and a bookmobile were planned.

The Board wrote to Morris service clubs and other organizations and was gratified to receive pledges totalling about $80,000 towards the projected purchase, renovation and stocking of the former 'Concepts on Main' store building (now the town of Morris Civic Centre). The Foundation also began the process of applying for a Community Places Grant. However, the three-municipality regional library plan fell through in early 1990 when the Rural Municipalities of Morris and Montcalm turned down the Foundation's $4.50 per capita funding proposal.

Acting on the suggestion of a community resident, Foundation members Barbara Shewchuk, Turid Milton and Claudia Schmidt looked into the possibility of establishing a library in a corner of the Morris School Library. They put together a very low-cost budget and eventually gained the agreement of the town of Morris and the R.M. of Morris, which passed bylaws and an intermunicipal agreement forming a regional library in 1992. In accordance with the Public Libraries Act, a Board was appointed by the town and R.M. to run the library. It included R.M. of Morris resident Barbara Shewchuk (chair from 1992) and Town of Morris resident Claudia Schmidt (secretary-treasurer from 1992 to the present).

The Valley Regional Library was set up in a 400 sq. ft. corner of the Morris School Library and opened on May 17, 1993. The service began with only restricted weekly hours of service and a collection of donated books, supplemented by newly-purchased materials. Despite its cramped quarters and limited hours, the demand for service grew rapidly. Within a few years, this little corner in the school library was bursting at the seams and a new location had to be found. Thanks in large part to an active, service-minded Library Board who were not afraid to ask for community support, area residents rallied behind the cause.

The second board of the Valley Library Foundation was elected at a public meeting held March 4, 1993. The Foundation's next job was to find a permanent location for the library. The board was pursuing the lease of the rear of the Busy Nest Day Care Centre when Bill Fitchett, a Morris resident and member of the Masonic fraternity, came forward with the possibility of donating the Masonic Lodge located on the town's main street.

The Foundation Board moved into high gear in the fall of 1992 as the donation of the 1,800 square foot, 43-year old building became a certainty. A Foundation-based building committee worked out the renovation plans while other members developed fundraising projects. Foundation members spent many hours applying for grants and soliciting donations; they eventually received a federal CEIC grant, funding from Community Places for exterior finishing, and a grant from the Thomas Sill Foundation for shelving and furnishings.

The King Solomon Lodge was handed over in a ceremony in March 1993 and renovations began the following week. Three Foundation members served as volunteer contractors, planning and supervising the entire project that cost more than $100,000. The official opening was held in September 1993.

As a result of the overwhelming success of their experiment, both supporting municipalities increased their levy and today, in its stand-alone centre-of-town location, the library is open 30 hours a week, has a collection of more than 10,000 items, and is enjoying a steady upswing in use by the public.

The Valley Regional Library is very much a grass-roots organization, run more "by the heart than the head" at times. Volunteers with a passion to establish and maintain this library are responsible for its existence and its success. Loyal patrons who donate as many books as they borrow are responsible for the extensive art and gardening collections. Board members (including current council member appointees) who are willing to fight for municipal grant money, together with helpful, enthusiastic staff and volunteers keep the library vibrant, forward-looking, creative and happy.

The board members, staff and volunteers describe themselves as "the most cheerful, gung-ho bunch of library nuts you might find in Manitoba". They realize they are running out of space, but not out of time. They want the library to always be welcoming and accessible to all. Currently, a few volunteers, assisted by the town of Morris Public Works staff, are creating a beautiful public park on the library grounds.

"Valley Regional Library was conceived, gestated, birthed, and grown in love. We know we're going to grow. We know we're doing a good thing."

Claudia Schmidt

Lord Selkirk Would be Proud:
The Story of the Selkirk Community Library

The Selkirk Community Library makes a vital contribution to its community. In addition to a collection of over 29,000 books, the Library offers an automated circulation system, interlibrary loan service, periodical files, a children's reading program and book block services from Public Library Services. The library welcomes the community by offering members free rental of a meeting room, and brings the world into the community by offering members free access to the Internet.

The town of Selkirk has had a public library for over one hundred years. In the 1880s, a reading society loaned books as part of its activities. In 1909, when the public wanted more books and an appropriate builiding, the town was fortunate to receive a grant of $10,000 to build a Carnegie Library. The building held a library with reading and meeting rooms and, in the basement, space for a gymnasium and a bathhouse. A later addition proved controversial. A 1916 hearing into liquor traffic in Selkirk heard witnesses complain of "the uncivilized behaviour of soldiers at the library where a bar had been fitted up in the basement."

Over the next four decades the Library was continually relegated to smaller and smaller spaces as other services and clubs took over areas once used by the Library. By 1956, the Library had been confined to a 30 ft. x 20 ft. room. In 1959, the Carnegie Library, condemned for structural reasons, was torn down and replaced by the new town civic centre. The Library was again relocated to a small space in the civic offices.

By 1973, library services were delivered a sharp blow when the town decided to eliminate them altogether. Fortunately, a dedicated group of citizens stepped in to rescue library services. The Library was divided between the local high school and a local elementary school. It remained there for almost a decade, kept afloat by the generous support of the Lord Selkirk School Division, which donated three-quarters of the public library's operating expenses.

This measure saved library service, but it was hardly an ideal situation. First, the collection was distributed among the two schools, meaning that patrons had to travel to both locations to get access to the full book collection. Adult fiction, for instance, was found in one school, while adult non-fiction was in the other. Adult patrons felt uncomfortable mixing with the students, and space was always a problem. By 1982, space limitations meant that more than 2,000 books had to be stored in boxes.

In the interim, a regional library system between the town of Selkirk and the Rural Municipalities of St. Andrews and St. Clements was proposed several times. The attempts failed repeatedly.

Library service in Selkirk emerged once again from the darkness thanks to the efforts of a resourceful community group. In 1981, a volunteer steering group calling intself "The Red River Region Library Fund" was formed to raise funds for a local library. Their efforts were successful, and on September 1, 1982, the Selkirk Community Library opened its doors to the public in space rented in a small shopping mall. The astounding success that resulted from this move boosted the Library's image as a desirable and essential service. People rushed to investigate the Library and use its services. Innovative programming for children and adults attracted people who had previously shown little or no interest in the Library. An interlibrary loan service was established and reference services provided at the library surprised and pleased people seeking information. Two hundred and seventy-four new memberships were taken out within four days of the Library's opening. Within a month, circulation increased 268% over the average circulation in the schools.

The highly visible store-front location which established the Library as an integral part of the community was soon overcrowded. The Red River Region Library Fund raised money towards the contruction of a new library building which had its official opening at 303 Main Street on November 12, 1987. The building is attractive, comfortable and well-used.

The Selkirk Library has suffered through many crises—fights for space, several moves to improve its location and at least two battles for its very existence. Its swift growth has challenged all who have worked for its development. The Library has overcome its difficulties and has proved its importance as a centre for information and culture within the community.

In 1998, the Library realized a long-time dream, when the town of Selkirk entered into a regional library agreement with the Rural Municipality of St. Andrews. The Library now calls itself the Selkirk and St. Andrews Regional Library. Lord Selkirk would be proud.

David Borowski

Public Libraries in Rural Manitoba: Creative Uses of Historic Buildings

Although Andrew Carnegie's Foundation provided funding to erect four public libraries in Manitoba in the early years of the 20th century, only one was built outside the city of Winnipeg. The Selkirk Carnegie Library, constructed in 1909, boasted two separate reading rooms (one for men, the other for women) and had provision for a bath house and a gymnasium in the basement. The Library was demolished to make way for civic offices in 1959.

Lacking funds to erect stately, new library buildings, the citizens of rural communities have made do with the buildings that were available. The Swan River branch of the North-West Regional Library was first located in the former Manitoba Telephone Building on 5th Avenue North, while the Biblio-thèque Ste-Anne got its start in a small room on the upper floor of the Grey Nuns' Convent. Bibliothèque St. Claude can, however, lay claim to the most unusual building conversion. Founded in 1990, the Library took over space in the first municipal building built in St. Claude in the 1960s. The renovations were done around a closet-sized room reinforced with steel that could not be gutted. That room, the former town jail, now houses the library's video collection.

Selkirk Carnegie Library, c1946

Many commmunities have converted historic buildings to new use as a public library. The Arborg Branch of the Evergreen Regional Library is located in a park-like setting on the Main Street of Arborg in a former Canadian Pacific railway station built in 1910. The exterior has been preserved while the interior has been renovated to provide a warm and inviting setting for the Library. The Brandon Public Library was housed in the former Merchant's Bank Building from 1946 to 1984, when it moved to new quarters in the Centennial Library/Arts Centre of Western Manitoba. The Boyne Regional Library has occupied the former Carman Post Office since 1972. The building was erected in 1915.

Manitoba's newest public library had its official opening June 19, 1998. It occupies one room in the former Emerson Court House and Town Hall Building. This splendid example of a small Neo-Classical style municipal building was designed by the John D. Atchison Company of Winnipeg. Erected during 1917–1918 by general contractors Grey and Davidson, it remains one of the outstanding buildings in Emerson.

The South Interlake Regional Library took over the former Stonewall Post Office in 1978 and occupied the building until 1994 when the Library moved to a new location. This building is Manitoba's foremost example of Prairie Style architecture and the only known surviving example of Prairie Style institutional architecture in Manitoba. It was designed by Francis Conroy Sullivan (1882-1929) who was a pupil of Frank Lloyd Wright (1869–1959), the renowed Chicago architect and originator of the Prairie Style which achieved widespread acceptance from 1900–1914.

The Emerson Court House and Town Hall Building, erected 1917-1918

The Boissevain & Morton Regional Library occupies one of the first general stores built in Boissevain at the turn of the century. The store was first known as McAvoy's and later as George King and Sons who operated the store from 1907 until 1959 when it was purchased for the Library. Some of the shelving units on the lower level were originally used in the store.

The Stonewall Post Office, erected 1914-1915, was the site of the South Interlake Regional Library from 1978 to 1994

The Pas Public Library is housed in a building of unique design: a town landmark for over seventy years. In 1975, the Library took over the town's former power house, a brick and concrete structure designed and built by Underwood and McClelland in 1928. Extensive renovations were done to the building with the aim of creating a warm, cheerful atmosphere for library users, as a contrast to the somber appearance of the building's exterior. Rather than hide the evidence of history in this older building, the designers had the ductwork painted in bright colors to complement the rest of the interior. The renovation has given citizens of The Pas a convenient and accessible Library located in the downtown area, and has given new life to an important historic building.

Boissevain and Morton Regional Library, Boissevain, Manitoba

The Pas Public Library

CHAPTER TWO

College and University Libraries in Manitoba

Introduction

University and college libraries provide a range of resources and services to meet the educational needs of students, teachers and researchers in university or other degree-granting institutions at a post-secondary level, or non-degree granting institutions, including community colleges, private colleges and vocational schools. Although the primary users of academic libraries are students and instructors, academic libraries make their resources available to the community through interlibrary loan.

In addition, members of the public may use materials on-site and apply for a membership card to borrow materials. Some libraries charge a fee for borrowing privileges. Generally, there are some restrictions placed on the types of materials external users can borrow.

One of the most important functions performed by academic librarians is teaching students and staff how to access library resources and facilities and helping users conduct literature searches to located needed information sources using online databases, CD-ROMs or the Internet. Several academic libraries are making the expertise of their reference and information staff available to the public as part of a fee-based information service. The Neil John Maclean Health Sciences Library and the E.K. Williams Law Library at the University of Manitoba are two libraries that have introduced such services.

This chapter features profiles of the libraries of Manitoba's universities and community colleges. Some of these institutions have very specialized collections that are of interest to the public. Profiles of a selection of these specialized collections, grouped by subject area, are described in Chapter Six entitled "Collections of Significance in Manitoba Libraries".

University Libraries

The John E. Robbins Library Brandon University

The George T. Richardson Centre at Brandon University houses the John E. Robbins

Library, the J.R.C. Evans Theatre, the S.J. McKee Archives, the Fine Arts Department and archaeology labs. An as-yet undeveloped section of the lower level will eventually be home to the B.J. Hales Museum of Natural History and a multi-purpose display area. S.J. McKee was the founder of Brandon College, (which became Brandon University in 1967) and will celebrate its 100th anniversary in 1999. Evans and Robbins were former presidents, serving for forty and seven years, respectively.

The George T. Richardson Centre, home of the John E. Robbins Library, Brandon University

The 50,000 sq. ft. building was opened in 1993, after a one and a half year construction period. The facility cost more than $7 million, of which approximately $4.5 million was provided by the Province of Manitoba, with the $2.5 million balance raised from private sources. The facility was a welcome addition to a campus which had relied on a thirty year old, overcrowded (20,000 sq. ft.) library which occupied the second floor of an adjacent building.

The combined facilities now extend to more than 70,000 sq.ft., and contain valuable collections which are used extensively by the university community and the public. Students from local and regional high schools, Assiniboine Community College, the University of Manitoba School of Nursing (located at Brandon General Hospital) and other community groups constantly make use of the facility. Library access by all regional residents can be obtained at no cost. The Library is a publicly-accessible facility with level access and an elevator.

The library system has more than one million holdings (books, journals, microfiche and other collection components). Significant assets include a music library with more than 7,000 sound recordings, Canada's largest collection of musical theatre scores and a modest rare book collection. Within the library system, several key specialist components are new or enhanced. Recently, the Library acquired the entire collection of the former Manitoba Health Psychiatric Nursing program to use in its School of Health Studies which now delivers a four-year Bachelor's degree program in Psychiatric Nursing. The University Archives is an important resource for local and regional historians, and the new location makes it more accessible to the public. The Film Services collection consists of a complete National Film Board collection and more than 3,000 films and videos, some of which can be withdrawn for home viewing.

The new building houses a computer lab and study carrels are being wired for Internet access. The entire catalogue system is computerized and accessible through the University's Web site. Recently, links have been made with providers of online journals to give students improved access to up-to-date research material.

The Library acts as the University's art gallery. Library visitors enjoy studying surrounded by original artwork produced by current and former students. The Evans Theatre was recently upgraded to allow for the showing of 35 mm movies in surround sound, comparable to larger commercial theatres. For more than twenty-five years, a local film group has hosted weekend movies and a yearly film festival at the Evans Theatre, which is also home to the University's drama performances.

Bob Cooney

Collège universitaire de Saint-Boniface Bibliothèque Alfred-Monnin

Mandat de la bibliothèque:
La bibiothèque du Collège universitaire de Saint-Boniface est avant tout une bibliothèque d'enseignement dont la fonction principale est de fournir à la clientèle étudiante et aux membres des facultés les ressources documentaires et les services connexes qui appuient les programmes d'études du Collège.

Description et historique de l'institution:
Les origines du Collège remontent au début de la colonisation de la Rivière-Rouge lorsque Mgr Provencher enseigna la grammaire latine aux garçons en 1818. En 1871, le Collège est incorporé par un acte parlementaire de la Province du Manitoba. Le Collège, avec le Collège St. John et le Collège de Manitoba formèrent l'Université du Manitoba en 1877. Les grades et diplômes universitaires obtenus au Collège sont encore aujourd'hui décernés par cette université dont il est le cofondateur. Au cours de ses premières 150 années d'existence, la direction du Collège est assurée par le clergé catholique, et en particulier par les pères jésuites de 1885 à 1969. La corporation du Collège est aujourd'hui dirigée par les membres de la communauté francophone du Manitoba.

Le Collège offre un vaste éventail de cours de premier et de deuxième cycles en arts (sciences humaines et sociales, littérature et langue française, anglais, traduction), en sciences (mathématiques, biologie, chimique, physique) et en éducation. Le Collège comprend également l'École technique et professionnel avec des programmes dans les domaines de l'administration des affaires, de la gestion de bureau, de l'éducation en services de garde, de l'aide en soins de santé et de l'informatique de gestion. La Division de l'éducation permanente offre un choix de programmes, de cours et d'ateliers non crédités aux adultes désireux de parfaire leurs connaissances, d'apprendre une langue seconde ou d'enrichir leur culture.

Description et historique de la bibliothèque:
Le Collège a eu plusieurs bibliothèques au cours de son existence dont une contenant au delà de 20,000 volumes qui fut complètement détruite par un incendie en 1922. Suite à ce sinistre, la bibliothèque du Petit Séminaire qui remonte à 1909, devenait le fondement de la collection actuelle, mais ce n'est qu'en 1960 que furent organisés les services qui se perpétuent à ce jour.

La bibliothèque du Collège porte le nom du 3e juge-en-chef francophone de la province du Manitoba. Elle abrite un édifice de trois étages construit en 1975. Elle possède une collection d'environ 110,000 monographies, est abonnée à quelques 485 périodiques et journaux, et possède des collections de microformes, de documents audiovisuels et sur disques compacts. La collection de la bibliothèque est à grande majorité en langue française, mais comprend aussi de nombreux textes en anglais. Depuis quelques années, des documents en espagnole y ont été ajoutés.

En 1986, la bibliothèque avait choisi le logiciel MultiLIS de DRA comme système intégré pour gérer ses opérations. Tous les documents de la bibliothèque ont été catalogués, sont inscrits dans la banque de données et peuvent être consultés via le réseau d'ordinateurs PC à la disposition des usagers. Un nouveau serveur Digital-Alpha est installé en août 1998 et un serveur client Z39.50 sera acheté prochainement. Il s'agit de consulter le site web de la bibliothèque pour connaître les détails des différents services et les ressources électroniques disponibles.

Le contrat d'affiliation du Collège permet aux étudiants universitaires l'accès à tous les services disponibles du réseau des bibliothèques de l'Université du Manitoba. En plus, des ententes de privilèges réciproques sont en vigueur avec les autres universités et collèges locaux ainsi que les bibliothèques membres de l'ABCDEF (Canada).

Marcel Boulet

The University of Manitoba Libraries

The University of Manitoba Libraries includes eleven libraries on the Fort Garry Campus, one on the Bannatyne Campus and one at the St. Boniface General Hospital Research Centre. Together they contain over 2,000,000 volumes, subscribe to 9,000 serials, hold a variety of materials in microform and multimedia formats and provide access to both local and remote databases.

William R. Newman Agriculture Library

The William R. Newman Agriculture Library is an electronic resource centre serving the Faculty of Agricultural and Food Sciences (including the School of Agriculture) in the disciplines of Agricultural Economics, Animal Science, Entomology, Farm Management, Food Science, Plant Science and Soil Science. The collection includes reserve material, reference material and the latest two years of current agriculture periodicals. The bulk of the agriculture collection is located in the Sciences and Technology Library.

The Library's focus is on electronic access to materials. Agricultural information is accessed through the Library's microcomputers. From the Library, students can access the University of Manitoba Libraries' online catalogue, several electronic indexes and databases, the Internet and agricultural and general software packages on the Agriculture LAN. A computer lab with 12 Windows NT computers and projection equipment is available for use by students or faculty and can be used on a drop-in basis or booked for instructional purposes.

The Library is named in honour of Dr. William R. Newman, a graduate of University of Manitoba who had a distinguished career as a geologist. Dr. Newman donated his collection of books to the University and made a generous contribution to the building fund for the new Agriculture facility.

The Architecture/Fine Arts Library

The Architecture/Fine Arts Library supports the teaching and research requirements of the Faculty of Architecture which consists of four graduate programs (Architecture, City Planning, Interior Design, Landscape Architecture) and two undergraduate programs (Environmental Design, Interior Design), and of the School of Art which offers undergraduate degrees in Art History and Studio Art. Service is also extended to members of the design and artistic community and to the general public. The Library includes the Slide Collection and the Product Catalogue Collection.

D.S. Woods Education Library

The D.S. Woods Education Library serves primarily the students and faculty of the Faculty of Education and the Faculty of Physical Education and Recreation Studies. Service is also provided to the general public. Collections include adolescent literature, child development, education, ERIC microfiche, higher education, instruction materials and recreation and sport sciences.

Elizabeth Dafoe Library

The largest of 12 libraries at the University of Manitoba, the Elizabeth Dafoe Library serves the research, study, and teaching requirements of the Faculties of Arts, Education (since July 1998), Human Ecology, Nursing, Physical Education and Recreation Studies and Social Work and provides service to the University community, off-campus students and the general public.

The Elizabeth Dafoe Library has a collection of approximately 900,000 volumes, 460,000 government publications, 654,000 microforms, 102,000 maps and two special collections supporting Icelandic and Slavic Studies. It also houses the Department of Archives and Special Collections which includes the university archives, manuscripts and rare books. The Library also provides access to a growing array of electronic resources including over 50 bibliographic and full-text databases on NETDOC (Networked Databases on Campus) and a wide range of Canadian and international primary data sets and geographical information products.

The Library is named after Elizabeth Dafoe, University Librarian from 1937–1960 and daughter of John W. Dafoe, editor of the *Winnipeg Free Press* and University of Manitoba Chancellor. Dafoe played a major role in library development in the University, was an active member of the Canadian library community and was instrumental in the establishment of the Canadian Library Association.

Donald W. Craik Engineering Library

The Donald W. Craik Engineering Library serves the Faculty of Engineering, which includes Electrical and Computer Engineering, Biosystems Engineering, Civil and Geological Engineering and Mechanical and Industrial Engineering. The collection includes reference material, standards and reserves, the latest four years of currently received engineering journal titles and new books. Other engineering materials, including the book collection and back issues of journals, are located in the Sciences and Technology Library.

Neil John Maclean Health Sciences Library/ Carolyn Sifton-Helene Fuld Library

The Neil John Maclean Health Sciences Library supports the teaching, research and patient care requirements of the staff and students of the University of Manitoba, Faculties of Dentistry, Medicine, Nursing, and the Schools of Dental Hygiene and Medical Rehabilitation. Neil John Maclean, for whom the Library is named, established a reputation as an illustrious pioneer surgeon in Western Canada. The Library was named in his honor as a result of a gift from his daughter, the late Mrs. Flora Margaret Ross.

The Carolyn Sifton-Helene Fuld Library, located in the St. Boniface General Hospital Research Centre, 351 Taché, is a satellite information centre of the Neil John Maclean Health Sciences Library.

These libraries support the research and patient care activities of staff and students at the Health Sciences Centre and St. Boniface General Hospital as well as those located at other University of Manitoba teaching sites in both Winnipeg and in rural Manitoba. The Library acts as a backup resource for health sciences information in the Province of Manitoba. Fee-based services are offered to external users in the form of MHINET and INFO-Rx.

The Neil John Maclean Health Sciences Library has an extensive collection of rare books and an Aboriginal Health Collection which contains resources on all aspects of Aboriginal health including epidemiology, community health issues, traditional medicine, self-determination and health care.

E.K. Williams Law Library

Primarily serving the teaching and research needs of the Faculty of Law and the University in general, the E.K. Williams Law Library is also an integral part of the legal resources of Manitoba, playing a prominent role in the delivery of legal information to the members of the legal profession, the judiciary, other professional groups and the public.

Albert D. Cohen Management Library

The Albert D. Cohen Management Library supports the teaching and research requirements of staff and students of the Faculty of Management's three departments (Accounting and Finance, Business Administration and Marketing), the Warren Centre for Actuarial Studies and Research and related programs. The Library's specialized collection includes company annual reports, trade directories and investment and marketing update services. ABI Power Pages, a full image/text management journal database, is also available from the Library.

In May 1987, the Library was renamed the Albert D. Cohen Management Library in conjunction with the Faculty of Management's move to the new Drake Centre for Management Studies. The Library was named after Albert D. Cohen, a prominent Winnipeg businessman, who is chairman and CEO of Gendis Inc.

Eckhardt-Gramatté Music Library

The Eckhardt-Gramatté Music Library provides library service to the School of Music and Winnipeg's musical community. In addition to monographs and periodicals, the library's specialized collections include music scores, performance music, phonorecords, compact discs, audiotapes and video cassettes.

St. John's College Library

St. John's College Library, established in 1849, was a founder, in 1877, of the University of Manitoba. Even before its recognition as a College, the Anglican Church had provided education to residents of the Red River Colony, with money and books being provided by donations, both personal and institutional. The College Library has existed, in one form or another, for almost two hundred years. While its mandate and collections have changed over time, it continues as a valuable resource to the University of Manitoba and the Anglican community.

At present, the Library exists primarily to serve undergraduates. Its collecting responsibilities focus particularly on Canadian studies (history, political studies, English-Canadian literature, French-Canadian literature) and religion (Old and New Testament studies, Pastoral studies, Anglicanism). As an integral part of the University of Manitoba Libraries' system, the full range of services provided by the other units is available.

St. Paul's College Library

St. Paul's College is a Roman Catholic Liberal Arts College and its Library gives special attention to philosophy, Catholic theology and Canadian history. The Library supports the Arts and Science courses offered by College, as well as the special Catholic Studies and Christian Ministries programs taught in the College. The Library is named in honor of Fr. Harold Drake, S.J. Under his direction, the Fr. Drake Library developed an excellent collection that serves not only the needs of the faculty and students but also the needs of the Catholic community at large.

Sciences and Technology Library

The Sciences and Technology Library, serving the teaching and research requirements of the Faculties of Science, Pharmacy, Agricultural and Food Sciences and Engineering, is the second largest library on the University of Manitoba Fort Garry Campus. The collection of 220,000 volumes includes books, government publications, periodicals, print and electronic indexes and abstracts, microforms, computer software, video tapes, interactive laser discs and CD-ROMs, science vertical files and women in science vertical files.

Source: The University of Manitoba Libraries Web Pages

The University of Winnipeg Library

The University of Winnipeg is a medium-sized, primarily undergraduate university with approximately 7,000 full- and part-time students. The university offers degree programs in Arts, Science and Education within a Faculty of Arts and Science, as well as a range of graduate certificates and degree programs through a Faculty of Theology. Students may take degrees in any of the 32 program areas. Joint programs in Communications, Applied Chemistry and Biology are offered in partnership with Red River College. Graduate studies are available in History, Public Administration, and Religious Studies through a joint masters program with The University of Manitoba. The University is undergoing a period of rapid technological change and is a leader in distance education and learning technologies.

The University of Winnipeg Library supports established programs of teaching and research at both the undergraduate and graduate levels. It also provides library support for Continuing Education and the Collegiate.

The University of Winnipeg Library is located on the fourth and fifth floors of Centennial Hall. It has a collection of approximately 500,000 bound volumes and maintains about 1,700 periodical subscriptions. The Library also offers access to 23 CD-ROM titles through work stations located in the Library and to eight online bibliographic services. Two terminals to access the Internet will be available in the Fall of 1998.

The primary languages featured in the collection are English, French and

German. The Library has several special collections, among them The Ashdown Collection of Canadiana and The Samuel J. Drache, Q.C. and Arthur B.C. Drache, Q.C. Legal Collection which is an integrated series of law books and documents that portrays the operation of law and the courts in Manitoba from the province's beginnings. Other special collections include the Rutherford Collection on British History, the Wanka Collection on Sudeten German, and the Asian Development Bank Collection on the Economy of Southeast Asia. There are also large collections of science fiction and children's literature and a growing collection on German-Canadian studies. The Library has a Rare Book Room which houses not only its own collection of rare books but also the United Church Archives for the Conference of Manitoba and Northwestern Ontario. The Institute of Urban Studies, which is directly associated with The University of Winnipeg, maintains a small library of urban studies material.

In 1996 the Library purchased INNOPAC, an integrated library system and has now implemented the acquisitions, fund accounting, cataloguing, circulation/reserve, serials, materials booking and online public access catalogue modules available through the system. Text and World Wide Web versions of this catalogue can be accessed through the Internet.

The Library is a member of COPPUL and the Manitoba Library Consortium Inc., and it participates in a number of the services and programs offered through these organizations. Reciprocal borrowing privileges exist with the University of Manitoba, Red River College, St.Boniface College, Brandon University, Concord College, Canadian Mennonite Bible College, William and Catherine Booth College and Providence College.

Linwood DeLong

Community College Libraries

Red River College Library

The main campus of Red River College (name changed from Red River Community College July 1, 1998) is located at 2055 Notre Dame Avenue, Winnipeg. With an annual student population of 26,000 to 29,000 full-time and part-time students, Red River College is the second largest post-secondary institution in Manitoba. The College offers over 90 diploma, certificate, advanced diploma and joint university programs in areas such as applied arts and sciences, business, health and technology and trades.

The Red River College Library dates back to 1948 and the creation of the Manitoba Institute of Technology. In 1949, the Library was located on the second floor of the Robert Fletcher building at 1181 Portage Avenue. It is presently located on the main campus of Red River College.

In 1981 the Library introduced BROWSE one of Manitoba's first online public access library catalogues. Since then, the Library has adopted new information technology as it has become available such as CD-ROM products, full-text journal databases, and Web-based Internet resources. BROWSE was replaced in December, 1996 by VOYAGER, an online intergrated library system from Endeavor Information Systems. VOYAGER is a client/server product using Windows clients and provides direct access to other online and CD-ROM information resources as well as the Library's catalogue from a single interface.

The Library's primary clientele is the students and staff of the College. Anyone enroled in a College day, Continuing Education or Distance program is a College student. Users other than students and staff are free to use the Library and its resources on site. External users are charged an annual fee (currently $10) for borrowing cards. Some restrictions (e.g., reserve material, audiovisual items) apply to these cards.

The Library exists to support teaching and learning in the College through a variety of resources, services and facilities appropriate to the needs of its primary clientele. The Library's book, periodical and audiovisual collections support the College's primary teaching areas, namely, business administration, technology and trades, communication, library and information technology, health sciences and early childhood education.

The Library has a well-established library instruction program to ensure that staff and students are given training to be able to make effective use in research assignments of the Library's resources, such as the online catalogue, Statistics Canada data and other online newspaper resources. Library instruction sessions are held in a variety of locations: the Library, classroom and labs, as well as the College's Lecture Theatres. In planning these assignments, Library staff work with College instructors to ensure that library instruction is planned in conjunction with a research assignment, focuses on the specific needs of the students, and is delivered at the time when students most need it. In the 1996–1997 academic year, Library staff delivered over one hundred instructional sessions to more than 2,000 College students.

The Library staff also research and produce an extensive collection of print and Web-based guides, workbooks and bibliographies that are targeted at specific courses and programs taught at the College. These sources are listed on the Library's Web page.

Norman Beattie

Assiniboine Community College Library

The main campus of Assiniboine Community College is located in Brandon, Manitoba. The Parkland Campus is located in Dauphin and there are regional centres in Russell and Neepawa. Originally named the Brandon Vocational Training Centre when it was founded in 1961, the College now has 75 full-time instructors and offers 24 full-time day programs and three apprenticeship programs to a full-time enrolment of nearly 1,500. However, many off-campus and evening programs contribute to an annual enrolment of over 10,000.

The Library's collection emphasizes book, periodicals and audiovisual resources in the following subject areas: business, hospitality and tourism, office administration, nursing, child development, agriculture, carpentry and automotive.

The Library has a large collection of interactive CD-ROMs to support courses in areas such as nursing and technical trades. The full-text periodical database, Ebscohost will be made available to students and faculty in the autumn of 1998. The Library's online catalogue is available for searching on the World Wide Web.

The Library also houses a Computer Centre which is open daily from 6 a.m. until midnight. Students can use the facility to access library CD-ROM materials and additional computer software. The Library provides staffing for this facility.

Sandra Armstrong

Keewatin Community College Library

Keewatin Community College is mandated to offer post-secondary education and training services to the vast area of Northern Manitoba. Founded in 1966, Keewatin Community College offers programming from its two main campuses in The Pas and Thompson, three regional centres in Swan River, Flin Flon and Churchill and in communities throughout Northern Manitoba. Over 3,500 students annually enroll in academic, career, trades, developmental, continuing education, and special programs.

The College offers programs unique to Manitoba including Band and Northern Community Administration, Natural Resource Management, Facilities Technician, Chemical Engineering technology, Ecotourism and Law Enforcement Career Preparation. The Trades department is responsible for all levels of apprenticeship for Welding, Industrial Mechanics, and Industrial Electrician for the province of Manitoba.

The Library at Keewatin Community College is committed to supporting the college programs by offering quality service and a variety of resources in different formats and media. The Library's main focus lies in meeting the educational, informational and research needs of its users. Resources held by the library include books, magazines, newspapers, government documents, company annual reports, career information, maps, vertical files, videos and films, audiotapes, microfiche and audio-visual equipment. Materials are collected in the following subject areas: natural resources, nursing, dental assisting, Aboriginal studies, process engineering, business administration, recreational leadership, automotive and trade and technology.

The Library issues cards to any adult resident of The Pas, Thompson and surrounding communities upon presentation of suitable identification.

Elena Ruivivar

CHAPTER THREE

School Libraries in Manitoba

Introduction

Under the direction of a teacher-librarian, the school library program assists students to become lifelong learners, critical thinkers and informed decision-makers. Support for this position appeared, surprisingly, in a 1997 issue of *Drive* magazine—a promotional publication put out by the automobile manufacturer, Subaru. In an article entitled "The Internet: Is It Replacing the Library", the authors argued that:

> Students need librarians and other educators to teach them the skills needed to locate and organize information in the face of a multitude of electronic sources. No matter how user-friendly interfaces and search engines appear, students must learn how to use them correctly and efficiently. They must understand how to define a research topic, how to conduct an effective search, and how to interpret and evaluate information resulting from that search. Once students attain these skills, the Internet can prove to be an excellent library resource.

According to an article in the May, 1998 issue of *Feliciter*, there are 975 schools in Manitoba. Approximately 200 of them have a teacher-librarian for at least some of the time. Most teacher-librarians are concentrated in urban areas; in rural areas, they are virtually non-existent.

This chapter begins with an article entitled "A Parent Looks at the School Library Program". Although the author, Carolyn Ledwell, is, herself, certified as a teacher-librarian, she has put on her parent's hat to give a clear and consise explanation of what resource-based learning is, and what the teacher-librarian's role is in implementing resource-based learning through the school library program. Carolyn Ledwell knows what education was like in the past: her article tells us what education is like today, and what it will be in the future. She concludes that all members of the community must become aware of the role of libraries in schools so that students will receive the education they need to prepare for, and survive, in the Information Age.

Several professional associations have recently been concerned with forging a national perspective on the future direction of school libraries in Canada. An invitational Symposium on Information, Literacy and the School Library in Canada was held at the National Library of Canada in Ottawa, November 19–22, 1997. The Symposium was sponsored by the Association for Teacher-Librarianship in Canada (ATLC) and the Canadian School Library Association (CSLA) in association with ASTED (Association pour l'avancement des sciences et des techniques de la documentation).

In this chapter, we reproduce the *Summary Statement* from this Symposium. Some commentators consider the Symposium to be a watershed for school libraries and teacher-librarians. The papers presented at the Symposium and the ensuing discussions have re-energized support for what teacher-librarians are trying to achieve. For teachers and administrators struggling to redefine educational expectations and outcomes in the face of decreasing budgets, the Symposium's declaration that school libraries are "an integral part of the fundamental quality of our schools and a fundamental right of all children" is an inspirational guidepost by which to chart future directions.

Manitoba is the home of many dynamic and creative teacher-librarians who have won recognition for their professional achievements at the provincial, national, and international level.

In the final two articles in this chapter, tribute is paid to two teacher-librarians, Judith Dueck and Michelle Larose-Kuzenko who have both received the Teacher-Librarian of the Year Award, presented by the Canadian School Library Association and the National Book Service. Ms Dueck was honored in 1996; Ms Larose-Kuzenko in 1998.

The purpose of the award is to honor individuals who have planned and implemented a school library program based on a collaborative model which integrates library and classroom programs. The award recognizes the responsible and influential role that school-based teacher-librarians play in promoting excellence in education, contributing to the development of independent and lifelong learners and providing leadership in the development of school library programs. Finally, the award stimulates interest in planning, implementing and supporting school library services which are essential to an effective educational program.

The descriptions of Judith Dueck's program at Gordon Bell High School and of Michelle Larose-Kuzenko's program at Sun Valley School provide details of the range and scope of programs that have been crafted by two very talented and creative individuals.

A Parent Looks at the School Library Program

We live in a complex world. It's a wild, exciting time. So much is happening: so many choices, so much richness and variety. So much information!

In all this excitement, many older parents harken back to simpler times, when we had lots of hard work and few windows to the wider world—a few books, maybe a telephone, and maybe a television. Neighbours, in the off-season, had time to exchange gossip and tell stores at the local hang-out. Our parents had lots of what we now call "down time" to chat, play cards, weave rugs, and hook mats.

Our schooling was highly structured and rigidly controlled. It placed a lot of emphasis on test results. Many children got lost in the shuffle and dropped out. Our experience of school often relied heavily on the talents and temperaments of our classroom teachers. Phys. Ed was not yet a course, let alone a program. We got our exercise chasing cows on the back forty. Classroom teachers had few resources other than textbooks. If schools were lucky, there would be a shelf at the back of the room with a few dog-eared copies of Nancy Drew books or the Hardy Boys. Some schools were luckier. They were the recipients of monthly deliveries of boxes of books from the provincial library.

Short generations ago, information was scarce or otherwise filtered, controlled, and sometimes even censored. Children were taught the basics—how to read, write, and do math, and the basics in a variety of subjects which gave them the foundation deemed necessary to choose a career and settle down to a lifetime of work in a chosen field.

We now live in an information-rich universe. Sometimes it appears overwhelming. Information is coming at us in such great amounts at ever-increasing speeds, from a variety of sources and directions. TVs and VCRs, telephones (pushbutton, portable, and cellular), computers with CD-ROMs and modems (with access to e-mail, Web pages, newsgroups, and the Internet), not to mention those resources of the "old" world, such as books and human beings.

Educators recognize that the needs of students in today's environment are changing rapidly. Our children will probably change careers and job functions more frequently and will be required to learn new skills for solving new problems throughout their lives. Continuing to teach children all the information we think they need to know is no longer enough. Our children will need to be taught skills to help them manage information: how to find and use information and make decisions about which information is best, or how to create new information to solve problems.

How are educators proposing to teach students the skills they will need to use information? Their method is down-to-earth and practical, and it is called resource-based learning. How does resource-based learning work?

Students use a variety of sources for information: books, films and videos, CD-ROMs, the Internet, and people.

Students learn where to look for information in their homes, their schools, and their communities.

Students become active learners who look for information themselves, with the guidance and help of their teachers or teacher-librarians.

Students get excited about being actively involved in their learning, and learning becomes fun.

Students learn to make decisions about what kind of information is helpful and what isn't.

Students transform information into knowledge and skills they will use throughout their lives.

Because resource-based learning requires more resources and the school library is where these resources—especially new technology resources—are housed, new and increased demands are being placed on the person who runs the library—the teacher-librarian. This is especially true of newer technologies. Some classrooms have computers but most of the computer resources are being networked in the school library.

Who is responsible for introducing teachers and students to resource-based learning? The Teacher-Librarian. In the past, teachers were teachers. They taught classes in classrooms. Librarians were librarians (or they were teachers who committed part of their time to signing out books and organizing the library's resources). New demands on libraries and new ideas about teaching information skills have created a new breed: the teacher-librarian, an information specialist.

Teacher-librarians no longer just keep track of books and check them out. They now are required not only to know how to use technology but also to work with classroom teachers to help students deal with the information it helps them access. They become participants in resource-based learning experiences, managers of a school library program, and leaders within the school community in teaching information skills. The system is new and improved!

For example, teacher-librarians are being trained in Faculties of Education to bring new approaches to teaching and learning to classrooms. They are required to be qualified teachers, first. To become teacher-librarians, they are taught not only how to run computers and select resources for libraries but also how to work with fellow teachers to help students learn to manage information.

Why is it so important to understand the role of libraries in our schools? As parents, we are aware of the enormous demands being made on educational resources—personal and financial—and of tough decisions being made. We are often asked to choose what is more important: more computers or more physical space in schools for students? Smaller class sizes or more CD-ROMs? Parents need to be ready to make informed comments when asked for opinions. We need a cooperative, informed community of learners of all ages and levels, in and out of school, to help make sure our children acquire the skills they need to prepare for and survive in the Information Age.

Carolyn Ledwell

Summary Statement of the National Symposium on Information, Literacy and the School Library in Canada

With the purpose of forging a national perspective on the future direction of school libraries in Canada, the Association for Teacher-Librarianship in Canada (ATLC) and the Canadian School Library Association (CSLA) in association with ASTED (Association pour l'avancement des sciences et des techniques de la documentation) convened an invitational National Symposium on Information, Literacy and the School Library in Canada at the National Library of Canada in Ottawa, November 19–22, 1997.

In an attempt to keep alive the incredible energy that was released by the symposium, the National Symposium Committee has produced the following Summary Statement, a distillation of some of the ideas and positions expressed in the proceedings.

School Libraries for Tomorrow
The school library is a unique idea in our educational system. It is seen as a critical resource for literacy and curriculum support; a place for collaboration and discovery and an integral part of the instructional program all students need in order to fully take part in Canadian society.

Almost every school in the country has a space that is called 'the library' or 'the resource centre', but their educational role has withered as other priorities push aside the perception that students need school libraries.

A unique meeting was called in Ottawa, November 19–22, 1997, to consider how best to sustain these institutions in the face of change wrought by the coming of the computer and its information highway, and new calls to reduce the overall cost of schooling. Sixty-five individuals representing a diverse range of interests gathered at the National Library of Canada for 'Forging Forward: the National Symposium on Information, Literacy and the School Library in Canada'. Created by the two groups who represent school libraries in Canada: the Canadian School Library Association (CSLA) and the Association for Teacher-Librarianship in Canada (ATLC), and supported by the Quebec-based Library Association—ASTED, this meeting marked a significant moment in public education in Canada.

At its simplest level, the school library is a collection of materials of interest and value to students and teachers in that school, coupled to systems that permit and encourage access to that information. The group gathered in Ottawa saw the school library as a vehicle for offering a wide range of materials related to the instructional programs in the school, supporting both instruction in the use of the new information tools, and in the critical use of information skills across the curriculum. This instructional use requires the expertise of a teacher-librarian as a 'knowledge navigator' in this information-intense world, who with his or her special training, is able to relate the objectives of the school and classroom curriculum to the rich variety of learning resources assembled in the school. Ironically, it is the teacher-librarian who is under fire everywhere as priorities shift, as resources (especially human ones) are reduced, and as the school moves away from developing truly independent learners.

There is a new myth floating in Education: 'The Internet and the Web can replace the old library in the school. The Internet can replace those boring books and stuffy ideas and costly specialists with lively, colourful, interactive action through the ether.' Just who will bring that wealth of information into play in the curriculum? Who will teach our young people how to discern propaganda from truth? Who will choose the best quality resources for use by our students and teachers? Who will help students and teachers connect information technologies with the skills associated with information literacy?

For many at the Symposium it seemed ironic that we are having this discussion in the public system when private schools have expanded their view of the teacher-librarian and the school library. Research on the effectiveness of the school library was shared by keynote speakers and it was shown that there is a strong correlation between student achievement and the quality of the school library programs in their schools. For parents in attendance at the Symposium this was particularly important since their concerns centred on how their children will be prepared for the future cultural, social and economic conditions.

School libraries have been on the forefront in their recognition of the electronic realities of our new society. Educational leaders have embraced the necessity of providing access to the new technologies and they must now recognize the fact that these technologies enhance and confirm the essential values provided by the school library. There is no longer room in the school for a quiet, bookish place caught in its standard stereotype. The new school library has embraced the new tools of learning as critical components in meeting the needs of citizens in this new world. The school library is an excellent symbol for the concept of self-directed learning, the notion of reading as an essential skill in our society, the recognition that visual and other literacies must be taught and nurtured through experience and that 'information literacy' may well be the new curriculum in the 'information age.'

The Symposium set many objectives and goals for its three day meeting in Ottawa. The agenda carried with it all the accumulated trials and anguish that have touched the specialty over the years. Across Canada, there is wide variation in the quality of service, the scope of collections, the provision of personnel and the training of specialists among provinces and regions. While the participants were unable to resolve all the problems, they did strongly reaffirm the fundamental values that our society still holds for the education system:

—that every child should have the opportunity to engage the best learning material we produce;

—that every child should leave the school equipped with skills—the literacies—that will open doors to a continuous learning process;

—that every child should be able to use the computer to connect with a wealth of information for which he or she can find the information needed, and;

—that every child should realized that the school is only a part of a learning environment that is the world.

The school library is not driven solely by teacher-librarians, administrators, teachers, technocrats, or budget balancers. It belongs to everyone. It is an integral part of the fundamental quality of our schools, and a fundamental right of all children in Canada.

> Don Hamilton, Convenor, National Symposium on Information, Literacy and the School Library in Canada

Sun Valley School Library Program

Sun Valley School was established in a residential area of Winnipeg eleven years ago and has a student body of over six hundred students. It is a dual track school with programs in English and French Immersion K to 6 and a Special Education program. There are four classes at each grade level.

The Library
The Library staff consists of one full-time teacher-librarian, Michelle Larose-Kuzenko, a full-time library technician and a half-time library clerk. Michelle designed the set up for the facility and trained a dozen volunteers to help make the Library functional before the official opening in January 1987. Michelle continues to work with parent volunteers for special activities such as the planning of a week-long book fair.

The library hours are from 8:15 a.m. to 3:45 p.m. although Michelle usually stays after five o'clock meeting with teachers for cooperative planning and conducting workshops. The days range from busy to hectic: often two to three groups use the facility simultaneously. Michelle might be storytelling with one group while a class works in the computer writing lab and small groups of students use the research area. On an average six-day cycle, approximately 2,000 books are borrowed and returned by teachers and students.

The Library has a collection of more than 13,000 books, CDs, audiovisual materials and miscellaneous resources in both French and English. This extensive quality collection has resulted from Michelle's efforts to seek the best information and fiction resources to support the curriculum. Canadian literature features prominently in the collection. Last year her budget for learning resources was $10,000. The Library is in the process of being automated, a formidable task given the level of on-going activities requiring staff attention.

Michelle promotes use of the collection by setting up several thematic displays during the year. Beyond the traditional themes of fall, Christmas, Valentine's Day and the like, she has set up exhibits of Canadian illustrators, mathematics story books, the Olympics, science fair ideas, and the Festival du Voyageur. She introduces new materials at monthly staff meetings. Library personnel provide resources, both in-school, and through inter-library loan, for teachers preparing classroom projects and supply thematic bibliographies upon request.

Michelle markets the Library by means of a flyer targeted at staff and through monthly columns in the school's newsletter sent to parents. She is active on the

Sun Valley Advisory Council and has provided many information sessions for parents on the integration of technology in the curriculum at Sun Valley. Every year she spends time with new teachers and student teachers, explaining the program of cooperative teaching, taking them on a tour of the library and outlining the services available to them.

The Program
The school library program at Sun Valley School, as mandated by the administration is three-quarters flexibly-scheduled time. The only scheduled classes are for grades K to 3.

A two-fold program of literature appreciation and learning skills is offered for children in grades K to 3. The learning skills program ensures that access to information resources is provided through planned learning activities. The children's literature appreciation program provides for exposure to a broad range of literature, with an emphasis on Canadian authors and illustrators. The children develop higher thinking skills in the process of enjoying stories. In a carefully planned sequential process, there is a close integration with the language arts curriculum in the classroom.

For grades 3 to 6, the library program focuses on strengthening and expanding the learning skills already developed in K to 3. The children learn how to access information through curriculum-based learning activities planned, delivered and assessed cooperatively with the classroom teachers. Some aspects of the research report require the use of computer technology.

Michelle's innovative reading, writing and research projects expose teachers and students to the most current library and information services, such as the use of digital hypermedia.

In 1997–1998, Michelle has cooperatively planned and taught to assessment more than 15 units in science, social studies and language arts in both French and English. Working with the teachers, she has created rubrics for evaluation based on the learning goals and expected outcomes of each unit.

To complement her program, Michelle holds noon-hour extracurricular activities based on student interests and needs. The D.E.A.R. (Drop Everything and Read) Club is held at different times of the year for K, grades 1 to 2 and for grades 3 to 4. The grade 5 Newspaper Club uses desktop publishing to produce a bilingual newsletter that reports on school happenings. The grade 6 Multimedia Club allows students to extend their integrated media production skills.

Through the years, Michelle has promoted reading through access to "living" authors and illustrators. She coordinates displays of the "author of the month" in the Library and has invited several artists to the delight of the students. Peter Eyvindson entertained the little ones. Jeni Mayer scared and thrilled the older ones. Margaret Buffie talked about the writing process with grade 6 students and Louise Lalonde took students through the making of a book.

Technology Integration
As chair of the school's technology committee, Michelle selects software to support resource-based learning and classroom-based programs (i.e., talking books, math-

ematics software and reference CDs). The extensive CD collection serves as a model for the school. She also selects computer hardware for the school.

As part of the Library program, students are expected to use technology for classroom-based and research-based projects. To that end, Michelle encourages the use of varied reporting formats. In the past years, students have been encouraged to create posters, charts, computer-produced journals and multimedia resources such as "talking books." Many have been produced for French Immersion where so few appropriate resources are available. She has also participated in a community access television series, where students presented their projects. Last year she had a CD pressed which contained some of her students' multimedia projects.

Michelle has also participated in outreach projects such as the Schoolnet Grassroots project called KidHost: Sightseekers Across Canada. In this project, she team taught with a grade five teacher and provided technical support for the creation of a World Wide Web site.

A joint project with another school on forces and motion used e-mail to share data and procedures. This project initiated the use of e-mail at Sun Valley as a resource to support the curriculum. Since then, Michelle has facilitated e-mail exchanges by training teachers in the use of this electronic resource and by setting up e-mail partnerships with teachers around the world.

The River East School Division believes that the new technologies such as Internet and CD-ROMs are a source of information and that the teacher-librarian, as an information specialist, is best suited to facilitate their integration into the resource-based learning program. Michelle has been in the forefront of this implementation at both the school and divisional level.

Sun Valley was the first elementary library in the division to have an Internet link. The school now has access to the Internet through the multimedia lab and from all the classrooms.

Her elaborate bilingual World Wide Web site for Sun Valley was chosen as a "model web page" by Peter Milbury of LM_Net in Technology Connection in 1996. She created this web page in 1995 and updates it regularly with school plans, current information and student projects. Her site can be visited at: (http://204.112.18.6/schools/sun.valley/Index.html)

Heather Panaschuk, Director of Libraries for River East School Division #9 praised Ms Larose-Kuzenko for modelling an exemplary "information age" school library program that has raised the awareness of the need for teacher-librarians to acquire technological skills.

Pat Gagné

Gordon Bell High School Library

A Profile
One indicator of a good school library program is the number of people using it. At Gordon Bell High School, an inner city school in Winnipeg, the numbers are

high. The Library averages nearly 200 students each day before classes begin. Judith Dueck is the teacher-librarian at Gordon Bell High School. She describes the library hours: "Officially, the library is open continuously from 8:00 a.m. to 3:30 p.m., although we often stay open until 4:30 p.m. (about when I leave). There is a writing circle which meets every Thursday, sometimes until 6:30 p.m. These keeners, who often come after school and will stay as long as I stay, are the same ones who wait for me on the stairs in the morning as early as 7:00 a.m. We occasionally open for special circumstances, for example, on a Saturday when Grade 12 students are preparing for English departmental exams."

Teachers, librarians and administrators have high praise for what Judith has accomplished in her school library program. Quoted in a recent interview in Winnipeg School Division #1's newsletter, *Our Schools*, Hart Sera, Principal of Gordon Bell High School described Judith Dueck as "the best teacher-librarian I know in terms of integrating technology, library and classroom programs. She is an outstanding teacher who commands respect from all who work with her. She is constantly on the look-out for new materials for both the library and the classroom. She goes out of her way to bring new resources to the attention of all teachers who could use them. She is a most dedicated person whose work is recognized the world over."

All students entering Gordon Bell get on the right track through a detailed orientation to information literacy in the library. This involves between 10 to 12 lessons at the beginning of the year for the grade 7 students. A similar program is offered for students who transfer to the school after grade 7. Judith takes this opportunity to focus on books that meet the needs and interests of her multicultural student population. For example, she has assembled an extensive collection of Aboriginal materials.

Reflections on Her Role as an Educator and Information Specialist
Judith recently reflected on her role as an educator and information specialist for the journal *Orana: Journal of School and Children's Librarianship*:

> I really do believe that information literacy is one of the most crucial skills that we can teach kids in terms of how to access information and what to do with it once they've got it. I also believe inner city kids have particular needs. Kids who come from well-to-do homes often have other ways—they have computers and Internet accounts at home, they have transportation to get to other libraries, they have encouragement from their parents to learn to read early and they have role models at home. I work pretty hard to make sure that there is at least a little bit of the equalising of the playing fields for our kids. I try to create a strong library program in this school, so the kids here will not feel that they don't know how to use a library . If they do go to university they can walk into the information world and know what they're doing. Those skills are important no matter where and in what occupations our kids end up. That's true not only of electronic information, but also of print information,

whether it be magazines or encyclopedias or books or the Internet. I think that on the technology side there is a danger of thinking that technology can do it all. I get a kick out of technology and I enjoy technology, but I make a point when I'm working with kids to ensure that it's only one of a variety of sources. I emphasize that the skills that you learn in one are transferable to the other. That's one of the things that people who are more heavily into the technology side of things sometimes miss. Just today I had a conversation with a teacher about the poor quality of some materials on the Internet and of the problems of easy, sometimes unintentional, access to pornographic material.

My approach has always been you just teach them the same kinds of principles when they are using the Internet that you teach them in terms of access to other materials. You teach them the quality principles: what to look for; how to choose; how to evaluate.

There is not the same notion of building a quality collection such as we do in our school libraries. On the Internet that's missing and so are really good, controlled search engines. Kids so often end up with a maze of junk.

My role in technology is important in the way I operate in this school. When we were setting things up, it would have been much easier for me just to say 'no, my area's the library' and not to get involved in technology but I didn't want that schism between technology and information access and use to develop in this school, so when I was asked to do various technology things I took them on with energy. I probably worked far more than I should have, but I think the result is that now when people think of me in this school, they're beginning to blend the two [technology and information specialist].

We have a technology education department, a business education department, a math department that do technology very well. But they approach technology development in a similar way to that of the Library and have merged it together. So I don't think the schism is as broad as if technology had just happened or development in one particular department.

Resource-Based Learning
In 1994, Manitoba Education and Training published a document entitled *Resource-Based Learning*. Resource-based learning is an educational model which involves students, teachers, and librarians in a meaningful use of a wide range of appropriate print, non-print, electronic and human resources. According to Manitoba Education and Training: "Students in Manitoba schools should have access to a school library program that is integrated with the school's instructional program. This integration of classroom and school library is fundamental to the resource-based learning model which is essential to student achivement."

Judith has implemented this model in her school library program. In the 1997–1998 year she participated in more than 20 teaching units. Her involvement ranged from providing resources and faciliting the students' research, to co-operative planning and teaching and evaluation. A sample of the topics covered include teenage pregnancies, historical novels in the Renaissance, Aboriginal justice, James Bay hydro electric power and human rights.

While most of these projects result in a written report, Judith encourages other means of reporting such as creating videos and developing teaching materials for future research groups. One project resulted in a five chapter, 100-page book spanning 100 years: *Perceptions of the Past: A collection of short historical fiction written by members of the grade 12 class at Gordon Bell High School.* The significance of this resource is heightened when one learns that several of the contributors were ESL students. A student and staff-created research book entitled *Tapestry* focussed on the history of the local neighbourhood over the last 100 years. The Manitoba Historical Society awarded this local history publication a certificate of recognition.

Book Talks and Storytelling
Although story time is not common in a high school, Judith feels that the multicultural population of the school benefits from story time, with her own creative twist. She has used the reading of multicultural folk tales as a way to enhance the English comprehension of ESL students. She constantly takes opportunities to do book talks on genres such as realistic fiction, fantasy, and and science fiction. She has also cooperatively planned and taught units on creation stories and the evaluation of picture books.

Judith's encouragement of reading extends to the youngest participants in the school. Joanne Pritchard and Marie Roznick, of the Gordon Bell Child Development Lab Program say that "parents in our on-site parenting program often comment with amazed pride that their toddlers expect to be read to during 'cuddletimes'. How lucky we are to have a Library that supports and encourages these fragile young families by strengthening bonds and building positive memories in an educational setting."

The Library at Gordon Bell is a busy and welcoming place at all times. Noon hours are especially hectic: the computer stations are always active as well as the modem-access computer. Students play chess and the 'Magic Gathering', a 15-member club, meets in the library classroom.

Judith spearheaded extensive renovations including new carpets, new shelving for the professional collection, the remodelling of the library classroom to facilitate the teaching of information technology and planned a student information technology area. A local furniture company donated two couches, three love seats and two chairs—soft furniture for two leisure reading areas. Student art decorates the library.

Judith applies for funding on a regular basis to add to her collection. She works in collaboration with departments to purchase materials. They often share costs for books as well as equipment, periodicals, audiovisual resources and computer programs. She actively particpates in her division's Book Review Program and involves her teachers as well. In return for reviewing books from publishers, she receives the copies for her Library.

Hart Sera, Principal of Gordon Bell High School, described the Library as "the dream classroom—a place where both teacher and student would like to spend their day surrounded by easily-accessible information. From well-stacked shelves with a variety of books on all topics to the Internet's world of global resources, the Library is one of the main hubs of Gordon Bell High School."

With contributions from Michelle Larose-Kuzenko and Marjorie Lobban.

References:

"Gordon Bell High School Library: A Collage," *School Libraries in Canada*, spring 1997, Vol. 17, No. 2, pp. 15–18.
"An Interview with Judie Dueck, Canada's 'Teacher-Librarian of the Year'" by Marjorie Lobban, *Orana: Journal of School and Children's Librarianship*, February 1997, Vo. 33, No. 1, pp. 12–19.

CHAPTER FOUR

Special Libraries and Information Centres in Manitoba

Introduction

Special libraries and information centres maintain specialized collections of resources designed to meet the information needs of their primary clientele. Special libraries and information centres are established, supported and administered by several types of organizations, including private corporations, business firms, associations, government agencies or other special-interest groups to meet the needs of their employees or members in pursuing the goals of the organization.

Special libraries emphasize their information function, which is to add value to the information collected. The Special Libraries Association describes special librarians as "information resource experts whose function in the organization goes beyond locating and collecting data. Using the Internet and other current technology, they also evaluate, analyze, organize, package, and present information in a way that maximizes its usefulness." SLA that the following list represents a sample of the diverse range of services that special librarians may perform:

Preparing research reports in response to staff requests for specific information;

Gathering competitive intelligence;

Identifying research done at other organizations to avoid unnecessary duplication;

Verifying facts for external and internal reports and publications;

Creating databases for organizations to access their internal information;

Searching patents and trademarks;

Evaluating and comparing information software and sources of data prior to purchase; and

Training other staff to efficiently and cost-effectively use online databases.

Many special libraries and information centres also offer their information services to external clients on a fee-for-service basis.

Special librarians and information specialists facilitate better decision-making within their organizations. The Canadian Association of Special Libraries and Information Services (CASLIS) recently prepared a brochure that provided evidence that the special library is a cost-effective way for organizations to meet their information needs. The following organizations offered these examples:

> One drug change as a result of a literature search can save 20 times the cost of the search. (Deer Lodge Centre, Winnipeg)

> Firms without libraries spend an average of 2 to 4 times more per professional for information than firms with libraries. (US Dept. of Energy)

> Use of libraries is positively correlated to productivity of professionals. (US Dept. of Energy)

> Employees decided on a course of action based on information provided by the library 91% of the time. (Calgary District Office, Revenue Canada).

Examples of special libraries include those in the "for profit" sector such as legal firms, banks and corporations, as well as those in the "not-for-profit" sector such as hospitals, museums and associations.

In this chapter we profile several government agencies and non-profit organizations whose special libraries and information centres are meeting the needs of scientists, researchers, inventors, entrepreneurs and the public. The profile of the NRC's Information Centre is a thoughtful account of a pioneering effort to create a 'virtual library' to meet the needs of researchers at Winnipeg's Institute for Biodiagnostics, while still retaining the best aspects of traditional library service. The International Institute for Sustainable Development is headquartered in Winnipeg, but its information services reach around the globe. Its resources are complemented by the newly-amalgamated federal/provincial Environment Library/ Bibliothèque de l'Environnement. The Library of the Industrial Technology Centre is unique in Manitoba with its focus on technology-based economic development.

Three special libraries are working to conserve Manitoba's rich historical resources, while at the same time, trying to increase the public's awareness of them: the Hudson's Bay Company Archives, the Library of the Manitoba Museum of Man and Nature, and the Western Canada Pictorial Index.

The Electronic Library
A Profile of the National Research Council Information Centre, Winnipeg

The National Research Council's Information Centre Winnipeg (NIC Winnipeg) is a regional branch of the Canada Institute for Scientific and Technical Information (CISTI). The branch was created in the fall of 1992 to support biomedical research at the Institute for Biodiagnostics (IBD) and to provide a regional service outlet for CISTI products and services in Manitoba. From the outset, the goal of the branch was to capitalize on rapidly evolving library and information science technology to provide information for our clients. To this end, the emphasis has been on access, rather than on building an on-site collection.

The collection consists of approximately 80 journals and newsletters and about 1500 monographs. These form a useful core for immediate access to documents, particularly in subject areas such as magnetic resonance where much of the research is concentrated in a handful of journal titles (examples include *Magnetic Resonance in Medicine* and *NMR in Biomedicine*). Beyond this core, however, the advantages of having a larger collection would have resulted in diminishing returns for NIC Winnipeg clients. The needs of researchers are increasingly multidisciplinary and wide-ranging, while paradoxically, also having a narrow but evolving focus. Single journal titles cannot meet these kinds of needs, so the decision was made to obtain articles as required from both CISTI and elsewhere, as identified by current awareness and retrospective literature searches and from article bibliographies. The result has been a consistent demand for articles, averaging about 600 per month for a total of 36,000 over a five-year period.

In retrospect, our initial means of providing this service was rudimentary: Articles were identified using DOS-based current awareness software and a stand-alone Medline CD-ROM station. Requests were made by manually filling out e-mail templates. Articles were delivered using a manually operated Ariel workstation in Ottawa. As our systems evolved, we developed more sophisticated means of performing all of these functions. Articles are now identified using various Web-based bibliographic databases, many of which permit ordering directly from the results screen. We have also developed a method of e-mail ordering using batches of downloaded references from other databases.

As for transmitting articles, we moved from a manually-operated Ariel station to a system whereby electronically transmitted requests are automatically matched with call numbers and Ottawa stack locations. Once manually retrieved, articles on request are scanned into CISTI's proprietary system and delivered to our Winnipeg fax or Ariel machines. In addition, special copy requirements were developed to accommodate particular needs such as the requirement for clean copies or even color copies. Turnaround time for our articles has remained constant at between 24 and 48 hours.

Recently, we have started to experiment with providing access to electronic journals. As of the summer of 1998, we have access to over 1,000 titles. Ideally, e-journals provide a consolidation of all steps in the process of identifying, retrieving and delivering relevant articles. Unfortunately, they do not yet fulfil this promise and, at NIC Winnipeg, they have been used primarily as a means of delivering articles quickly. It can take 15 minutes to burrow into a Web site and retrieve and print an article, but this is considerably better than the time it would have taken to have this article delivered from a a remote site. Certain e-journal publishers are starting to take advantage of HTML by integrating bibliographic databases, full-text and bibliographic links.

As our electronic resources to clients became richer and more diverse, the World Wide Web was the natural way to organize and provide access to these services. A local Web presence was initiated in 1995 and has been evolving since then. In 1997 a national Web site for NRC clients was established, known internally as the Virtual Library. An already impressive collection of resources, it is currently undergoing extensive redesign to further facilitate client use.

Much of the literature searching that takes place in the Institute is done by end users. Library staff promote, organize access to and train users to make the best use of these resources. As an extension of this database searching, CISTI is considering providing access to a whole suite of databases from a major online vendor, rather than limiting end user searching to the current selection of databases.

The response from our users has been enthusiastic. In a 1996 survey of all our users, 99% of them rated library services as either excellent (70%) or good (29%). Almost all recommendations from users for improving our services were suggestions for improving electronic access. Two findings were of particular interest: most users still used books as one of their most important sources of relevant information, and those users who were more likely to embrace electronic library habits were also more likely to avail themselves of more traditional library services such as mediated searching and consulting the on-site reference collection.

It is this mix of old-fashioned service and exciting innovation that has made NIC Winnipeg a valuable resource to its users. CISTI and NIC Winnipeg continue to explore innovations in supplying information for scientific researh and to support the customer service that users have come to expect.

David Colborne

International Institute for Sustainable Development Information Centre

Located in the heart of downtown Winnipeg, on the sixth floor of the Bank of Canada building, the IISD Information Centre is a relative newcomer to the local library scene. A thoroughly modern and technologically advanced facility, the Centre was established in 1990 as an integral part of the International Institute for Sustainable Development (IISD) and, as such, supports the not-for-profit, Winnipeg-based corporation's mandate to promote the use of sustainability principles in public and private decision-making.

Acting as a clearinghouse for sustainable development policy research and analysis, the IISD Information Centre maintains a highly focused collection and database on sustainable development, provides international access to the collection, responds to requests for information and research inquiries and informs decision-makers about the latest information and materials on sustainable development.

The Centre's reach is extremely long. A typical client would be a researcher from somewhere in North America working on sustainable development issues, but the Centre also responds to requests for information from around the world. Plugged into many networks, several of them international in scope, the Centre provides Manitobans and Canadians with access to global networks and, in turn, reflects Manitoban and Canadian experience back to the international sphere. In a very real sense, the Institute and its Information Centre provide the local community with a window on the world.

As part of its Information and Research Service, the Information Centre provides both quick fact-finding and information searches, research assistance and consultations. Information packages can be customized to the client's needs and may include current awareness information, contact organizations, annotated bibliographies and reading lists. The IISD's Information Centre operates on a cost-recovery basis and charges do apply in some cases. Please contact the Information Centre for more information.

The IISD Information Centre is open to the public, but is not a lending library. Access is by appointment only. Library hours are from 8:30 a.m. to 5:00 p.m., Monday to Friday.

Marlene Roy

Environment Library/Bibliothèque de l'Environnement

Located in Winnipeg's historic Union Station, just off the main rotunda, the newly-integrated federal-provincial Environment Library boasts high arched ceilings and terrazzo floors. It is also one of the first joint federal-provincial libraries in the country, providing services to federal and provincial environment departments.

The Environment Library is noteworthy not only because of its extremely attractive and convenient location, but also because of the redefinition of government working relationships that it reflects. The Library is part of the larger co-location project of the federal and provincial Environment Departments and the Canadian Council of Ministers of the Environment. (CCME). The project, one of the first of its kind in Canada, is a direct result of the Canada-Manitoba Agreement for Environmental Harmonization signed in 1994. The agreement is based on the framework for Environmental Assessment Harmonization adopted by CCME in 1992.

When the provincial and federal departments and CCME decided to co-locate, the Library was identified as one of the areas to be shared in order to reduce duplication of service. Although the concept is excellent, the details of the new venture took a long time to work out. The process is, in fact, an ongoing one. The new central location with its proximity to the Forks has resulted in a large increase in public use, as has the recently completed integration. The grand opening of the new Library took place in August 1997.

The Environment Library maintains a collection of books, reports, periodicals, legislation and electronic products on a wide variety of environmentally-related topics. In addition, the Library distributes brochures and information bulletins produced by Environment Manitoba. The Library also maintains the Public Registry, a collection of development proposals filed under the Environment Act, and the Contaminated Sites Registry.

Although the public does not have borrowing privileges, the Environment Library is open to the public, and work space is available for visitors. Interlibrary loans can be arranged through other libraries.

Shelley Penziwol

Manitoba's Gateway to Worldwide Technical Information: Industrial Technology Centre Library and Information Services

The Industrial Technology Centre is a special operating agency of the Manitoba government's Department of Industry, Trade and Tourism and serves as Manitoba's primary industrial technology resource for business, industry and government. ITC is located on Niakwa Road East in St. Boniface.

In support of technology-based economic development, ITC provides a full range of technical services to Manitoba companies in various industrial sectors and to federal, provincial and municipal government departments and agencies. ITC has facilities to help in the creation of a prototype of an invention, as well as the capability to test new products. Clients include start-up entrepreneurs, existing small companies and large corporations seeking specific complementary assistance.

The Library and Information Services of the Industrial Technology Centre provide access to sources of technical information for industry and small businesses, entrepreneurs, inventors, manufacturers and engineers. The full-service Library specializes in the provision of applied technical information, that is the "how-to" stuff. There are over 5,000 sources of information, including 4,000 technical reports and books and 150 technical and scientific journals. Subject areas collected include industrial engineering, manufacturing, fabrications, mechanical engineering, electrical engineering, instruction and product design. The Library's online catalogue is available for searching on the World Wide Web.

Clients may borrow materials from ITC's collection. Being a full-service library for Manitoba business and industry, the ITC Library provides document delivery and interlibrary loan services for clients. With an extensive network of libraries and other document suppliers, ITC is able to meet the information needs of clients. Various partnerships, reciprocal arrangements, document suppliers and alternative sources of information are constantly being reviewed for cost and timeliness of delivery. Clients who require these services should first check the Library's Service Statement on the ITC's Web site. Although the library professional's time is not charged to the client, any additional costs incurred on behalf of a client are charged back.

Two information services offered by ITC deserve special mention. Budding inventors are one category of clients who make use of ITC's Preliminary Patent and Trademark Searching Service. ITC believes that intellectual property, particularly patents, plays an important role in the research and development of new products, as well as providing an excellent source of scientific and technical information to assist in problem-solving. ITC's Library acts as an intermediary for the Canadian Intellectual Property Office (CIPO) which is responsible for all intellectual property rights in Canada, including patents, copyrights, industrial designs, trademarks and integrated circuit topographies. The Library distributes the brochures published by CIPO and, for a fee, will perform preliminary patent and trademark searches.

Betty Dearth

Hudson's Bay Company Archives Library

The Library of the Hudson's Bay Company Archives (HBCA Library) consists of about 5,500 titles catalogued following Library of Congress standards. It is divided, for reasons of physical format and security, into four divisions: the Library, the rare book collection, the papers and pamphlets collection and the periodicals. Particular strengths of the collection are the fur trade in all its aspects, Native peoples and the exploration of the Arctic and Western North America.

For the purposes of understanding the history and content of the Library, the Library should be considered under two categories: libraries created in Canada and those created in London.

In Canada

The libraries created in Canada before this century are now one of the most interesting parts of the Library. For an overview, see Judith Hudson Beattie, *My Best Friend: Evidence of the Fur Trade Libraries Located in the Hudson's Bay Company Archives*, Epilogue, Vol. 8 No. 1 & 2 (1993), 1–32.

In the 20th Century, the Company continued to supply the recreational and educational reading needs of its employees in the fur trade. Few, if any, of these post library books seem to have survived, but the post libraries themselves are fairly well documented. The Edmonton Store Executive Library, now in the HBCA, appears to be the one surviving example of a modern "Fur Trade Library".

Several different libraries seem to have been maintained at the Company's Canadian head office in Hudson's Bay House, 77 Main Street, Winnipeg. Some of these books, identified as "Canadian Committee Office", "Land Department", and so on, are now in the HBCA library. The Radio Laboratory also maintained a library of volumes on topics such as radio, SONAR and LORAN. Many of these items are now in the HBCA.

The Library of *The Beaver* magazine, formerly at 77 Main Street, is now in *The Beaver*'s office.

In London

The two earliest catalogues of the library in London (HBCA A.64/7 & 20) date from 1802 to 1819 and from 1819 to 1871 respectively. They were not just catalogues but included information on book borrowings. The first catalogue lists approximately 65 titles, the second approximately 270.

Although it is not possible to tell from these catalogues when books were acquired, it is tempting to speculate that the increase in the size of the library shows the influence of Sir John Henry Pelly. A Fellow of the Royal Society and a keen supporter of Arctic exploration, Sir John was Deputy Governor from 1812 to 1822 and Governor from 1822 to 1852.

In the 20th century the Company maintained two libraries in London. One, known as the "Archives Library", was created to support the work of the archives staff as they researched the Company's history on behalf of the Hudson's Bay Record Society and patrons of the archives. By 1964 the size of the "Archives Library" was said to be 3,700 volumes. The "Board Room Library" was the nucleus of the "Archives Library," which forms the largest part of the HBCA Library.

The other library, set up in 1932, was known variously as the "Staff Library", "Staff Technical Library", "Technical Library", and "Beaver House Library" (to distinguish it from the "Archives Library" which was in Hudson's Bay House, Bishopsgate, until 1955). The "Technical Library" was divided into a lending library and a reference library. As its name implies, the purpose of this library was to provide the London staff with educational reading, concerning both their work and the Company's activities, and also with leisure reading. This library numbered a few hundred volumes at most.

The Company received gifts of books over the years, which is still true today. Many of these come from individuals who have had some connection with the Company, who had been assisted by it in their travels, or who had used its archives. The largest donation came from P.R. Poland, a London fur merchant. In 1949, he presented the Company with 234 books from the library of his late father. Divided at the time between the Archives and the Technical Libraries, these books deal mainly with the fur trade, fur-bearing animals and British history, particularily that of the City of London.

When the Library was transferred to Winnipeg in 1974, the process of uniting all the Company's libraries into one began. Since the Edmonton Store Executive Library was accessioned only in 1992 and the Fur Trade Libraries were not acquired until the 1980s, it is possible that more of the Company's books are yet to come.

The component libraries of the HBCA Library have combined to create a Library which is rich in research value for students of the Hudson's Bay Company, the fur trade and the history of Western and Northern North America. The Hudson's Bay Company Library also contains a number of items of high bibliographic and monetary value.

Anne Morton

Manitoba Museum of Man and Nature Library and Museum Archives

The Manitoba Museum Library and Archives support the mission of the Museum to "encourage discovery, appreciation and understanding of Manitoba" through its service to the staff and volunteers of the Museum, Planetarium and Science Centre.

The Library started out as a small collection of books located in the old Manitoba Museum that was located in the former Winnipeg Civic Auditorium, now the Manitoba Archives Building. When the new museum was in the planning stages in the 1960s, Kay Gillespie, the first librarian at the new museum recognized the need for a more extensive library. She helped build a comprehensive collection of materials through purchases, exchange and donations as well as through correspondence with other museums across Canada.

Today, the Library houses more than 20,000 books and subscribes to over 300 journals and newsletters. Other materials include over 8,000 photographs, 700 oral history tapes, vertical files (consisting of pamphlets and newspaper clippings), maps and microfilm.

The Library contains many unique items such as the Ashdown Company and Eaton's catalogues from as far back as 1900, city street directories dating back to World War I, and a collection of early Manitoba newspapers such as the *Nor'Wester*, an early Red River Settlement paper, and the original *Winnipeg Sun*. The rare book collection includes some exceptional volumes such as a seed catalogue from the 1880s filled with beautiful color prints of flowers, fruits, vegetables and trees.

Museum staff and researchers can draw on an extensive collection of materials pertaining to the human and natural history of Manitoba. The subject areas collected by the Library include archaeology, botany, ethnology, geology and Manitoba history. Although borrowing privileges are available only to Museum staff and volunteers, members of the public may consult materials in the cheerful, well-lit surroundings of the Library's reading room.

The Manitoba Museum Archives were established in 1994 as part of the Museum's Information Service. The Archives, when complete, will provide access to records from the province's museological beginnings in the early 1900s. The collection describes the foundation of this institution in 1932 and the provincial museum community. It contains documentation concerning organizations that the Museum housed and/or established. These papers contain important records of historical, scientific and ecologically-based research and consequent programming activity in Manitoba.

The Manitoba Museum Library and Archives are open to the public, the scholarly community and Museum members and volunteers. Hours are from 8:30 a.m. to 4:30 p.m., Monday to Friday. Appointments are preferred.

Cindi Steffan

The Western Canada Pictorial Index, Inc.

The Western Canada Pictorial Index, Inc., located in Room 404–63 Albert Street, is an independent, non-profit organization devoted to the preservation of the visual history of Western Canada, from the Lakehead to the Rockies, and from the Arctic to the Missouri Basin. The collection includes records of Aboriginal rock paintings and petroforms, as well as drawings left by the Elizabethan explorers. Reproductions of the paintings of Paul Kane and A.J. Miller form part of the collection as do images captured by the camera from 1858 until the present.

Residential School, c1900, Oblate Fathers' Collection, Western Canada Pictorial Index

The Western Canada Pictorial Index Inc., founded by Eric Wells and Thora Cooke, was established in the Media Department at the University of Winnipeg in 1978 with the support of the University of Winnipeg and the generosity of the Mrs. James A. Richardson Foundation. Many people at the University of Winnipeg including Dr. R.O.A. Hunter, Mr. Ronald Riddell and Mr. Lionel Ditz contributed enormous support in setting up the Index.

The concept of the W.C.P.I. was somewhat different from traditional archives where original collections are catalogued and stored. At the W.C.P.I., selected originals are copied, made into negatives and slides and returned to source. This policy permits the Index to incorporate material that would otherwise be unavailable. The research of many is deposited in the common pool for all to appreciate.

The ease of access found at the Index is unparalleled in pictorial research. Each image is available for instant viewing through a system of cross-indexing by category, by date, as well as by description. Researchers can view the images through the use of contact sheets and slides.

Recent technological developments have permitted the photographs to be scanned into a computer database, joining them to the descriptions already recorded. Scanning of the entire collection is well underway.

The Index includes a number of special collections. Western Canada's agriculture is reflected in photographs of research stations, universities, experimental farms, museums, grain companies and the Canadian Wheat Board. The Oblate Fathers' Collection records the history of the North West Territories, the Native people and residential schools. The James A. Richardson Collection provides a record of the early aviation history of Canada. The Canadian Broadcasting Corporation Collection includes images of early television programs and personalities who have become distinguished in their profession. The Canadian National Railway Collection tells the story of the railroad in Western Canada. The Reverend R.T. Chapin Collection provides vivid illustrations of the life of the Native people in Island Lake, Manitoba during the 1920s. Finally, the *Winnipeg Free Press* and *Winnipeg Tribune* collections record the lifestyle of Western Canadians.

The Index has provided images for publications of all kinds, for television programs in Canada and abroad, for costumes and set designs for live theatre, cinema and videos, as well as photographic exhibits and advertising displays. Staff at the Western Canada Pictorial Index are available to assist individuals who are interested in learning more about the extraordinary people and events from Western Canada's past.

Thora Cooke

CHAPTER FIVE

Government Libraries Serving the Citizens of Manitoba

Introduction

The Manitoba Government Libraries Council represents libraries and resource centres that serve the executive, legislative and judicial branches of the Manitoba government, crown corporations and the multitude of client groups from all walks of Manitoba life. The MGLC provides leadership in library and information services to support the cost effective and efficient functioning of the Government of Manitoba and its agencies, boards and commissions. A list of all Manitoba government libraries can be found at the MGLC Web site: (http://www.mb.ca/leg-lib/mglc.html#mglc).

This chapter provides descriptions of four government libraries or agencies that have wide-ranging responsibilities to the community. The Legislative Library, founded in 1870, is Manitoba's oldest library, serving as a major source of information for Members of the Legislative Assembly, government personnel and the general public. The Legislative Library also acts as the keeper of the published historical record of the province.

Public Library Services is a specialized agency of the Department of Culture, Heritage and Citizenship that has responsibility for ensuring that all Manitobans have access to public library services.

The Department of Education and Training provides resources and services to the province's teachers, administrators and other members of the educational community through two libraries. Service in English is provided through the Instructional Resources Unit located at 1181 Portage Avenue. French services are provided through DREF (Direction des ressources éducatives françaises), located at Room S208–200 rue de la Cathédrale. Contact information for both these resource units is included in this chapter.

Manitoba Legislative Library

The Manitoba Legislative Library is located in the Manitoba Archives Building on Vaughan Street in downtown Winnipeg. The Legislative Reading Room, a dignified old-style library, is located in the Legislative Building on Broadway, and is the main service point for the Members and staff of the Legislative Assembly.

The Legislative Library traces its beginnings to the Red River Settlers who first established a library in 1848. Some of their books formed the nucleus of a collection begun in 1870 when A.E. Archibald, Manitoba's first Lieutenant Governor, chose some 2,000 additional books suitable for the new Legislature. Over the years, the Library's collections has grown to over 1,500,000 items. The first Legislative Librarian, J.P. Robertson, was appointed in 1884. For much of its history, the branch included responsibility for archives and services to public libraries. In the 1970s, these functions became the separate branches of the Provincial Archives of Manitoba and Public Library Services. The Library has retained its role as a prime source of information for Members of the Legislative Assembly, government personnel, and the general public, and as the keeper of the published historical record of the Province.

The Library's mandate is to support the conduct of public affairs and the development of a well-informed society by providing efficient, effective, and impartial access to specialized information resources for the Legislature, government and people of Manitoba, and to ensure current and future access to Manitoba's published heritage.

The Library holds extensive collections of books, government publications and serials emphasizing subject areas such as political and social sciences, economics, public administration and management, law and legislation and Manitoba history.

The major collections of the Main Library include:

Government Publications:
The Library holds extensive collections from Manitoba, Ontario, and the federal government as well as selected publications from other Canadian provinces and the U.S federal government.

International Organizations' Documents:
As the official deposit library in Manitoba, the Library receives documents of the United Nations and its main organs, commissions and agencies. These include official records, resolutions, proceedings, reports, treaties and many other documents. It also receives documents from the Food and Agriculture Organization (FAO) and the International Labor Organization (ILO) on partial deposit as well as selected publications from the Organisation for Economic Co-operation and Development (OECD) and the World Trade Organization (WTO).

Newspapers:
All newspapers currently published in Manitoba are collected. The Library also has the most complete collection of historical Manitoba newspapers. Dating back to 1859, the newspaper holdings are available on microfilm for on-site research and most may be borrowed on interlibrary loan. Current issues may be used in the

Library. Newspapers are invaluable tools for community and family histories.

A large collection of newspaper clippings from Winnipeg's daily papers dating back to 1885 are kept in scrapbooks and file folders. The subject areas covered are biography, local history, and Manitoba politics. A card index provides access to the historical and biographical clippings.

Books and Reports:
Books and reports are selected primarily to fill the information needs of the Legislature and government in areas of law and legislation, politics and government, economic and social issues, and public administration and management. To alert government personnel to its collections, especially in areas of current concern, the Library publishes selective reading lists on current topics and issues.

The Library houses the most complete collection of materials published in Manitoba. Under provincial legislation, Manitoba publishers are required to deposit their publications with the Library.

Rare Book Collection:
Established by the first Legislative Librarian, J.P. Robertson, in 1884, this collection includes the 350 volumes that remain of the Red River Library which served the Red River Settlers until the 1860s, as well as histories of Manitoba communities, early accounts of the exploration of the North-West and the Arctic, and major historical series such as that of the Champlain Society, Hudson's Bay Record, and the Manitoba Historical Society. The majority of the collection relates to the history of Manitoba ,but it also serves as a valuable source of information on famous Manitobans such as J.S. Woodsworth, E. Cora Hind and Nellie McClung.

Quality and Innovation Centre:
The QUIRC (Quality & Innovation Resource Centre) collection is a central repository of publications and reports on quality service, as well as unpublished materials describing innovative government projects. This collection supports Manitoba government programs and services.

The Legislative Reading Room:
The Reading Room, located in Room 260 of the Legislative Building, is the main service point for the Members and staff of the Legislative Assembly. All materials housed in the Reading Room are available for use by the general public as well, but reference service may be limited when the Assembly is in session.

The principal collections at this location include: government legislative publications from the Manitoba Legislature; all other provincial legislatures and the federal Parliament; all newspapers currently published in Manitoba; major daily newspapers from across Canada; periodicals dealing with current affairs, legislation, and parliamentary activities; and Manitoba press clippings of articles about provincial government activities selected from the *Winnipeg Free Press*, the *Winnipeg Sun*, the *Brandon Sun*, and *La Liberté* for the current year and the two previous years.

Manitoba Government Publications Monthly Checklist:
The Legislative Library is responsible for the publication of this checklist which includes Manitoba government publications received during the month by the Library under the terms of its deposit requirement with all provincial government departments and agencies. Departments, together with their branches and subdivisions, and boards, committees and other agencies are listed in each Checklist in alphabetical order under the minister to whom they report. All publications are listed under the issuing body.

Items listed in the Checklist are available for consultation at the Main Library at 200 Vaughan Street. Most titles are available for circulation to Manitoba government personnel or to the public through interlibrary loans. The Checklist is available by subscription or free through the Library's Website (http://www.gov.mb.ca/leg-lib).

Members of the public may use all materials in the Library and may borrow circulating items through interlibrary loan.

Rick MacLowick

Public Library Services Branch
Department of Culture, Heritage and Citizenship

History and Mandate:
The Public Library Services Branch ensures that all Manitobans have access to public library service. The Branch fulfills this role by administering departmental policy and provincial legislation, by maintaining a central resource collection for the use of all Manitoba residents and by providing a variety of support services to libraries.

Provincial involvement in public library development began in 1893 when libraries were permitted to be established under the Municipal Act. The first library act in Manitoba was passed in 1899. In 1918, a Travelling Library Service was initiated by the Department of Agriculture and then transferred to the Department of Education in 1923. In 1948 the current Public Libraries Act was passed and a Public Library Services Branch was developed within the Department of Education. In 1955 the University of Manitoba took over Open-Shelf (a books-by-mail program) and Travelling Library services. A 1960 amendment to the Act permitted library regionalization.

In 1974, a Public Library Services Branch was recreated within the Department of Tourism, Recreation and Cultural Affairs and the University of Manitoba returned the Extension service to the Branch. Since then, Public Library Services has undertaken several initiatives and has guided the establishment and development of many new rural and Northern public libraries. In 1992, the Branch was decentralized from Winnipeg to Brandon. Since relocation, and in response to the Public Library Advisory Board's recommendations, the Branch's main thrusts have been the development of a state-of-the-art public library computer network

(MAPLIN), imimprovements to the central collection and better funding for libraries.

Programs and Services:
The Branch provides library establishment and operating grants, special grants to library-related organizations and consultation and training on all matters pertaining to public libraries, primarily for rural and Northern public library staff and trustees. Extension and collection support services include reference and interlibrary loans, books-by-mail (a travelling library program to areas not served by a a public library), and block rotations of specialized library materials to rural and Northern public libraries. Public Library Services catalogues non-fiction materials for client libraries and provides technological support to them, including maintenance of MAPLIN which is the electronic version of Manitoba's public library holdings.

Collection:
A central collection of approximately 140,000 items serves all citizens of the Province. It includes a range of items that would normally be found in a large urban public library, including a substantial reference collection. The Branch also holds special collections such as local history and Manitobiana, French language materials, large print books and materials related to the library profession. A portion of the multilingual collection formally held by the National Library of Canada is housed at the Branch. An extensive collection of audiovisual materials includes both public performance and home-use-only videocassettes, Talking Books for the print impaired, audio books and 16 mm films. Audiovisual material includes both French and English titles. The Branch maintains a large vertical/pamphlet file and publications from various levels of Canadian governments, including annual reports from libraries and library organizations. The Branch also utilizes commercial electronic databases and the Internet to answer reference queries.

Louise Shah

Manitoba Education and Training Instructional Resources Unit

The Instructional Resources Unit provides Kindergarten through Senior 4 educators with curriculum implementation support, educational research and professional development materials, Department of Education and Training staff with essential library services, teachers-in-training with library services as preparation for teaching and all of the above clients, including the general public, with library services to facilitate lifelong learning and parental involvement.

All the Unit's activities focus on the following educational outcomes: involvement in teaching practices and student learning, the increased use of educational research and practice to improve decision making in the classroom and in educational administration and an increased emphasis on resource-based learning as an educational model in schools.

The Library specializes in resources on curriculum implementation, educational theory and practice, educational research for Kindergarten to Senior 4 and professional development. Resources in multicultural education include language education, heritage languages, English as a second language, intercultural understanding and anti-racist and human rights education.

Phyllis Barich

1998-1999 Contact Information for Teachers

Instructional Resources Unit, Manitoba Education and Training
Main Floor, 1181 Portage Avenue, Winnipeg, MB R3G OT3
Fax: (204) 945-8756
Telephone Toll Free: 1-800-282-8069 + extension number (last four digits of phone number)
Toll Free (Media Booking Only): 1-800-592-7330
Internet Mail: iru@minet.gov.mb.ca
Online Public Access Catalogue: (http://library.edu.gov.mb.ca)

Information and Reference Services

Subject Inquiry/ERIC and other CD-ROM Searches
Diane Dwarka 945-4015 e-mail: ddwarka@edu.gov.mb.ca
Rita Braun 945-7851 e-mail: rbraun@edu.gov.mb.ca
Carol Sawatzky 945-7851 e-mail: csawatzky@edu.gov.mb.ca

Multicultural and Anti-Racist Information
Diane Dwarka 945-4015 e-mail: ddwarka@edu.gov.mb.ca

School Library Services
John Tooth 945-7833 e-mail: jtooth@edu.gov.mb.ca

Main Floor Meeting Room Inquiries and Bookings
Diane Dwarka 945-4015 e-mail: ddwarka@edu.gov.mb.ca

Old Manitoba Textbooks/Departmental Publications
John Tooth 945-7833 e-mail: jtooth@edu.gov.mb.ca

Collection Management
Lorrie Andersen 945-7823 e-mail: landersen@edu.gov.mb.ca

Bibliographic Management (Cataloguing)
Atarrha Wallace 945-7834 e-mail: awallace@edu.gov.mb.ca

Access Services

Loans, Registration, Overdues/Extensions
Lucy Malo 945-5371 e-mail: lmalo@edu.gov.mb.ca
Sandra Richardson 945-7832 e-mail: srichardson@edu.gov.mb.ca

Media Booking
Mary Barg 945-7849 e-mail: mbarg@edu.gov.mb.ca
Robyn Bruneau 945-7849 e-mail: rbruneau@edu.gov.mb.ca
Media Booking Toll Free: 1-800-592-7330

Media Distribution/School Division Courier Depot
Anita Gaudry 945-6166 e-mail: agaudry@edu.gov.mb.ca

Video Duplication
Dave Stimpson 945-7880 e-mail: dstimpson@edu.gov.mb.ca

Inter-Library Loan (lending)
Betty Seidel 945-2271 e-mail: bseidel@edu.gov.mb.ca

Unit Coordinator
John Tooth 945-7833 e-mail: jtooth@edu.gov.mb.ca

Assistant to the Coordinator
Vacant

Human Resources/Work Experience/Bulk Mailing
Betty Seidel 945-2271 e-mail: bseidel@edu.gov.mb.ca

Copyright
John Tooth 945-7833 e-mail: jtooth@edu.gov.mb.ca

Tours, Publications and Displays
Phyllis Barich 945-5764 e-mail: pbarich@edu.gov.mb.ca

Linking Libraries Initiative
Phyllis Barich 945-5764 e-mail: pbarich@edu.gov.mb.ca

Direction des ressources éducatives françaises (DREF)
Bureau de l'éducation française of Manitoba Education and Training

The Direction des ressources éducatives françaises (DREF), which is a branch of the Bureau de l'éducation française division of Manitoba Education and Training, is located in the community of St. Boniface in Winnipeg. Doris Lemoine is Director of the Library, which serves all educators involved in French education in the province of Manitoba: teachers, curriculum consultants, university professors, student teachers and home schooling parents.

The collection of approximately 40,000 French language items includes print and non-print teaching resources—books, posters, multimedia kits, compact discs, maps, read-along books, audiocassettes, video cassettes, CD-ROMs and filmstrips which support Français, French-Immersion and Français de base programs. Media booking services allow for loans of videocassettes to clients.

DREF recently installed a Z39.50-compatible version of the Best-Seller Library program, which allows patrons to access the catalogue on the Internet at (http://bibliotheque.edu.gov.mb.ca). DREF also provides dubbing and production services to teachers. French language television programs are made available to rural schools lacking cable television through the program Cable in the Classroom. The Mediamobile coordinators promote the library collection and services to rural Franco-Manitoban and Immersion schools

Doris Lemoine

1998-1999 Contact Information for Teachers

Manitoba Education and Training
Direction des ressources éducatives françaises (DREF)
Room S208 200 de la Cathédrale, St. Boniface, MB R2H OH7
Fax: (204) 945-0092
Telephone: (204) 945-8594
Toll Free: 1-800-667-2950
Electronic Mail: ldoucet@,omet/gpv/,b/ca
Online Public Access Catalogue (http://bibliotheque.edu.gov.mb.ca)

Information and Reference Services:
Norma Rocan 945-4782 e-mail: nrocan@minet.gov.mb.ca
Huguette Dandeneau 945-6859 e-mail: dandenau@minet.gov.mb.ca
Doris Lemoine 945-8554 e-mail: dlemoine@minet.gov.mb.ca

Technical Services:
Gemma Boily, cataloger 945-0816 e-mail: gboily@minet.gov.mb.ca

Collection Development:
Huguette Dandeneau 945-6859 e-mail: dandenau@minet.gov.mb.ca

Acquisitions/Technology:
Nicole Baudry 945-2743 e-mail: nbaudry@minet.gov.mb.ca
Dubbing Services:
Thongsay Phanlouvong 945-3824 e-mail: phanlouv@minet.gov.mb.ca

Loans, Registration, Overdues, Extensions:
(204) 945-8594

Media Booking:
(204) 945-2467
Toll-Free: 1-800-667-2950

Director:
Doris Lemoine 945-8554 e-mail: dlemoine@minet.gov.mb.ca

Library Coordinator:
Huguette Dandeneau 945-6859 e-mail: dandenau@minet.gov.mb.ca

MediaMobile Coordinators:
Martyne Laliberté
(French Immersion/Rural Schools) 945-8526
e-mail: mlaliberte@minet.gov.mb.ca
Jacques Frenette
(Franco-Manitoban/Rural Schools) 945-8526 e-mail: jfren@minet.gov.mb.ca

CHAPTER SIX

Collections of Significance in Manitoba's Libraries

Introduction

In his keynote address to the Canadian Library Association's national conference held in June 1998, Canadian author John Ralston Saul spoke on the topic of "Libraries and the Public Good". Saul challenged the popular notion that library collections are becoming unaffordable and will be replaced by electronic alternatives that are powerful, broad-ranging and efficient in retrieval. Saul argued that:

> If the library is the key to public memory, people have to act as if it is. What is the central job of the library? First of all, libraries create collections; they preserve the memory bank, the local memory. You have an obligation to put it together; no one else is going to do it. Management is a minor part of what you do. If you believe management is more important than building collections and serving citizens, then you will have no money for books or for serving the public.
> —(*Feliciter*, July/August 1998, vol. 44, no. 7/8, p. 33).

Several outstanding collections held by Manitoba's libraries are featured in this chapter. These collections include materials in all formats: print, audiovisual and electronic. The subject areas covered are those that have special significance in terms of Manitoba's history, culture and economy: agriculture; business; Canadiana and Canadiana-Manitoba collections; fine arts, architecture and urban studies; First Nations; French language and multicultural collections.

These specialized collections are located in public, academic and special libraries and information centres. Although each of these types of libraries may be collecting resources in the same subject area, there will be differences in terms of the specific focus of the collection, the depth and breadth of the collection, and the target audience. Members of the public are usually able to use on-site, and to borrow, via the interlibrary loan system, materials owned by special and academic libraries. The directory section located at the end of this book provides details of such arrangements under the heading "external users."

From Field to Table
Agriculture Collections in Manitoba's Libraries

The agri-food industry is one of the top five in Canada and accounts for about nine percent of the Canadian gross domestic product. Within Manitoba, food and beverage processing contributes close to one-quarter of the province's total manufacturing output. It is not surprising, therefore, that in Manitoba we have a range of libraries providing information services to those involved at all levels of the agri-food industry.

Agriculture and Agri-Food Canada, Manitoba Research Centres

There are twenty-three Agriculture and Agri-Food Canada libraries in Canada, all members of a national resource-sharing network involving the free exchange of information, monographs and journal articles. Three of these libraries are located in Research Centres in Manitoba. The Research Centres concentrate on basic research intended to improve agricultural production such as developing new crop varieties or new farming techniques. The library collections are similar in that they are tightly focused and emphasize academic material, particularly journals. However, each of the Centres concentrates on research in a different area and these differences are also reflected in the library collections.

Winnipeg Research Centre Library

Located on the University of Manitoba campus, the Winnipeg Research Centre is also known at the Cereal Research Centre. The mandate of the Centre is to develop enhanced wheat and oat cultivars and to improve methods for controlling insect pests and ensuring grain quality during storage. The Library provides research support through its collection in plant breeding, plant pathology, biotechnology, cereal chemistry, entomology and mycology.

The Centre houses the Buller collection, bequeathed to the library by A.H.R. Buller whose research was rust epidemics in wheat and who helped found the first Dominion Rust Laboratory. The collection includes scientific books, Buller's personal collection and early article reprints in the areas of plant pathology and plant breeding.

Morden Research Centre Library

The Morden Research Centre is linked administratively to the Winnipeg Research Centre, but it has a slightly different research focus that is reflected in the in-house collection. The Morden Centre concentrates on the development of flax crops, pulse crops (such as peas, beans or soybeans) and woody ornamentals (landscape plants). Support for these crops includes information in the areas of plant breeding, plant pathology and biotechnology.

Brandon Research Centre Library

Scientists at the Centre focus on beef production systems, barley breeding and land resource management. The barley breeding program, as with the plant breeding programs in the other Research Centres, requires a collection strong in genetics, heredity, and bio-technology. The beef production systems research uses information on calving, feeding, pasturing and grazing of cattle. The land resource management program is involved in the development and assessment of agricultural production systems. This is a multidisciplinary program requiring information in a wide variety of areas, including soil processes, crop physiology and pathology, manure management, weed ecology, micrometeorology and systems agronomy.

The Inglis Elevator Row, terminating at Inglis, Manitoba, is significant as the last surviving line of old style 'standard' prairie grain elevators. These landmark structures, one of Canada's newest National Historic Sites, will be restored to their former architectural glory as monuments to the agricultural industry in western Canada.

Canadian Grain Commission Library

Established in 1912, the Canadian Grain Commission regulates grain handling in Canada and establishes standards for Canadian grain quality. The Library collection primarily supports two operating divisions of the Canadian Grain Commission: the Grain Research Laboratory and Industry Services.

The Grain Research Laboratory concentrates on grain and oilseeds chemistry and technology. Research covers aspects of processing grains and oilseeds from the post-harvest stage, but does not extend to new product development and marketing. In support of this mandate, the collection includes information on processes such as baking, milling and brewing; testing for chemical or rheological properties of grain products; and screening for enzymes which can affect the quality of various end-products, such as pasta, chapattis, or Chinese steamed breads.

The Industry Services Division deals with all aspects of grain handling and grain quality, including inspection and grading, weighing and registration. Support from the Library for this Division involves supplying general grain industry information, such as newsletters, annual reports and reports from grain elevators.

The focus of the Divisions on the development of efficient varietal identification techniques and grain inspection techniques has resulted in a library collection which is particularly strong in the areas of analytical chemistry (including near-infrared techniques, spectroscopy, and chromatography), genetic techniques for DNA identification and entomological information related to grain infestation control.

Canadian Wheat Board Library

Established in 1935, the Canadian Wheat Board markets wheat and barley grown in Western Canada. With over five billion dollars in export earnings, it ranks as one of the top Canadian exporters. The Canadian Wheat Board is involved in only a very small part of the broader agricultural scene—exporting wheat and barley. This narrow mandate, however, requires the support of a wide spectrum of information.

In order to effectively export grain, Canadian Wheat Board employees need information that will help them identify potential buyers, estimate demand and keep on top of market conditions around the world. To respond to these needs, the Library has information on grain production and trade, worldwide weather, current political events, global finance, transportation information (such as vessel statistics or data on ports) and anything else that may have a bearing on grain prices.

Some of the materials in which the collection is particularly strong include Western Canadian crop reports, annual reports from grain companies, US Department of Agriculture reports, a wide variety of trade statistics and economic studies of foreign countries. The Library also houses a historical collection on the grain trade in Western Canada.

Food Development Centre Library

The last step in the agricultural process is bringing the agricultural products from the farm to your table. In Manitoba, the Food Development Centre focuses on the food product development aspect of agricultural production.

Located in Portage La Prairie, the Food Development Centre is an operating agency of Manitoba Rural Development. The Centre helps individuals and companies to establish or expand food processing initiatives that may involve developing a new food product, including the process development, packaging, evaluating, testing and marketing the product.

The Library in the Food Development Centre supports the Centre's mandate with a strong collection covering a wide variety of foods as well as related agricultural products such as animal feeds, neutraceuticals, herbs and even perfumes and fragrances. To support the evaluation and testing initiatives at the Centre, the Library carries information on analytical chemistry and microbiology, including standard test methods for identifying food constituents, such as nutrients or vitamins or contaminants such as pesticides and pathogenic bacteria. Canadian, US and international food-related standards and regulations are also available in the Library.

William R. Newman Library

Opened in November 1996, the William R. Newman Library serves Agricultural and Food Sciences faculty and students at the University of Manitoba. There are six departments within the Faculty: Agricultural Economics and Farm Management,

Animal Sciences, Entomology, Food Science, Plant Science and Soil Science. Emphasis is on supporting faculty and graduate student research in these departments.

The Library collection is very broad since it must cover six very diverse areas within agriculture. The Library has an extensive collection on the development and processing of canola, from breeding to seed drying and storage, oil extraction, fertilizer recommendations, pollination technique and utilization of the meal. Other areas of emphasis include the forage industry, conservation-tillage cropping systems, non-chemical pest control and sustainable agriculture.

The Library's focus is on electronic access to information. Agricultural information is accessed through the Library's microcomputers. From the Library, users can access the University of Manitoba Libraries' online catalogue, several electronic indexes and databases, the Internet and agricultural and general software packages on the Agriculture LAN. The hard copy collection includes the most recent two years of periodical issues and reference books. Back issues of periodicals and much of the book collection is located in the Sciences and Technology Library located on the University of Manitoba campus.

Karen Clay

Services to the Business Sector

Increasingly, libraries of all types in Manitoba are playing a significant role in providing much-needed information to the business sector in a timely manner. With the advent of electronic resources, and with knowledgeable and trained personnel, many libraries are now better equipped than ever to serve the business community effectively and efficiently. Three libraries of varied types are described here to illustrate this growing trend. Each library offers a unique strength in meeting the vital information needs of the corporate sector.

Albert D. Cohen Management Library, University of Manitoba

As a partner in the mission of the University, the University of Manitoba Libraries are an essential information resource for the province of Manitoba. One of the goals of the University, in addition to teaching and research, is to serve the community directly by making its expertise available to individuals and institutions, and by providing as much access to the University's intellectual, cultural, artistic and physical resources as its primary teaching and research responsibilities permit. This commitment extends to the University's libraries. The University of Manitoba Libraries have established an information service designed to meet the information and research needs of professional groups, business, government, researchers and the general public. Corporate Information Services, operated on a non-profit, cost-recovery basis, enables groups and individuals outside the academic community to have access to a wealth of material contained in the University's 12 libraries.

The Albert D. Cohen Management Library supports the teaching and research needs of the Faculty of Management and the Transport Institute and provides information services in all management, transport and business-related subjects. The book and bound periodical collection consists of approximately 30,000 volumes; the journal and newspaper collection of 450 current subscriptions. This collection is augmented by access to 400 journals in full image on a CD-ROM database called ABI Power Pages. The Management Library houses one of the largest company annual report collections in the province, numbering over 1,000 Canadian and American companies. The collection also includes an extensive collection of Canadian, American and international trade and company directories and financial investment services.

The services offered by the Management Library are co-ordinated with services available through all libraries in the University of Manitoba system. For example, NETDOC is a network of database information available to all microcomputer users on campus that provides access to over 45 databases in management, psychology, law, science, education, medicine, agriculture and the social sciences. Professional library staff provide consultations and seminars on bibliographic information management and the use of computerized information resources.

The Canada/Manitoba Business Service Centre/Centre de services aux entreprises du Canada/Manitoba

The Canada/Manitoba Business Service Centre, or CMBSC, is the newest member of a national network of business service centres in Canada. The CMBSC is an economic development agency that opened April 1, 1998 as a result of a partnership between 28 federal government departments, 13 provincial departments and several private sector organizations including the Manitoba and Winnipeg Chambers of Commerce, Winnipeg 2000, the Association of Manufacturers and Exporters Canada and the University of Manitoba. The Centre delivers an array of programs and services to the Manitoba business community.

The Centre is the primary resource for market research and other business information and services in the Prairie region and is particularly helpful for starting or growing a small business. The Centre is composed of a Telecentre, a consulting unit, the services of business and trade officers and a business research library.

The Library includes five public access workstations where users can scan the information world using a keyword searching method. Access is provided to Industry Canada's national business database, STRATEGIS, and more than 32 additional online databases. The Centre offers free access to the Internet. The Library's Web site has a menu-driven business planning module that allows the user to document market research findings on-site to produce a hard copy business plan. The Library has a hard copy business reference collection of more than 10,000 documents, a journals collection of 150 current titles and a CD-ROM tower that covers 7,000 major magazines published from the early 1990s to the present. The CD-ROM tower permits users to do keyword searching on all 7,000 titles and to print selected articles, free of charge. More than 700 training videos may be used on site or loaned for a seven-day period.

An exciting new development is the Canada/Manitoba Business Service Centre's establishment of twelve regional satellites in rural Manitoba. It is anticipated that by September 1998, the Centre will have successfully removed the geographic barriers to business information that have previously existed in Manitoba. These regional satellites will provide a core business collection in hard copy and computer access to the Canada/Manitoba Business Service Centre. The philosophical basis for this decision is that the citizens of Manitoba are to be served first in the communities where they live and work. When the regional core collection is not adequate to answer specific queries, the Centre will provide the necessary information from Winnipeg.

This action will increase the visibility of business services in remote areas and in rural Manitoba and further the role of the Centre in meeting the needs of business in this province. The merger of the Business Library and the Canada Business Service Centre in April 1998 has already doubled the volume of use and speaks well to the role of libraries in business and economic development. The Centre is currently working with the Winnipeg Library Foundation to bring to Winnipeg in 1999 a conference on the role of libraries in economic development.

The Centre's hours of operation are 8:00 a.m. to 5:00 p.m. Monday through Friday, except for statutory holidays. The Centre is located at suite 250–240 Graham Avenue in downtown Winnipeg.

Winnipeg Public Library Centennial Branch

The Winnipeg Centennial Library, located at 251 Donald Street, houses Winnipeg Public Library's largest collection of business materials and resources. The Information and Reference Department at Centennial Library provides a variety of resources and services to meet the business information needs of investors searching for investment advice, public and private sector managers seeking information about job performance and evaluation and of business owners and managers trying to improve their company's performance. This specialized collection is also helpful to individuals researching employment and career options, to university and college students completing assignments and to the general public who are looking for biographical information about well-known business people.

Reference staff offer telephone assistance to locate quick facts such as addresses and other information on companies, as well as in-person and telephone assistance to locate books and data on business-related topics. When the requested information is not available at the Centennial Library, clients are referred to other libraries, agencies or associations.

A variety of sources are available to help staff respond to in-person or telephone queries. The Library's collection of investment information includes newsletters, business periodicals and books on investing. Employment and job information can be found in business directories and in a Business Card File describing local Manitoba companies. The Library also has a good collection of books on writing resumes and the job search process and subscribes to newsletters highlighting employment opportunities across Canada. The Centennial Library has an extensive collection of telephone books for North American cities, as well as city directories for selected Canadian locations. The Business Directory Centre houses a collection of manufacturing and service industry directories that help users locate companies by the type of product manufactured or service offered. The circulating collection contains books on a variety of business topics such as bookkeeping, marketing, advertising, starting a small business, staff development and performance appraisal.

Ganga Dakshinamurti with contributions from
John Giesbrecht, Gail Doherty, Eric Hunt and Dennis Felbel.

Canadiana and Canadiana-Manitoba Collections

"The Acquisition of a Canadiana Collection" was the subject of a paper written by John S. Russell, Chief Librarian, St. James Public Library, for the Manitoba Library Association Bulletin in 1965. His article began with a lengthy quote from Lorne Pierce's *An Outline of Canadian Literature*, written in 1927:

> There will always remain the barriers of mountains and lakes, and the sectional interests which they create, but already it is clear that our destinies lie together. How, then, are we to acquire a greater cohesiveness? It cannot be through the influence of foreign capital any more than through the supremacy of foreign magazines. It must be through the intensive study of our history, its romantic events and inspiring personalities, as well as an increasing devotion to our national literature. Here, for better or for worse, speaks the soul of Canada; here is the highway, broad and beautiful, which shall cross every divide, and create the only enduring entente cordiale.

In his conclusion to this extensive bibliographical essay, Mr. Russell urged even the smallest libraries in the province to make a special effort to assemble collections of Canadian materials: "Librarians have a clear duty to develop the national consciousness by making available to as wide an audience as possible the materials that play such a significant part in the understanding of our place as a people occupying the northern part of this continent."

Eleven years after this article was written, the Commission on Canadian Studies released the first two volumes of its report, entitled *To Know Ourselves*. In these volumes, it examined some fifty academic areas and suggested that in each of these areas, in both teaching and research, there was need and opportunity for greater attention to be paid to Canadian content and to the Canadian context.

Speaking at a Conference on Canadian Studies held in 1994 at the University of Manitoba, Professor Thomas Symons, who had chaired the Commission on Canadian Studies observed that:

Archives and libraries provide the foundations for Canadian Studies. Scholars with an interest in Canada, wherever they may be located, can assist in strengthening these foundations by working together to help to identify, preserve, share, and enhance relevant archival and library resources. And there is much to be done by librarians and archivists, and by those who are indebted to them, in promoting the health and development of these two vital professions. Canadians need a fuller understanding of the value of their own archival and book heritage.

The province's Legislative Library, the Winnipeg Centennial Library, and the Department of Archives and Special Collections at the University of Manitoba have as part of their mandate the collection and preservation of materials relating to Canada's culture and heritage.

Manitoba Legislative Library

The Legislative Library traces its beginnings to the Red River Settlers who first established a library in 1848. Some of their books formed the nucleus of a collection begun in 1870 when A.E. Archibald, Manitoba's first Lieutenant Governor, chose some 2,000 additional books suitable for the new Legislature. Over the years, the Library's collections have grown to over 1,500,000 items. Under the terms of legal deposit, the Library receives copies of all new books published in Manitoba.

The Legislative Library's Rare Book Collection was established by the first Legislative Librarian, J.P. Robertson, in 1884. This collection includes the 350 volumes that remain of the Red River Library which served the Red River settlers until the 1860s, as well as histories of Manitoba communities, early accounts of the exploration of the North West and the Arctic, and major historical series such as that of the Champlain Society, Hudson's Bay Record and the Manitoba Historical Society. In addition to books about the history of the province, the collection also includes biographies, autobiographies and the writings of famous Manitobans such as E. Cora Hind, Nellie McClung and J.S. Woodsworth.

The Reading Room of the Legislative Library located in the Legislative Building

The Library has two special Manitoba Heritage Collections. The Library's collection of Manitoba Newspapers and its collection of Manitoba Community and Family Histories are used extensively by historical and genealogical researchers from Manitoba and abroad. The Library receives all newspapers currently published in Manitoba and also maintains the most extensive historical collection of Manitoba newspapers published since 1859. Most have been microfilmed and are available on interlibrary loan to those who are unable to visit the Library.

The Library also maintains a large collection of local histories from municipalities and communities throughout the province, as well as biography and history scrapbooks of newspaper clippings and vertical files.

Winnipeg Centennial Library

As far back as 1917, the number of Canadiana items acquired during the year was documented in the annual report of the Winnipeg Public Library. The Canadiana collection, housed at the Winnipeg Centennial Library, 251 Donald Street, was established to assist research into various aspects of Canadian society, past and present. Materials for this collection are selected to offer a "snapshot" of a particular time and are evaluated for potential historical value as well as current use. The collection emphasizes topics and subjects of interest to Winnipeggers and and Manitobans.

The collection covers a wide variety of topics from politics and economics to sports and entertainment and includes biographies and autobiographies of individuals who have achieved local or national prominence. Fiction and poetry are no longer collected for this area. Older fiction and poetry titles can be found in the collection.

While the Library does collect material of national significance, regional materials are purchased only if they relate to Winnipeg or Manitoba. Local history items will often be purchased and housed in the Canadiana area to ensure that a copy remains available within the system. Most of these materials have small print runs and there might be only one opportunity to add them to the collection. The Library purchases between 200 and 300 items a year for the Canadiana collection. Generally, a circulating copy of each item will also be purchased.

Canadiana materials are interfiled in the library's online catalogue and are identified by a "Ca" designation. in the call number. They are not available for interlibrary loan and may only be used in the Centennial Library. Request slips for Canadiana materials must be presented to the Micromedia and Periodicals Department located on the third floor of the Library.

Micromedia and Periodicals staff receive 15 to 20 requests a day to retrieve items from the Canadiana collection. Popular topics include the history of Manitoba towns, materials about World War II (particularly information about local medal holders and regimental history) and biographical information on local figures. In 1997, staff answered many questions relating to the flood, including other famous floods in the province's history. Reference and Information staff also make extensive use of this collection in answering queries received by telephone, mail, or electronic means.

Department of Archives and Special Collections, Elizabeth Dafoe Library

As part of its mission to acquire, catalogue and preserve research collections which foster the teaching and research aims of the University of Manitoba, the Department of Archives and Special Collections manages a special collection of rare books and various other printed materials. The 35,000 volumes in the Department constitute a valuable and popular scholarly resource.

The subject strength of the collection is Canadiana, particularly the works on the history and development of Western Canada, early Arctic exploration and the search for the North West Passage. First editions of John Palliser, Alexander Mackenzie, Henry Youle Hind, John Franklin, James Cook, John J. Bigsby, George Heriot and scores of other explorers, pioneers and settlers are represented in the collection. Other major holdings are in Canadian Prairie literature and the history of agriculture in Western Canada.

Several private research libraries have been acquired, including the Marshall Gauvin library of free thought and anti-religionist literature, the Desmond Smith Canadiana collection, and the Ralph Estey library of Canadian agricultural history and plant pathology.

An outstanding collection of literature was recently donated to the University of Manitoba Libraries by Charles and Elizabeth Bigelow. The collection consists mainly of the works of Canadian, American and British authors, and of works about these writers. Most of the books are first editions. The works of most contemporary Canadian writers such as Margaret Atwood, Margaret Laurence and Mordecai Richler are well represented in the collection.

Dr. Michael Angel, recently retired Associate Director of Collections at the University of Manitoba, observed that the addition of this large collection of works to the University of Manitoba Libraries will greatly enhance the strength of our literature collections. The donation of books by Charles and Elizabeth Bigelow, together with an earlier significant donation of Canadian literature by Judge Roy St. George Stubbs, has gone a long way toward making the Canadian literature collection one of our premier collections. In fact, this collection, along with the continually growing archival collection in English Canadian literature, distinguishes the University of Manitoba Libraries as one of the major centres for English Canadian literature.

One of the most popular resources located in the Department of Archives and Special Collections is the large *Winnipeg Tribune* collection. The collection contains the *Tribune* research "morgue", that is, files consisting of personality and subject folders of newspaper clippings from the 1930s to 1980. There are approximately 2,500,000 clippings, divided over some 11,000 subject categories and 60,000 personality folders. Together they provide ready-made information packages on people and events in Winnipeg, Manitoba, Canada and abroad. The collection is also well documented pictorially with over 500,000 photographs. The collection's subject listings can be searched using the Libraries' online catalogue.

With contributions from Sue Bishop, Gail Doherty,
Darlene Wusaty, and Mike Mooseberger

Consumer Health Information

In April 1998 the Manitoba Health Libraries Association adopted a position paper entitled *Access to Knowledge-Based Health Information in Manitoba* that was prepared by a sub-committee of MHLA in response to recent changes in the health care environment. The paper addressed the issue of the public's demand for more information about health care and documented the importance of libraries and information services in providing consumer health information to the community.

The authors of this paper quoted from a 1993 article published in the *Bulletin of the Medical Library Association* by A.M. Rees, author of *The Consumer Health Information Sourcebook*:

> The most promising approach to the present health care crisis lies in educating consumers to improve their self care practices and reduce health risk factors... It bears repeating that educated, well-informed, and empowered consumers can do more for improving [health] than a massive investment in buildings and expensive medical technology.

Depending on the specific medical topic being researched, and the user's reading level, Manitobans seeking consumer health information have several options: public libraries, medical libraries affiliated with the University of Manitoba and special libraries dedicated to specific health care issues.

Flin Flon Public Library

Consumers seeking health care information written for the layperson can access Manitoba's system of public libraries. The Flin Flon Public Library has taken a leadership role in the provision of consumer health information through its participation in the Healthy Communities Manitoba Project that was aimed at fostering the overall well-being of the community. Flin Flon was the winner of The Healthcare Forum's 1996 International Award for Healthy Communities. Gretta Redahl, Library Administrator of the Flin Flon Public Library, also served as Co-Chair of the Manitoba Healthy Communities Network and represented Manitoba at the national level.

The establishment of a Consumer Health Information Centre in the Flin Flon Public Library was one of the initiatives of Healthy Flin Flon. This facility provides a central location where local people, both consumers and providers of health services, can access health and wellness information. The information coordinator who runs this facility develops and distributes consumer surveys, gathers local health and wellness data and researches consumer requests for information.

The Flin Flon Public Library is developing a strategic plan to respond to several challenges including community-based health reform initiatives and the needs of an aging population. In the fall of 1998, the Library will be launching its "Info Pod", which houses a Community Informatics Centre. The Info Pod contains all-media technology, including state-of-the art computers (Macintosh and IBM, cross-platform), high-speed modems, as well as a photo-quality printer, a scanner and a VHS video camcorder. Users can connect to the Internet and send e-mail with attachments, including scanned photos, text or speech. Projects are currently being developed to utilize this technology in health promotion and community-based programming.

Neil John Maclean Health Sciences Library and the Carolyn Sifton-Helene Fuld Library

The Neil John Maclean Health Sciences Library is located on the Bannatyne Campus of the University of Manitoba in downtown Winnipeg. The Library's collection is the primary resource for health sciences information for the University of Manitoba, affiliated teaching hospitals and health care professionals in the province of Manitoba. The collection consists of materials in the areas of clinical medicine, biomedical sciences, dentistry, dental hygiene, nursing, rehabilitation and Aboriginal health.

The Library also has a growing consumer health collection and offers reference services to consumers. Literature searches, search seminars and extensive consultation are available through the Library's fee-based service, INFO-Rx. Pamphlets describing the INFO-Rx service are available from the Neil John Maclean Health Sciences Library.

The Carolyn Sifton-Helene Fuld Library, a satellite information centre of the Neil John Maclean Health Sciences Library, is located in the St. Boniface General Hospital Research Centre.

The J.W. Crane Memorial Library of Gerontology and Geriatrics

The J.W. Crane Memorial Library of Gerontology and Geriatrics is one the largest specialized libraries on aging in Canada. The Library was established in 1962 by the Canadian Geriatrics Research Society, one of the first organizations to focus specifically on research issues related to the aging process. The collection of the late Dr. J.W. Crane, a former Dean of Medicine at the University of Western Ontario, formed the nucleus of the Library and gave it its name. When the Toronto-based Research Society began to wind down its operations in 1989, it issued a request for proposals to acquire and develop the Library. The Deer Lodge Centre entered the national competition and was the successful applicant. The Library moved to Manitoba in 1990, and has continued to develop and expand since then.

The Deer Lodge Centre has always tried to share its resources with the larger community. In the late 1980s, with a grant from the Winnipeg Foundation, the Centre began providing services and resources to nursing homes and health care workers across the province. Without this service, many had little access to such a range of specialized information. It was this tradition of accessibility that may have been the deciding factor in the Research Society's decision to place the Crane Collection at Deer Lodge, rather than at another institution in Canada.

The collection includes resources on the following topics: the medical, social and psychological aspects of aging; chronic disease and disability; the planning, administration, organization and operation of long-term care systems and services; and the economics, demographics and philosophy of aging. A particular emphasis is placed on collecting Canadian resources. The Library also houses the "Reading Room", a consumer health information resource for seniors, their families and friends.

The Library provides resources and services to the staff and clients of Deer Lodge Centre, the Riverview Health Centre and long-term care facilities throughout the province. The Library is also used by students, researchers and the public from across Canada. External users may use materials on-site or may borrow items through interlibrary loan.

The Family Information Library of The Children's Hospital of Winnipeg

In the early 1990s, family resource libraries were emerging in the United States, but there were few in Canada. At the Winnipeg Children's Hospital, the Multi-disciplinary Patient Education Committee felt that a resource centre for families that would provide information about their children's health was not only needed, but absolutely necessary. The Committee sur-

The Children's Hospital Family Information Library

veyed physicians, nurses, allied health staff and parents to assess the need for a family resource centre that would provide pediatric health information at the lay level. The response was overwhelmingly in favor of such a project.

Only one out of 110 responses cited the danger of providing medical advice without medical expertise. The Committee, however, knew that this would not be the function of the Llibrary. Rather, in order to enhance the parent-professional relationship, we would educate and inform families. We wanted to open lines of communication between parent and professional, and believed that our goal could be more readily accomplished if families were educated about their children's health.

The Children's Hospital Family Information Library opened its doors on May 20, 1993, with funding provided by the Children's Hospital Book Market, the Winnipeg Foundation, the Junior League of Winnipeg and McDonald's Restaurants of Canada. It is the third such facility in the country.

With the belief that parents need and want an understanding of their children's growth, development and medical condition, we have established a collection of materials related to children's health. This collection is aimed at the layperson, and supports and supplements information provided by health care professionals. The subjects covered in the collection include child development, nutrition, parenting, children in hospital, childhood cancer, diabetes and asthma. All materials in the library are screened by professionals in the field to ensure that they are written for the layperson, are accurate and up-to-date, and comply with Children's Hospital guidelines.

When the Library opened, there were about 200 items in the collection. Presently, there are about 2,000 books with a separate collection of approximately 100 French items. (Winnipeg has one of the largest French speaking communities in Canada outside of Quebec. The Children's Hospital, as the only pediatric hospital in the province, has a mandate to provide service in French). About 200 videotapes are also part of the collection. Besides materials on specific diseases, there are extensive collections on death and dying, parenting and normal growth and development. Sources for selecting material included hospital staff, *The Consumer Health Information Sourcebook* by A.M. Rees, and other family resource centres.

To ensure that facts are current and accurate, all material is reviewed by a health care professional before being included in the collection. However, we did run into a problem with this policy. When health care personnel were asked to review controversial materials, they would not recommend them. Yet we had parents, especially the families of cancer patients, requesting this information. The Library Advisory Committee agreed that the Library should be providing the information, and obtained permission from the Child Health Program Management Team to house controversial information. We felt that if patients and their families really wanted certain types of information, they would obtain it by whatever means they could. At least we could attempt to ensure that the information they obtained was current. At this point, we added a disclaimer to all of the materials housed in the Library, not only the controversial ones.

The Family Information Library also maintains a pamphlet clearinghouse for the entire Children's Hospital. Presently, the clearinghouse contains about 750 pamphlets covering asthma and allergies to vaccinations, and accident prevention to substance abuse. All pamphlets go through the same review process as the books; they are reviewed every few years to ensure accuracy and currency. Any Children's Hospital staff can order pamphlets through the Library.

The Family Information Library, as a resource for the entire Children's Hospital catchment area, mails and sends material by fax to Northern Manitoba, Northwestern Ontario and the Keewatin District, the Northwest Territories, and to nursing stations on First Nations reserves.

We have recently gained access to the Internet. In addition, funding has been received from the St. John's Guild for an Internet workstation for families to access children's health information. This workstation will also be available to inpatients who would like to communicate with other children concerning similar health issues.

Every year we mail brochures and posters to pediatricians and family practice clinics in the catchment area. As a result, more and more physicians are referring their patients to the Library and calling for information.

We have come a long way. The Library has become firmly established as a necessary component in providing family-centered care with the most important commodity of all in mind: the children in hospital. The Family Information Library is a province-wide resource for parents and caregivers, children and teenagers, inpatients and outpatients of Children's Hospital, and agencies and professionals.

The William Potoroka Memorial Library of the Addictions Foundation of Manitoba

The collection at the William Potoroka Memorial Library of the Addictions Foundation of Manitoba is one of the most comprehensive of its kind in Manitoba. The Library serves as the information resource for addictions and related issues for all of Manitoba. It was originally established in 1952 as an information centre serving the Committee on Alcoholism for Manitoba. In 1956, the committee became the Alcoholism Foundation of Manitoba. Beginning with a small nucleus of books, by the 1970s the Library was firmly established in providing services to AFM staff, funded agencies and the public. Since that time, the modest collection has increased dramatically and library services have expanded.

The Library collects and disseminates alcohol, drug and other addictions information. It offers a selection of accurate and current resources on issues, trends and research in the addictions field, including topics such as alcohol, drugs, gambling, counselling, stress, anger management, family violence, sniff, communication, fetal alcohol syndrome, smoking, co-dependency, compulsive behaviors, doping in sport, and drinking and driving.

The collection represents Manitoba's largest collection of adiction-related books, government documents, reports, statistical publications and academic/professional periodicals. The Library has an extensive audiovisual collection, including audiotapes, VHS videotapes and kits. The vertical file collection includes more than 140 subject files, each containing up-to-date reference materials, pamphlets and a subject index to journal articles and newspaper clippings.

Borrowers can access information by phone, fax, mail, e-mail or in person. During the academic year, the Library is open three evenings a week. The collection is available province-wide and membership is free.

MFL Occupational Health Centre Library

The Library of the Manitoba Federation of Labour is open to all Manitobans who are interested in learning about workplace health and safety issues. In addition to a book and periodical collection, the Library maintains an extensive vertical file on topics dealing with occupational medicine, safety and toxicology. The publications of the U.S. National Institute of Occupational Safety and Health are available for consultation. The collection is non-circulating. Library staff help on-site visitors to locate and interpret materials and respond to information queries by telephone, fax or mail. Library hours are Monday, Tuesday, Thursday and Friday from 9:00 a.m. to 5:00 p.m., and Thursday from 9:00 a.m. to 8:00 p.m.

With contributions from Gretta Redahl, Carol Cooke, Judy Inglis, Liz Price, Morag Belliveau and Pat Hebert.

Fine Arts, Architecture and Urban Studies

Manitobans seeking information about fine arts, architecture and urban studies—with a special emphasis on Canadian content—are well-served by the collections of the Winnipeg Art Gallery, the Architecture/Fine Arts Library of the University of Manitoba, and the Institute of Urban Studies at the University of Winnipeg.

The Clara Lander Library and Winnipeg Art Gallery Archives

The Winnipeg Art Gallery Library and Archives seek to promote public access to information documenting the visual arts created by Canadians, and particularly by Manitobans, for the citizens of Manitoba. This is the only resource centre in Manitoba with this mandate. Named in honor of a founding member of what was then called the Women's Volunteer Committee of the Winnipeg Art Gallery, the Library supports the research needs of gallery staff and volunteers, gallery members, fine arts students, artists, teachers and interested members of the general public.

The Winnipeg Art Gallery

For the researcher of Canadian art, the Art Gallery Library is the best source of information in the region. The nearest alternative is the Glenbow Museum to the West, and the Art Gallery of Ontario to the East. The Library houses a collection of approximately 24,000 books and exhibition catalogues and subscribes to hundreds of art journals, art newsletters, calendars and gallery bulletins. A resource-sharing partnership with over 120 art institutions worldwide has been established by the library. The Clara Lander Library maintains biographical files on almost 10,000 artists. Online documentation on these files is provided to the Canadian Heritage Network (CHIN) which, in turn, provides online access to these files and to those held at other participating institutions.

The Library is also home to the Institutional Archives of the Winnipeg Art Gallery and to a fully catalogued collection of 20,000 slides. The Library is open Tuesday through Thursday from 11:00 a.m. to 4:30 p.m.

Architecture/Fine Arts Library at the University of Manitoba

The Architecture/Fine Arts Library at the University of Manitoba supports the teaching and research requirements of the Faculty of Architecture, which consists of five graduate departments: Landscape Architecture, Architecture, City Planning, Interior Design and Facility Management; two undergraduate departments, Environmental Design and Interior Design; and the School of Art which offers undergraduate degrees in Art History and Studio Art.

The Architecture/Fine Arts Library collection, which contains approximately 61,000 volumes including 443 current periodical subscriptions, covers architecture, art history, interior design, graphic design, environmental design, facility management, city planning and studio art. The collection serves the students, faculty and staff of the University of Manitoba, the professional community and the general public.

With over 114,000 35mm slides, the Architecture/Fine Arts Library Slide Collection's holdings are international in scope and cover time periods ranging from prehistoric to the present. The emphasis of the collection is on art and architecture, with particularly strong holdings in photography and local Winnipeg architecture.

Other special collections in the Library include the following:

> Architectural Drawings: The collection consists of drawings of Winnipeg buildings, along with a small sampling of drawings of buildings from other towns in Manitoba.
> Art Reproductions: This circulating collection consists of over 800 reproductions of both Western and other drawings and paintings that span the history of art.
> Historic Urban Plans: This is a collection of over 200 historic urban plans of major cities from around the globe.
> The Product Catalogue Collection: This collection contains over 8,000 design and building product samples, catalogues and brochures. The collection is arranged according to the building product classification system, and is non-circulating.
> The Winnipeg Building Index: This is an ongoing project to identify buildings in Winnipeg and some of the sources of information available in the Architecture/Fine Arts Library. The Index is available in the Library and through the Library's homepage.
> Winnipeg Photograph Collection: This is a small collection of 128 historical photographs documenting key churches, banks, hotels and other buildings significant to Winnipeg's architectural heritage, including a

selection of buildings on the University campus.

Vertical Files: The primary focus of the non-circulating vertical file collection is on Manitoba artists and architects, galleries and planning issues/sites.

The Institute of Urban Studies Reference Library

The Institute of Urban Studies, established in 1969, was created by the University of Winnipeg to respond to the problems and concerns of the inner city of which the University was, and remains, a vital part. From its inception, the Institute has been both an academic centre and a centre of applied research, committed to examining a wide range of urban issues.

The Institute of Urban Studies Reference Library originated as a collection of reports prepared by IUS staff, or donated by various sources such as Canada Mortgage and Housing Corporation and the Canadian Council on Urban and Regional Research. It was officially organized in 1985 under a grant from the Social Sciences and Humanities Research Council of Canada. Over the past 10 years, the IUS Library has grown considerably and has become a valuable resource for the University of Winnipeg and the wider community. Significant book donations have been received from Manitoba Urban Affairs, the Social Planning Council of Winnipeg, and numerous former provincial and civic officials. In 1994, the Institute of Urban Studies, including the IUS Library, moved from the University of Winnipeg campus to its present location at 346 Portage Avenue in downtown Winnipeg.

The Library has a dual function as a university research library and a community resource centre, specializing in the multi-disciplinary field of urban studies, with a specific focus on Canada and Winnipeg. The main users include university faculty and students, community organizations, government research consultants, and private consultants.

The Library collects materials in the areas of city planning, inner cities, urban transportation, municipal government, urban Aboriginal issues, housing, sustainable urban development and urban policy. Significant holdings of the Library include the Institute of Urban Studies publication collection which dates back to 1969 and includes *Research and Working Papers, Occasional Papers, Bibliographica*, and special series on *Canadian Prairie Inner Cities, Urban Resources, Urban Sustainability, Native Issues* and *Health and the Community*. The Library also houses a large part of the Winnipeg Core Area Initiative office collection that includes progress reports, status reports, consultants' reports, and program evaluations.

The Library is open, by appointment, to the public during regular hours, Monday to Friday. Borrowing privileges are restricted to faculty and students of the University of Winnipeg.

With contributions from Catherine Shields, Kenlyn Collins, Mary Lockhead and Nancy Klos.

First Nations

The release of the *Final Report of the Royal Commission on Aboriginal Peoples* in 1996, and the publication of the *Report of the Aboriginal Justice Inquiry of Manitoba* in 1991 have heightened the public's interest in the history, culture, and social and economic conditions of Manitoba's First Nations peoples.

First Nations resources come in many formats, including oral, written and visual. Manitoba has several significant resource collections of materials; some, such as the People's Library of the Manitoba Indian Cultural Centre, the Treaty and Aboriginal Rights Research Centre of Manitoba, Inc., and the Library of the Centre for Indigenous Environmental Resources are under the direction of boards of directors drawn from the First Nations.

A resource centre dedicated to North American Native heritage resources was recently opened as a special collection within the Boissevain and Morton Regional Library. Other significant collections of materials are located in the Elizabeth Dafoe Library at the University of Manitoba and the Multicultural Resource Collection in the Instructional Resources Unit Library of the Department of Education.

"Catching the Sun", Mixed media installation by Colleen Cutschall (1993), John E. Robbins Library, Brandon University

The People's Library and Resource Centre, Manitoba Indian Cultural Education Centre

The Manitoba Indian Cultural Education Centre, located at 119 Sutherland Avenue, is a non-profit educational organization that works to promote an awareness and understanding of the First Nations culture to First Nations and non-First Nations people. Founded in 1975, the Centre is solely funded by Indian and Northern Affairs under the Cultural Education Centres Program. The administration and management of the Centre are under the direction of a Board of Directors who are members of the Assembly of Manitoba Chiefs.

The focus of the collection is on contemporary, traditional, historical and social issues related to the First Nations. Formats collected by the Library and Resource Centre include books, films, videocassettes, educational kits, slide-tape presentations, audiovisual tapes, music, art and handicrafts.

Over the past 20 years, the Library has served more than 20,000 patrons, including students, teachers and the public. Part of the mandate of the Library is to provide assistance to First Nations communities that have expressed interest in establishing library programs, and to provide further assistance to those First Nations communities that have established libraries. Library staff assist in developing educational kits, pamphlets and brochures and provide displays of resource materials to groups wishing to learn more about the First Nations culture and heritage.

Treaty and Aboriginal Rights Research Centre of Manitoba, Inc.

The Treaty and Aboriginal Rights Research Centre of Manitoba, Inc. (T.A.R.R.), which has a regional office at 300–153 Lombard Avenue, provides historical research services to the majority of the First Nations of Manitoba. Incorporated independently on April 1, 1982, T.A.R.R. originated in 1969 when it began as a research program of the Manitoba Indian Brotherhood. Later, it was part of the Four Nations Confederacy. Through the years, the focus of research has been on Indian rights such as Treaty land entitlement, Treaty rights, hunting, fishing, trapping and gathering rights, and on Indian lands (reserve surrenders, leases, expropriations). The Centre is directly responsible to its member First Nations. One of several Indian Research units in Canada, T.A.R.R. is funded by the Department of Indian Affairs and Northern Development.

T.A.R.R. possesses a large collection of historical materials on the First Nations of Manitoba. These documents have been organized for easy access for T.A.R.R. researchers and First Nations organizations. Others may use the material by appointment.

The Research Centre owns significant microfilm collections including selected Department of Indian Affairs records relating to Western Canada (RG10 Black 1862-1959); the Adams Archibald and Alexander Morris Papers, Lieutenant Governors of Manitoba (1872-1877); and the Church Missionary Society records (1829-1930). The Research Centre's library also has an extensive collection of maps and a smaller collection of photographs and videocassettes.

T.A.R.R. also operates a regional office in Thompson. That collection is not as extensive as the one in Winnipeg, but it attempts to provide duplicate copies of significant items.

Library of the Centre for Indigenous Environmental Resources

Founded in 1994, the Centre for Indigenous Environmental Resources (CIER) is a First Nations' organization created and directed by a Board of First Nations' leaders from across Canada. CIER was created for the purpose of establishing and implementing environmental capacity-building initiatives for First Nations. CIER accomplishes this mandate through the provision of services in environmental assessment and remediation; through its post-secondary environmental education and outreach programs; through the development of environmental models, processes and techniques for utilization by First Nations at the community level, and through furthering an understanding of the relationship between First Nations' perspectives and sustainable development approaches.

CIER also works to initiate and promote First Nations' input in the deliberations and resolution of all environmental issues and to develop and enhance the links between all First Nations in Canada and indigenous peoples throughout the world.

The CIER Library, located in the Johnson Terminal at The Forks, is a repository of First Nations' environmental knowledge. The role of the Library is to nurture, preserve and honor traditional ways of knowing and conserving the environment and to represent research that integrates traditional knowledge with Western scientific theory. More narrowly, the function of the Library is to support the research of CIER students, faculty, staff and visiting researchers in the work in education, policy development and technical consulting services. It is hoped that the resources of the Library may eventually be made available to First Nations' communities across Canada through its Web PAC. The mandate for the next phase of the Library's development is to foster the network of Aboriginal libraries in Winnipeg and across Canada.

The CIER collection contains environmental material from both an Aboriginal and western perspective available in a number of different formats: books, periodicals, newspapers, CD-ROMs and Internet files. The CIER Library, along with the Environment Canada/Manitoba Library, the Information Centre of the International Institute for Sustainable Development, and the emerging Eco-Network collection, is one of four environment libraries located in the downtown area.

The subject areas covered by the collection are environmental law, natural resource management, environmental assessment, environmental sciences, biodiversity, sustainable development, Aboriginal law, First Nations culture, indigenous knowledge, forestry, water quality, agriculture, economics, and community development.

The Métis Resource Centre

The Métis Resource Centre, located at 506–63 Albert Street, started as a pilot project in March 1995. It is membership-based and was incorporated as a non-profit organization in September 1996. The Centre focuses on cultural, educational and social programming and offers the following services: classroom visits, cultural materials, workshops and seniors programming. The mandate of the organization is to help preserve, share and promote the culture and history of the Métis people and to help define and highlight the richness of the Métis experience for all interested people.

The Library's collection contains books, audio-visual materials and oral history tapes. The collection is for reference use only during the Library's hours of opening, Monday to Friday, 9:00 a.m. to 4:00 p.m.

The W.J. (Joe) McDonald North American Native Heritage Resource Centre

The W.J. (Joe) McDonald North American Native Heritage Resource Centre was established in September 1996 as a special collection within the Boissevain and

Morton Regional Library. The centre is funded by a generous bequest from the estate of W.J. (Joe) McDonald (1948-1993), a former Boissevain resident who spent many hours at the Boissevain Library and was always appreciative of the information offered there.

The Centre's opening ceremony featured speeches by dignitaries including Manitoba's Lieutenant Governor Yvon Dumont, a descendant of Métis hero Gabriel Dumont. He opened the dedication ceremony by stressing the importance of preserving Canada's heritage for generations to come. Cultural diversity is what has made Canada great in a little more than a century, he stated, but he also pointed out that it was important to remember that the foundation was in place when Europeans arrived to find civilizations that had existed for centuries. Those first people built homes, fed themselves, healed their sick with medicine and governed themselves. The Lieutenant Governor complimented the community of Boissevain for its contributions to the preservation of Canada's heritage through its murals, the Moncur Gallery and the new Native Heritage Centre at the Library.

Joe McDonald graduated from Brandon University and in his adult years, his association with, and studies of Indian peoples, their awareness of nature, the life circle, culture, history and spirituality had a profound effect on his life. It was his wish to donate a generous gift from his estate to the Boissevain and Morton Regional Library for the preservation and positive promotion of North American Indians and Indian culture, spirituality and history. A committee with representatives from the community and the Library was struck to consult with the McDonald family, and to advise the Library on developing the Centre.

The W.J. (Joe) McDonald North American Native Heritage Resource Centre consists of books, videos, CD-ROMs, magazines and some display articles collected by Joe McDonald. Over time, many new materials will be added. Because the materials in the McDonald Heritage Centre are part of a public library, they are available to all of North America through the interlibrary loan network.

Elizabeth Dafoe Library, University of Manitoba

The Library collects materials to support undergraduate teaching and faculty research in Native Studies, and undergraduate and graduate teaching and research in other departments such as linguistics, geography, history, anthropology, and law. The major emphasis of the collection is placed on the Cree and Ojibwa languages and literature, Aboriginal peoples and the law, and the history, art and culture of the Aboriginal peoples of North America. A significant part of the collection consists of publications issued by the Smithsonian Institution and other major American museums dating back to the 1870s. The Elizabeth Dafoe Library collects all publications related to Aboriginal peoples put out by the major university presses.

Multicultural Education Resource Collection at the Department of Education

The Instructional Resources Unit Library has a significant collection of materials in the areas of multicultural education, anti-racist education and human rights. Part of this collection includes resources about Aboriginal peoples, together with some materials in the Cree and Ojibwa languages.

Other sources of materials on First Nations peoples include the Provincial Archives of Manitoba, the Hudson Bay Company Archives, the Archives of the Archdiocese of St. Boniface and of the St. Boniface Historical Society and the United Church Archives. Both Brandon University and the University of Winnipeg have extensive collections regarding First Nations peoples.

With contributions from Violet Chalmers, Ralph Abramson, Naomi Lloyd, Lorraine Freeman, Phyllis Hallett, Jim Blanchard and Diane Dwarka.

Collections et services en français au Manitoba

On retrouve au Manitoba bon nombre de bibliothèques qui offrent des collections, des programmes et des services en langue française; certaines d'entre elles sont bien connues, d'autres le sont moins. La Bibliothèque publique de Winnipeg, la bibliothèque du Collège universitaire de Saint-Boniface, la Direction des res-sources éducatives françaises du Manitoba et l'Association des municipalités bilingues du Manitoba mettent toutes à la disposition de leurs divers publics des collections de matériel français.

Collège universitaire de Saint-Boniface

Bibliothèque publique de Winnipeg

La Bibliothèque de Saint-Boniface est la principale ressource du réseau des bibliothèques publiques de Winnipeg en matière de services et de collections d'ouvrages en français. La succurale de Saint-Boniface fournit un service d'information et une collection de référence, un service de programmation ainsi qu'un service bilingue d'aide aux lecteurs qui se présentent en personne ou qui utilisent le téléphone.

Le service aux adultes offre l'accès à une collection de plus de 60 000 livres traitant d'une grande variété de sujets. On y retrouve des romans historiques et policiers, des oeuvres de science fiction, des biographies ainsi que les titres les plus récents d'éditeurs manitobains, canadiens et européens; une vaste collection de revues et de journaux canadiens et européens; une collection populaire de documents généalogiques; et des publications gouvernementales, y compris *la Gazette du Manitoba, la Gazette du Canada* et les publications de Statistique Canada.

Le service aux enfants propose aux lecteurs débutants des trousses, des revues, des romans, des documentaires, des livres d'images et même des jouets. La programmation à l'intention des enfants, qui s'étend sur l'année entière, comprend l'Heure du conte pour les enfants âgés de 3 à 5 ans, ainsi que des activités saisonnières et un programme estival de lecture pour les enfants d'âge scolaire.

La succursale de Saint-Boniface propose également une collection de vidéocassettes françaises qui comprend des longs métrages, des documentaires, des films d'instruction et de voyage, ainsi que des productions de l'Office national du film. On peut aussi se procurer des cassettes et des disques compacts de musique, des partitions musicales, des bandes d'apprentissages des langues et des livres sur cassette. La bibliothèque comprend une aire de visionnement et une centre d'écoute.

Les personnes retenues à la maison peuvent prendre des dispositions pour que le personnel de la bibliothèque choisisse des livres pour elles sur une base régulière. Des bénévoles s'occupent de les livrer à domicile. On offre également du matériel et des services adaptés aux malvoyants.

La bibliothèque loue des salles de réunion (d'une capacité de 12 à 60 personnes) et du matériel tel que des magnétoscopes et des projecteurs de films et de diapositives.

Collège universitaire de Saint-Boniface

La bibliothèque Alfred-Monnin du Collège de Saint-Boniface s'affiche aujourd'hui comme la plus grande bibliothèque académique de langue française à l'ouest des Grands Lacs. La bibliothèque du CUSB est avant tout une bibliothèque d'enseignement dont la fonction principale est de fournir à la clientèle étudiante et aux membres des facultés les ressources documentaires et les services connexes qui appuient les programmes d'études du Collège.

La bibliothèque du Collège possède une collection d'environ 100 000 monographies, est abonnée à quelques 485 périodiques et journaux et possède des collections sur microforms ainsi que des documents audiovisuels et sur disques compacts. La collection de la bibliothèque est à grande majorité en langue française, mais comprend aussi de nombreux textes en anglais. Depuis quelques années, des documents en espagnol y ont été ajoutés.

Le contrat d'affiliation du Collège permet aux étudiants universitaires l'accès à tous les services disponibles du réseau des bibliothèques de l'Université du Manitoba. En plus, des ententes de privilèges réciproques sont en vigueur avec les autres universités et collèges locaux ainsi que les bibliothèques membres de l'ABCDEF Canada.

Direction des ressources éducatives françaises du Manitoba

La Direction des ressources éducatives françaises (DREF) a le mandat de mettre en oeuvre la mission d'Éducation et Formation professionnelle Manitoba. La bibliothèque, qui compte près de 46 000 documents (livres, affiches, trousses multimédia, discs compact, cartes, cassettes, vidéocassettes, CD-ROM et films fixes), a pour but premier la diffusion de matériel auprès de 5 000 usagers. Plus précisément, elle fournit des ressources pédagogiques et des services aux éducateurs de la maternelle au secondaire 4 des écoles franco-manitobaines, des écoles d'immersion française et des écoles offrant des programmes de français de base. La bibliothèque dessert également le personnel du ministère, les conseillers pédagogiques, les professeurs et les enseignants en formation à l'Institut pédagogique au Collège universitaire de Saint-Boniface, la Faculté d'éducation de l'Université du Manitoba ainsi que d'autres intervenants du réseau scolaire. La Direction offre également aux écoles de la province certains documents qui ne sont pas disponibles sur le marché, ainsi que des services de polycopie de documents audiovisuels pour lesquels elle obtient les droits de reproduction. De plus, la Direction enregistre des émissions éducatives en langue française qui sont diffusées sur TV5, RDI et CPAC afin de les rendre disponibles aux écoles n'ayant pas l'accès au cable. La Direction offre aussi de deux médiabus aux écoles en régions éloignées.

Enfin, la bibliothèque de la DREF possède un centre de prévisionnement, où les conseillers pédagogiques et enseignants en formation peuvent évaluer des logiciels et CD-ROM éducatifs avant d'en faire l'achat.

Fédération des municipalités bilingues du Manitoba

La Fédération des municipalités bilingues du Manitoba, qui fait partie des services de bibliothèques publiques du Manitoba, regroupe des bibliothèques qui ont été établies dans les municipalités suivants: Montcalm (St-Jean-Baptiste, Letellier et St-Joseph), Ritchot (St-Adolphe, Île-des-Chênes et Ste-Agathe), La Broquerie, Ste-Anne, Notre-Dame-de-Lourdes, St-Léon, St-Claude et de Salaberry (St-Pierre et de Salaberry). La fédération compte parmi ses ressources la collection complète des films de l'Office national du film ainsi que des collections en langue française.

Bruno LeGal NDLR: L'auteur remercie Marcel Boulet e Doris Lemoine de leurs contributions à la rédaction de cet article.

Multicultural Collections

Manitoba's libraries, historical societies and archives contain extensive collections that document the heritage and culture of the many ethnic groups that have settled this province.

The Icelandic Collection at the University of Manitoba

Unique in Canadian university libraries, the Icelandic Collection located in the Elizabeth Dafoe Library contains nearly 26,000 volumes. It is the largest collection of Icelandic materials in Canada and the second largest such collection in North America. The Collection is celebrating its 60th anniversary in 1998.

Immigrants who came to Canada from Iceland late in the 19th Century brought with them thousands of precious books that have since found their way into the Icelandic Collection. The nucleus of the collection was the Arnljotur Bjornsson Olson library of about 1,300 volumes, which was presented to the University of Manitoba by Mr. Olson of Gimli, Manitoba, in May 1936. The future of the collection was assured in 1939 when the government of Iceland designated the collection as an official depository of all Icelandic publications. This continued in varying degrees until 1978 when the collection was redesignated as a selective depository. It currently receives, at no charge, a limited number of the more important publications to come of out Iceland each year.

Meanwhile, the University of Manitoba Libraries, recognizing the collection's value and research potential, assumed the responsibility for funding the collection, so that it might continue to receive most books, periodicals and newspapers published in Iceland annually.

The collection includes books, periodicals, newspapers, manuscripts, microfilms and audiovisual materials. Icelandic is the primary language of the collection. Selected items in Danish, Norwegian and Swedish are included, together with translations from these languages into English. Geographically, the collection covers mainly Iceland, but also Scandinavia, Greenland, the Faroe Islands and the Arctic, and acquires available material by and about Icelanders in North America.

Among the prized possessions of the collection are the personal libraries of two of the Icelandic-Canadian community's foremost poets, Stephan G. Stephansson and Guttomur J. Guttormsson.

The Icelandic Collection is located on the third floor of the Elizabeth Dafoe Library. Service is available from Monday to Friday, 9:00 a.m. to 5:00 p.m.

The Slavic Collection at the University of Manitoba

The Slavic Collection is a separate language collection of over 56,000 volumes of books, periodicals, newspapers and microforms. It is located on the third floor of the Elizabeth Dafoe Library at the University of Manitoba. The collection, one of the best in Canada, contains material on a wide range of subjects, mainly in the humanities and the social sciences. Most material is in Russian, Ukrainian and Polish, although all 14 Slavic languages are represented.

The Slavic Collection supports courses and research in the Department of Slavic Studies, the Centre for Ukrainian Canadian Studies, Soviet and East European Studies and other departments. Materials are also used by multilingual members of the university community and general public.

The majority of the catalogued materials are listed in BISON, the Library's online catalogue. BISON lists Cyrillic titles in the Latin alphabet, using the Library of Congress transliteration system. Materials located in the Slavic Collection are distinguished by the prefix Slav in the call number.

Periodicals, reference materials, rare books and fragile books do not circulate. Any other items in the collection may be borrowed for 60 days at the circulation counter on the main floor of the Library.

The staff who manage the Slavic Collection will provide assistance in locating materials.

The Shastri Indo-Canadian Institute Collection at the University of Manitoba

The Shastri Indo-Canadian Institute (SICI) is a unique educational enterprise that promotes understanding between India and Canada, mainly through facilitating academic activities. The Institute funds research, links institutions in the two countries, and organizes seminars and conferences. It is named after Lal Bahadur Shastri, Prime Minister of India from 1964 to 1966, and a distinguished mediator and statesman.

The University of Manitoba joined the Shastri Indo-Canadian Institute in 1969, and became a member of its Library Programme in 1973. Within Manitoba, there are few collections on India or South Asia. The collection in the Elizabeth Dafoe Library, acquired through the Shastri Indo-Canadian Institute, supports an interdisciplinary undergraduate major and minor program in Asian Studies. Material acquired through the Institute is restricted to titles published and available in India through rupee funds given by the Indian Ministry of Education.

The collection of South Asian/Indian material in the Elizabeth Dafoe Library is predominantly in the subject areas covered by Asian Studies and interdisciplinary courses. Material in the collection is predominately in English, Sanskrit and Hindi, with selected titles in Urdu. The geographical focus is the Indian subcontinent, South Asia, Pakistan, Bangladesh, Nepal and Tibet. Current titles predominate, with selected titles in reprint from 1847. The chronological focus of the collection is the Colonial period after 1847, the 20th Century and post-independence India. Monographs, journals and serial publications from India are included with the occasional non-print materials, such as microforms and music tapes.

The Centre for Mennonite Brethren Studies

Canadian Mennonite Brethren have long recognized the need to collect and preserve valuable historical records in order to continue to nurture the faith and identity of the church. It was not until the 1960s, however, that Herbert Giesbrecht began to collect and preserve the materials in a more systematic way. In 1969, the Canadian Conference formally established an archival centre, and by 1975 the Centre for Mennonite Brethren Studies was designated as one of three North American centres, each of which accepted specified responsibilities (the others were the Centres at Fresno, California and Hillsboro, Kansas). The facilities were initially inadequate, but in 1979 the Centre moved to its new facility which it still occupies at Concord College.

The Historical Committee of the Canadian Mennonite Brethren Conference Board of Communications is responsible for the ongoing operation of the Centre. The regular staff includes the Director and the Archivist. In addition, volunteers and student assistants make valuable contributions to the work of the Centre.

The Centre collects and preserves historical records, such as Canadian Mennonite Brethren conference records, including minutes, and correspondence of various boards, staff, congregations and institutions; personal papers of influential leaders; periodicals, audio and video tapes, photographs, maps and other media relating to Mennonite history and theology; and genealogical records pertaining to Mennonite Brethren members.

It develops and maintains special collections, such as the John A. Toews Historical Collection (consisting of some 4,000 published volumes) relating to Mennonite Brethren history and the Ben and Esther Horch Music Collection (comprised of about 1,000 hymnals and other music materials). Other special collections include the Katie Peters Genealogical Collection, photo collections and a large collection of periodicals and journals.

Staff members assist individuals engaged in research and writing family and congregational histories, theses and dissertations. The Centre publishes the *Mennonite Historian* in cooperation with the Mennonite Heritage Centre.

The Jewish Historical Society of Western Canada

The Jewish Historical Society of Western Canada is dedicated to recording the history and culture of the Jewish people of the Western Canada. In addition to developing the collection, the Society presents public lectures and issues publications on topics of Jewish interest. The Genealogical Institute assists with research into family roots. The Society's archives are open to everyone.

Founded in May 1968, the Society functions as the standing committee on history, research and archives of the Canadian Jewish Congress, Manitoba region and gathers, records, preserves and presents the history and the religious and cultural heritage of the Jewish People of Western Canada. To this end, the Society collects documents, photographs and religious and community memorabilia, and engages in a continuous oral history program. To date, over 550 interviews have been completed.

The research room, located in the Asper Jewish Community Campus in Winnipeg, contains a comprehensive selection of books pertaining to the history of the Jewish people in Western Canada, as well as several important periodicals and encyclopedias. Holdings include back issues of local Jewish newspapers beginning in 1911, when they were first published. Indexes to the archival holdings, oral history tapes, a picture collection, and the vertical file of miscellaneous materials and clippings are available. There are also many reference works, books, and periodicals of specific interest to genealogists.

One of the major resources the Society has developed is the newspaper database, a searchable computerized index of information taken from the local Yiddish and Anglo-Jewish press from 1911 to the present. With well over 40,000 categorized entries, this database has proved to be an invaluable source for genealogy and family histories.

The archival collection has grown to over 4,600 photographs, more than 550 taped interviews with summary transcripts, and many hundreds of manuscripts and other documents.

Ukrainian Cultural and Education Centre Library

The colourful personality and lively spirit of the Ukrainian people is well represented in the Library of the Ukrainian Cultural and Educational Centre, located at 184 Alexander Avenue East. The Library is a little-known gem located in the heart of Winnipeg. Its contents include over 40,000 volumes, 10,000 periodicals, and 350 Ukrainian newspapers from North and South America, Europe and Australia. Established in 1945, the Library has been a centre, not only for scholars, but for anyone with an interest in anything Ukrainian. Holdings include works on Ukrainian history, culture, ethnography, art, music, literature, and Ukrainians in Diaspora. About sixty percent of the Library's holdings are in the Ukrainian language, although English, French, German and Italian titles are also available. The many volumes of Ukrainian titles translated into English provide an English-speaking audience with a glimpse of the various components of Ukrainian life.

Private collections of prominent Ukrainian community figures such as Alexander Koshetz and Dr. Paul Macenko have been deposited in the library.

Perhaps one of the Centre's most precious assets is the children's collection. Composed of numerous volumes by authors from Ukraine and North America, the children's collection provides an added sparkle to the vast array of valuable heirlooms.

Also located in the Library is the rare book collection. The oldest volume is a copy of the *Nomocanon (Book of Church Canons)*, in Old Church Slavonic, dating from 1624. Other rare books include works on history, religion and classical Ukrainian literature. The works are of special interest to those studying linguistics and the development and metamorphosis of the Ukrainian language.

The vertical file collection includes information on topics such as ceremonial breads, costumes, Christmas and Easter traditions, dancing and weddings, Chernobyl and the Great Famine of 1932–33. The Library relies heavily upon the generous support of the public for its acquisitions. Professional staff is available to assist with reference requests, and with recommendations of materials for research purposes.

With contributions from Sigrid Johnson, Nevia Koscevic, Bob Lincoln, Abe Dueck, Bonnie Tregobov and Larissa Tulchinsky.

Chapter Seven

Towards the Virtual Library: The Future and Manitoba's Libraries

Introduction

The convergence of computer and communications technologies has revolutionized the way libraries do business and has provided library users with access to unprecedented amounts of information, much of it available only in electronic formats. The virtual or networked library allows libraries to supplement their on-site collections with electronic access to other libraries' catalogues and to online databases generated anywhere in the world. The precursor to the networked library is the system of interlibrary loans by which libraries are able to borrow from other libraries materials not held in their own collections.

  The library and information profession continues to address the issue of resource sharing within Manitoba in the context of newly-available technolgies, and in relation to pressures such as shrinking budgets and increased user demands. Resource sharing describes the following kinds of activities: arrangements for reciprocal borrowing, document delivery and interlibrary loan, and electronic networking and interlibrary communications. Examples of these services described in this chapter include the Library Express Service coordinated by the Manitoba Library Consortium, Inc., the Manitoba Public Libraries Information Network (MAPLIN), and the Virtual University Library of the Council of Prairie and Pacific Universities (COPPUL).

  This chapter begins with profiles of Canada's National Library and the national science library known as CISTI, the Canada Institute for Scientific and Technical Information. The resources of these world-class institutions are available to citizens of Manitoba through the system of interlibrary loans offered by public, academic and special libraries.

  Looking towards the twenty-first century, the Winnipeg Public Library has begun planning for the Millennium Library which is a proposed expansion to the Centennial Library, opened in 1977 in downtown Winnipeg. This chapter concludes with an overview of the project and describes the work of the newly-created Winnipeg Library Foundation, Inc. which will be raising funds for the expanded library facility.

The National Library of Canada

The National Library of Canada is a federal institution located in Ottawa, established by Parliament in 1953, whose main role is to acquire, preserve and promote the published heritage of Canada for all Canadians, both now and in the years to come. The most comprehensive collection of Canadiana in the world— books, periodicals, sound recordings, manuscripts, and electronic formats—can be found at the National Library.

Interlibrary Loan and Location Service
The National Library plays a major role in encouraging the development of library resources and services throughout the country, and facilitating resource sharing among Canadian libraries as outlined in the National Library Act. It is the National Library of Canada's policy to respond to a request for material either by lending a copy of the requested item, providing a photocopy, or giving a list of other libraries from which the item might be obtained. The service is provided for specific titles, not for subject requests, and is offered to libraries or similar organizations. With a few exceptions such as rare books, manuscripts, reference materials and most sound recordings, the National Library will arrange to lend material to any library in the country or the world.

The National Research Council's Canada Institute for Scientific and Technical Information (CISTI)

The National Research Council is an agency of the Government of Canada whose mission is to support national science and engineering activities, perform and stimulate investment in research and development, and develop vital expertise and knowledge. CISTI began over 75 years ago as the Library of the National Research Council of Canada, the leading agency for R&D in Canada. The NCR Library became the National Science Library in 1957. The change to the Canada Institute for Scientific and Technical Information came in 1974 to reflect the wide scope of services provided and the increasing role in the development of electronic information products and services for the scientific and technical community. CISTI is located in the J.E. Brown Building, Montreal Road, Ottawa.

CISTI is one of the world's major sources for information in all areas of science, technology, engineering and medicine. The collection consists of more than 54,000 serial titles, 700,000 books, conference proceedings and technical reports and over two million technical reports on microfiche. Through its Web-based catalogue, CISTI provides direct links to many scholarly electronic journals.

Document Delivery
CISTI offers a sophisticated document delivery service to provide clients with access to its own collections and to those of its partners, the Canadian Agriculture Library, the British Library Document Supply Centre, located in Boston Spa,

England, and the Science and Technology Information Centre in Tapei, China. As part of its Global Supply Service, CISTI will supply a document in any subject and in any format from anywhere in the world. CISTI's automated document delivery system, IntelliDoc, uses a Novell-based network to produce copies of requested document and scanners generate image files that are sent electronically via Ariel, Fax or Internet (FTP).

The Manitoba Library Consortium, Inc.

The Manitoba Library Consortium, Inc. is an incorporated non-profit organization designed to plan and manage cooperatively projects and activities which will provide the citizens of Manitoba with faster and more equitable access to the library/information resources of the province. The purpose of the Consortium is to facilitate effective and efficient resource sharing among libraries in Manitoba in order to strengthen the library services provided to the residents of the province. Over 30 libraries have membership in the organization.

Library Express
Library Express is a project of the Consortium that provides the clients of participating member libraries with the timely delivery of materials and information available within the City of Winnipeg. Under the terms of the project, requests for materials are handled on a priority basis, with the requested item, if available, being shipped within 48 hours. The Library Express service delivers books, microfilm, audiovisuals and articles. Fax or other electronic delivery methods are also used as part of the service. Currently, eight libraries in Winnipeg are part of the regularly scheduled service; other participating libraries use the service on a call-in basis.

Licensing of Electronic Information Resources
MLCI has recently negotiated a licence with EBSCO Publishing Co. to provide access to online materials for member libraries. The agreement allows participating libraries to offer full-text journal articles from five databases: Academic Search FullTEXT Elite, Master FILE FullTEXT 1500, Canadian MAS FullTEXT Elite, Middle Search Plus and Primary Search.

Academic Search FullTEXT Elite provides full-text for more than 1,000 journals, with indexing and summaries for more than 3,200 journals. Canadian MAS FullTEXT Elite provides full-text for more than 150 journals, with indexing and summaries for more than 430 general interest and research periodicals. Participating members include three public library systems, two university libraries, three community college libraries, Public Library Services, the Legislative Library, the Industrial Technology Centre and seventy-one schools and resource centres in eleven school divisions.

The benefits of such a license include:
—by using the Internet, library clients gain timely access to the full-text of copyrighted journal articles;

—the information is up-to-date; and,
—libraries acting together can offer users more content than any single institution could afford.

The Consortium will continue to seek out licensing opportunities which will provide equitable, expanded and cost-effective access to information resources for the citizens of Manitoba.

MAPLIN: Manitoba Public Libraries Information Network

Libraries around the world have been using computers to handle routine procedures for several decades. Manitoba's library community was quick to recognize the benefits of using computers to streamline repetitive and labor-intensive operations such as library cataloguing. MAPLIN, a made-in-Manitoba library computer catalogue application has been evolving over the past decade.

For many years Public Library Services had been cataloguing its own material and much of the material owned by the rural libraries in order to create a union catalogue, that is, a centralized, combined catalogue listing holdings of several libraries. One of the main purposes of this union catalogue was to facilitate interlibrary lending, primarily among rural libraries.

In 1988, after considerable research and planning, Manitoba Public Library Services Branch began using computers and a library computer cataloguing standard known as MARC (Machine Readable Cataloguing) to catalogue its own collection and the non-fiction collections of rural and Northern libraries that subscribed to the Branch's cataloguing service.

Midway through the 1990s, a major investment in computer technology both at the Branch and throughout rural and Northern libraries brought Manitoba's public library system closer to realizing the full potential of library computer applications. The result was that by 1998, nearly all of the rural and Northern libraries had been fully automated and their card catalogues discarded, as had the central card catalogue created and maintained by Public Library Services. Its electronic replacement is called MAPLIN.

MAPLIN contains records of the holdings of all the rural and Northern public libraries, all of Public Library Services' central collection and a major portion of the Manitoba Legislative Library's holdings. MAPLIN is accessible through the World Wide Web. Libraries and individuals with Internet access can now search this electronic database from locations far removed from the UNIX computer that holds the records.

MAPLIN is a major tool that facilitates interlibrary loan and provides the foundation for a "one library" concept among the more than 50 public library systems in the province.

MAPLIN has emerged as a leading illustration of the advanced technology now in use in libraries around the world. It also demonstrates how computer technology can reduce the barriers of distance and isolation that are often cited as an issue by many rural and Northern Manitoba communities. When a library patron in Flin Flon needs to wait only a few days to receive a book from the library in Morris, one can easily see how beneficial MAPLIN is to all Manitobans.

The Council of Prairie and Pacific University Libraries (COPPUL)

The Council of Prairie and Pacific University Libraries is a consortium of 15 university libraries in Western Canada, established in 1968 at the request of the Council of Western Canadian University Presidents. Through its established resource-sharing agreements and cooperative projects, COPPUL provides a powerful example of inter-university and interprovincial cooperation in higher education. Its original purpose of "resource sharing" remains to this day, although that resource sharing is conducted in a very different environment: one of technological sophistication, fiscal restraint, and "let's make a deal" potential.

The primary focus of COPPUL libraries is to provide the information infrastructure and research needs of faculty and students, while building an information base that serves as an underpinning of knowledge-based economic development throughout Western Canada.

During the past two decades of library automation, the focus has been on the automation of bibliographic and citation information. Collectively, libraries have substantially improved access to their collections by implementing online catalogues, converting the data from catalogue cards into electronic format, and by making citation and abstract databases available either in CD-ROM format or online. The challenge of the 1990s and into the 21st century is not only the provision of bibliographic information electronically, but also the provision to the desktop of full-text information in an electronic format. This challenge is not limited to textual data, but also includes providing graphic images, numerical databases, sound and moving images.

Virtual Western Canada University Library

Recent trends in society, technology, education and libraries have led COPPUL to propose and develop the Virtual Western Canada University Library as both a response and a solution to the challenges posed by these trends. The creation of a virtual library is not unique to COPPUL, but is becoming increasingly recognized as a viable strategy to provide scholars with a single, user-friendly point of entry into a vast array of information. The virtual library builds on several important initiatives that the COPPUL libraries have taken in the last few years.

As a secondary benefit, this virtual library has the potential to be expanded to reach all citizens of Western Canada, ensuring quality of access to information, and meeting provincial and national government initiatives towards building an information infrastructure to support and promote knowledge-based economic activity. The intent is to deliver information to people as efficiently as possible in order to enable the lifelong learning essential to support economic development in the

Information Age, and to assist in the creation of an informed citizenry.

As of Fall 1998, the development of the virtual library is well underway, and, when fully-implemented, will provide a single system of easy-to-understand menus, a powerful search mechanism, and other design features that users can easily follow as they seek information. Users are now able to search for their material without regard to its location, seamlessly moving through the Internet to the appropriate site of the information. By means of an electronic request, the necessary information is delivered to the user via the library.

The Winnipeg Public Library's Millennium Library Project

In an effort to remain relevant to the community it serves and to chart a course for the future, the Winnipeg Public Library recently commissioned several reports and studies that examine its programs and services. These studies have articulated the Library's strategic vision for the future and incorporate the views of the community at large, members of City Council and staff of the Winnipeg Public Library.

Part of the impetus for this re-examination comes from the approaching millennium. With its accompanying technological, demographic and socio-economic shifts, the millennium will have a major impact on both the Centennial Library— which is the central library in the Winnipeg system—and on the neighbourhood branches.

When the Centennial Library opened in March 1977, the tremendous increase in the use of materials and services and the increased size of the collection were not anticipated. Nor could the technological developments that have revolutionized library operations have been foreseen. The Centennial Library is the most heavily used library branch in the library system, with over twenty-one million visits since its opening 21 years ago. Over one third of Winnipeg Public Library's 300,000 card holders borrow from the Centennial Library which houses the system's largest collection of materials and offers the most extensive reference and information service.

As part of its long-term planning process, the City of Winnipeg solicited proposals from library consultants in December 1996 for a planning study of the Winnipeg Centennial Library. The library consultants were asked to reassess and consolidate previous planning efforts and to evaluate the effectiveness of the current services and systems. They were also asked to make recommendations concerning Centennial Library's future needs and to detail a facility program that would meet the challenges facing libraries in the twenty-first century.

In March 1997, the RPG Partnership, a firm specializing in library consulting, was selected by the City of Winnipeg to undertake the planning study. RPG conducted visioning exercises with the Winnipeg Public Library Board, the Winnipeg Library Foundation, community representatives and Library staff. RPG produced a document called *Planning Parameters* that included a review of current systems at the branch level, including operations, delivery of services, and technical infrastructure, and outlined recommendations concerning the library's future needs. RPG also developed *A Facility Program* that detailed specific functional, operational and spatial requirements for an expanded library. The City of Winnipeg's Civic Buildings Department carried out an existing building assessment that evaluated the current condition and the constraints and opportunities of the Centennial Library building, located at 251 Donald Street. RPG's *Concept Plan* provided detailed capital cost information and illustrated how the proposed Millennium Library Square could be developed.

In its final report, the RPG Partnership observed that "the City of Winnipeg deserves a central library which enhances the city's quality of life and enriches the vitality of the community. The overall recommendation is to transform the existing Centennial Library into a world-class information centre and meeting place, reflective of Winnipeg's unique cultural identity and diversity. The rejuvenated library should be the heart of the library's branch network. The Centennial Library of the future will provide opportunities for individuals, a sense of community for the city and economic vitality for the region."

RPG concluded that the present Centennial Library was grossly inadequate to meet the needs of a community of Winnipeg's size in the twenty-first century. They argued that the Centennial Library should be larger, better equipped, better staffed and better organized to effectively and efficiently meet the needs of its numerous stakeholders, while continuing to build on its historical role as an intellectual and cultural cornerstone of the community. The expanded Centennial Library should facilitate the rapid and cost-effective exchange of information and provide broad-based access to information technology and lifelong learning opportunities. RPG also recommended that the Canada/Manitoba Business Service Centre be re-located to the expanded Centennial Library.

RPG recommended that the current floor space be doubled to 259,000 sq. ft. to accommodate both a substantial increase in materials as well as a larger number of technology workstations. The additional space would also provide for expanded public accommodation in the form of additional seating and meeting/learning spaces.

At the same time as the Winnipeg Public Library was undertaking its examination of the Centennial Library, the Winnipeg Public Library Board was working to establish the Winnipeg Library Foundation Inc. The impetus for this initiative came from the "Forward Thinking Process" carried out in 1996. The authors of the resulting report, *Winnipeg Public Library Plan, 1996–2000*, observed that the Winnipeg Public Library was in need of additional sources of funding to support and enhance its services and collections in order to meet the changing needs of its clientele.

The Winnipeg Library Foundation Inc., a non-profit organization, was incorporated in 1997 to develop and manage fundraising campaigns on behalf of Winnipeg Public Library. It is one of the first foundations of its kind in Canada. The mandate of the Foundation, working in collaboration with library staff, is to provide the people of Winnipeg with a leading edge public library system. Monies raised by the Foundation will be used to fund new technology, special projects, collection development and capital projects, but not ongoing operating expenses.

The Rt. Hon. Edward Schreyer is the honorary chairman of the Foundation.

Mrs. Dee Buchwald and Mr. Abe Anhang serve as co-chairs. Many prominent Winnipeggers and business people are serving as directors.

With the completion of the RPG report, the Library Department had a project worthy of the Foundation's efforts. Following a series of focus groups and presentations, the Library Foundation became convinced that their first fundraising endeavour should be the revitalization and expansion of the Centennial Library. The Foundation is committed to raising $25 million to cover the costs of the proposed Millennium Library as outlined in the RPG report. A significant portion of the funding will come from the private sector and the three levels of government.

The Foundation has been very active since it was established in 1997. Meetings with the Library Department and the Library Board to assess the needs of the library and to set future goals are held on an ongoing basis. The Foundation commissioned Coopers & Lybrand to produce business plans for the Millennium project. A case study has been prepared for prospective donors. Finally, two feasibility studies have been conducted to determine the viability of raising the necessary private sector capital.

Architect's conception of the proposed Millennium Centre of Knowledge, (RPG Partnership, April 9, 1998)

With the completion of the feasibility studies, the Foundation is set to enter the next phase of the project, which is the hiring of a fundraiser. In the months ahead, the Library Services Division will be working closely with the Foundation to ensure that the Millennium Library becomes a reality.

The Foundation's future plans call for the establishment of an endowment fund to benefit other branches in the Winnipeg Public Library system, and to fund special projects proposed by the Library Services Division.

With contributions from Patricia Bozyk, Louise Shah, Hazel Fry, Rick Walker and Vera Andrysiak.

CHAPTER EIGHT

The Library and Information Profession

Schools educate people. Libraries work to keep them educated.
—Library Association of Alberta

People, not machines, facilities or equipment bring libraries to life, interpret collections, bring together user and library materials, and cope with change.
—*Canadian Library Association Strategic Plan* (1991)

Introduction

Today, there are very few sectors of the workplace where the acquisition, management and dissemination of information do not play a significant role. Information technology, that is, the application of computer and communications technologies to the management of information, has transformed many workplaces, including libraries and information centres.

The role of libraries has always been to connect people with information. The emergence of the Internet has not replaced the library: it has simply provided additional challenges and opportunities as libraries strive to fulfil their role. Job titles in the profession have changed to acknowledge the impact of the new technology on library operations. Yesterday's 'librarian' may today be known as an 'information specialist', 'information manager', or 'knowledge manager'.

This chapter will describe the skills and qualifications of the people working in libraries in Manitoba: librarians, library technicians, library assistants and library clerks, and describe the nature of work these skilled individuals perform in public, academic, school, and special libraries and information centres.

Functions Common to All Types of Libraries

The following functions are generally performed in all types of libraries: information technology has, or is in the process of, transforming all these functions. For example, libraries were one of the first organizations to undergo automation when their printed card catalogues were transformed into online bibliographic databases known as OPACs (online public access catalogues). Similarly, the wide-spread availability of national catalogues in electronic form has resulted in many libraries 'outsourcing' their cataloguing and classification functions to the private sector as a cost-saving measure:

1. Collection development involves the selection of materials to ensure that the library's collections are developed to meet the needs of library users in a timely and economical manner.
2. Acquisition is the process of purchasing materials for the library from publishers, booksellers and agents.
3. Cataloguing is the process of building the bibliographic database which contains records of the library materials, such as the title, author's name and call number.
4. Circulation refers to the library's lending services and includes registration of library members. Issuing, renewing and returning of library materials, overdues and fines handling, and processing of lost items on loan are all part of this service.
5. Reference and Information Services are one of the most important functions of a service-oriented library. Library staff provide value-added services to users through provision of personal reference assistance, including in-depth research investigation; indexing and abstracting of information content; compilation of booklists and bibliographies; and dissemination of information, including current awareness and alert services.
6. Interlibrary Loan and Document Delivery Services include processing of requests, locating documents, making copies of documents, and arranging for either the physical or electronic delivery of items. Libraries in Manitoba may contact other libraries across the world to obtain materials needed by their patrons.
7. Audiovisual and Multimedia Services and Internet Access. These services are important as they provide other dimensions of information presentation. The library has moved from reliance on one media (print) to add newer formats: audio, video, image, graphics, and electronic formats.
8. Promotion and User Education. Most libraries have an ongoing user education program to promote and encourage the use of library materials, facilities and information. Examples include library instruction programs, author talks, forums, workshops, storytelling to children and class visits by schools.

Classification of Library Personnel

To most people, anyone who works in a library is a librarian. However, libraries have different levels of employees. Although the titles may vary from library to library, there are primarily four classifications of library personnel:

1. Librarian/Information Specialist/Teacher-Librarian
2. Library Technician
3. Library Assistant
4. Library Clerk

A summary of the minimum educational qualifications for each level:

Position	Minimum Level of Education Required
Librarian/Information Specialist	Master's degree in Library Science (MLS) or Bachelor's degree in Library Science (BLS), from an American Library Association accredited program. Note: the BLS is no longer granted.
Teacher-Librarian	Bachelor's degree in Education, plus additional specialized courses in school librarianship. Must also possess a valid teacher's certificate. Some teacher-librarians also have an MLS.
Library Technician	Two-year diploma or one-year certificate (no longer offered) from community colleges or technical institutes. Programs should follow guidelines established by the Canadian Library Association.
Library Assistant	High school diploma. Some libraries may prefer or require a library technician diploma or certificate or Bachelor's degree in any discipline.
Library Clerk	No level of education required for part-time positions. For full-time positions, some libraries might require a high school diploma.

Profiles of Library and Information Professionals

Librarians and Information Specialists

Librarians and information specialists are graduates of post-graduate degree programs in library or information science. Librarians plan, develop and coordinate all aspects of library and information services. They are involved in the selection, acquisition and organization of materials (such as books, cassettes, magazines, audiovisual and computer software). They assist people in locating sources of information using online dataabases, CD-ROMs or the Internet, and provide instruction in research techniques and independent learning skills. Experienced librarians may obtain managerial positions which require administrative skills such as financial planning and human resource management. Library managers develop policies and ensure that they are implemented consistently and appropriately.

Additional information about librarians/information specialists working in public libraries, academic libraries, school libraries and special libraries and information centres can be found in Chapters One, Two, Three and Four, respectively.

Teacher-Librarians

Qualified teacher-librarians have a Bachelor of Education degree, together with supplementary course work in the field of school librarianship. The Faculty of Education at the University of Manitoba offers such courses. The School of Library & Information Studies at the University of Alberta offers school librarianship courses which may also lead to a specialized degree in library and information studies.

Teacher-librarians work as partners with classroom teachers in planning, teaching and evaluating instructional programs, and in promoting literacy among students. They also carry out a variety of administrative functions, such as collection development and supervision of support staff.

Library Technicians

Training and Qualifications
Library technicians are graduates of programs such as the Library and Information Technology Program offered by Red River College. In 1962, Red River College established the first library technician program in Canada.

Most library technician programs are two years in length and are available at community colleges or technical institutes. A high school diploma or equivalent is required for entry into the program which should be completed within seven years for those pursuing part-time studies.

The program inludes between fifty to sixty percent technical courses, such as cataloguing and classification, online database searching, word processing and business communication, and between forty to fifty percent academic courses such as children's literature and human behavior in organizations. Students are required to spend a minimum of five weeks in field placements in order to apply their skills in actual library settings. Through this post-secondary training, library technicians are prepared to perform the specialized support staff functions unique to the library and information services environment.

Nature of Work
Library technicians support professional librarians or teacher-librarians and perform duties requiring specialized library training, such as bibliographic verification, answering basic reference questions, or instructing library clientele in the use of the online public access catalogue, CD-ROM resources, or library equipment such as microfiche readers. Library technicians often supervise other staff members, including library technicians or library clerks. They may be responsible for a section or department within a library, or be fully responsible for a library within a school, private business or industry.

Library Assistants and Library Clerks

Training and Qualifications
Library assistants and clerks are usually high school graduates. Other educational

requirements vary with the employers and the position, but range from clerical courses to library technician certificates or university degrees.

Nature of Work
Library assistants and clerks work in various library settings. They participate in acquisitions and technical services in ordering, processing, and cataloguing materials. In the circulation department, they provide public service to patrons in charging out materials, and in sorting and shelving materials. Those classified at higher salary levels may supervise a branch or section, or provide readers' assistance, working under supervision of a librarian.

Further information about working in special types of libraries is available from the following library associations in Manitoba, and from the national organization, the Canadian Library Association.

With contributions from Jo Ann Brewster, Pat Routledge and Gerald R. Brown

Chapter Eight

The Library User

This chapter provides some answers to questions that librarians are often asked, and which, because of their education and experience, they are well-positioned to answer. The questions range from the very basic, "how can I obtain books that my local library does not have" to the more complex, "how can I go about setting up a library?" and "how can our community establish its own public library?"

The Internet has revolutionzed the way the average person can access information. Staff in libraries and information centres are also making use of this resource to supplement their print, audiovisual and other electronic resources. This chapter provides guidelines for evaluating sources of information located on the Internet; gives ordering information for a primer for parents who are dealing with Internet access issues with regard to young children; and points to an excellent Web-based tutorial for individuals who want to learn how to navigate through the resources available on the World Wide Web.

The chapter concludes with some guidelines for parents who want to know what resources and services are available through the public library to help them develop their children's interest in reading and books.

How can I obtain resources that are not available in my local library?

You should inquire about the interlibrary loan service available through the public library system. Interlibrary loan is the process by whch another library requests materials from, or supplies materials to, another library. Materials in all formats may be requested; however, it is the supplying library that determines whether the material can be provided.

How do I go about setting up a library?

It is not as easy as it might seem to set up a library. Often the collection you are trying to organize is specialized and requires subject expertise. Today, libraries contain a wide variety of materials in audiovisual and electronic formats, not just books and magazines. Management of such a diverse collection may require technical expertise.

As a starting point, contact one of the professional library associations listed in Appendix 1. These associations will provide you with contacts in your area who will be able to provide you with help and advice. Many professional librarians now work on a freelancer basis to set up libraries and information centres on a fee-for-service basis.

You could also check the catalogue in your local library for books on library administration. A wide range of books is available on this topic, many of them published by library associations. Another source of information is publishers' catalogues, many of which are available on the Internet.

Some useful titles, aimed largely at special libraries and information centres, are:

Creating an Information Service by Sylvia P. Webb. 3rd edition. London, UK: Aslib, 1966.

Handbook of Special Librarianship and Information Work edited by Alison Scammed, 7th edition. London, UK: Aslib, 1997.

Managing Information Services: An Integrated Approach by Jo Bryson. Aldershot, UK: Gower, 1997.

New Steps to Service: A Common-Sense Guide to Managing School Library Media Programs by Ann M. Wasman. Chicago: American Library Association, 1998.

Special Libraries: A Guide for Management, 4th edition. Washington, DC: Special Libraries Association, 1997.

How can our community set up a public library service in our town?

Louise Shah, a former consultant at Manitoba's Public Library Services Branch describes the procedure for establishment of a tax-supported public library: In Manitoba, library establishment is governed by the Public Libraries Act.

> This Act is administered by the Public Library Services Branch of Manitoba Culture, Heritage and Citizenship, located in Brandon. The first step in any effort to establish library service should be a toll free phone call to Public Library Services. The Branch's consulting team can assist citizen groups and councils in the establishment process. Phone 1-800-252-9998 or (204) 726-6590.

> The road to establishment is often a long one, requiring sustained grass roots organization and careful economic and demographic analysis. Knowledge of the specific requirements and procedures contained in the Public Libraries Act and its regulations should be ascertained early in the process. However, patience and a talent for consensus building and persuasion are, by far, the most crucial prerequisites in any attempt to establish. Therefore, the second step in a successful establishment drive will be to assemble a core of dedicated community leaders who are committed to the idea and who have both the time and a flair for community

development work.

Public libraries are created through the passage of municipal bylaws, which, once passed require municipal governments to fund the library on an annual basis. In the end, no establishment drive will be successful unless the municipal council is convinced municipal property owners are willing to pay more taxes. In many areas of the province, population decline and a restrained economic climate discourage further public expenditure. In areas around Winnipeg, where population growth has been substantial in recent years, municipal governments have had to grapple with increased demand for basic services such as water and sewer, fire protection and municipal road maintenance. A request for public library service will be weighted within this context.

Often a neighbouring library board will make the first bid at a municipal council meeting, hoping to convince the council to join the library. However, as with any elected body, the council's own electorate, the municipal ratepayers, will usually receive a more sympathetic hearing than a delegation from outside the municipality. Therefore, a small nucleus of citizens from the municipality itself, working in close cooperation with Public Library Services (and with a neighbouring library, if a regional library is envisaged) has the best chance in creating a movement that leads to establishment. The core group of citizens often most interested in seeing library establishment through to fruition may be the library's non-resident members from the municipality in question. Library boards wishing to expand municipal membership are well advised to begin by talking to this group of people. Patrons of Public Library Services books-by-mail service could also be key allies, especially if they are made aware that the material they now have access to will still be available to them and much more in addition.

Once an organizing group is assembled, research begins. A meeting with a Public Library Services consultant is a good place to start. The legal and financial requirements and strategies for gaining support from municipal ratepayers are among the first things that need to be discussed. If the ultimate aim is to join an existing library system, certain members of the existing library board must be involved in planning any further strategy.

The development of two or three alternative models for library service should be undertaken. For example, both of the two options outlined in the Public Libraries Act, that of joining an existing system or developing a stand alone municipal library, should be seriously explored. Areas where compromises or reciprocal agreements between municipal authorities or between neighbouring libraries might be beneficial, need to be identified. Examples from other library systems in the province should be investigated. If joining an existing library is the favoured approach, the question of whether and where to have a branch library needs to be explored.

A careful analysis of the cost of delivering service to the municipality needs to be made. Regulations require that municipalities establishing for the fist time must contribute no less than $3.75 per capita. An existing library board, wishing to bring in another municipal member, may consider this too low. On the other hand, the minimum per capita contribution required to deliver the service may be more than the municipal ratepayers are comfortable with. Some compromise may be required. Arguments justifying the rates need to be developed to overcome taxpayer resistance. Public Library Services can also help with both the cost analysis and the 'winning' arguments. The Branch can also assist with demographic and other types of data.

The core organizing group needs to solicit the support of local service clubs, school boards and other community groups. If these groups can be approached and brought on side, organizers will not only have the strength of numbers behind them, but may also tap into sources of funding and partnerships.

At some point, the municipal council needs to be informed of the organizers' intentions. To receive a sympathetic ear from the council, the committee must demonstrate it has solid support from a wide cross section of the community. Good research and a clear understanding of all potential issues that may interfere with the intended goal are required to build that support.

In any grass roots movement, persuasion is always better than confrontation. Councils will appreciate being informed as the movement gains steam; however, that is no guarantee that they will take the petition seriously if the committee cannot demonstrate it has wide support and has done careful research.

Throughout the province there are many examples of libraries that started in modest surroundings with the hard work of many volunteers. After a few years councils are convinced that the service offered is worth the expenditure. Increased levies and newer, expanded facilities often result.

Grass roots organizers must bear in mind that library service will continue to grow and develop after bylaws are in place, and should perhaps, be ready to accept small beginnings as the first of many steps to come. In any case, any effort toward community development, which is what library establishment would be, can take many years to bear fruit. No one should be discouraged if first efforts do not bring about immediate results.

Can you recommend a good source for learning how to navigate through the wealth of resources available on the Internet?

An excellent Web-based tutorial is located at:
(http://lib.berkeley.edu/TeachingLib/Guides/Internet/FindInfo.htm)

Can you provide some guidelines for parents whose children want to have access to the Internet?

The Canadian Library Association has recently published a pamphlet entitled *Have a Safe Trip! A Parent's Guide to Safety on the Internet* (1998). This pamphlet gives an overview of what the Internet is and discusses parent's responsonsibilities with respect to their children's use of this information resource. The topic of Internet filters is explored and further sources of information are provided.

The pamphlet can be purchased from the Canadian Library Association at the following prices: 25 copies for $5.00; 100 for $10.00, and 500 for $45.00; 1,000 for

$75; 2,500 for $175; and 5,000 for $300.00. Please add taxes, shipping and handling. Orders may be sent to: Canadian Library Association, Suite 602–200 Elgin Street, Ottawa K2P 1L5

Can you provide some guidelines concerning how to evaluate resources that have been located on the Internet?

The following guidelines were prepared by Karen Hunt, Coordinator of Access Services at Red River College for the use of students working on assignments:

How to Evaluate Internet Resources
The following guide may help you evaluate any information (whether an Internet site, article in a magazine, book, or matchbook cover).

> ...there is an extremely wide variety of material on the Internet, ranging in its accuracy, reliability, and value. Unlike most traditional information media (books, magazines, organizational documents), no one has to approve the content before it is made public. It's your job as a searcher, then, to evaluate what you locate, in order to determine whether it suits your needs."
> —*Evaluating Internet Research Sources*, by Robert Harris, http://www.sccu.edu/faculty/R_Harris/evalu8it.htm

What are your needs?
Check with library staff to help you determine the most appropriate sources. The quality of the information within a document is related to what you require.
 The range of information services available on this topic (for example, books and articles)?
 Is the information sufficiently current to meet your needs?
 Does the document provide any new information on the topic?
 Are there obvious gaps or omissions in the coverage of the topic?

Why is the information being provided?
There are many motivations for publishing on the Web: to attract users and therefore advertisers, to sell something, to enhance service, to advocate a personal position, or even for altruistic reasons. Web pages can be divided into five groups:

1. Advocacy Web Pages (for example *Lifesite Canada* at htttp://www.lifesite.net/).
2. Business/Marketing Pages (for example *Ultra White* at http://www.ultra-white.com).
3. Information Web Pages (for example *Strategis* by Industry Canada at http://strategis.ic.gc.ca/engdoc/main.html). Some information sites are provided by governments, business or organizations as a service and some are provided to attract users and therefore advertisers (for example *Yahoo! Autos* at http://autos.yahoo.com).

4. News Web Pages (for example *Canoe* at http://www.canoe.com/).
5. Personal Home Pages (for example *Doreen's Home Page* at http://www.escape.ca/~doreen/index.html)

See "Evaluating Web Resources" (http://www.science.widener.edu/~withers/webeval.htm) for criteria to evaluate each type.

You can tell a little about a document by the address. Common domain name suffixes are: .com (for a commercial enterprise); .gov (for government—U.S. only); .org (for organization). Canadian domain names often end in .ca, but do not necessarily have to end in .ca.

Who is the author?

What is the author's training or experience with the topic?

Is the author a recognized authority on the topic of the document?

Is the author affiliated with an educational institution, research laboratory, government agency, or other reputable organization related to the topic of the document?

Is the information valid?

Is the methodology used to develop the resource described and appropriate to the content?

Has the document been linked to or referenced by recognized authorities? (for example, does the document show up on more than one list or resources on the topic?)

Is the document a primary (original, unfiltered material) or secondary (modified, selected, or rearranged information about primary materials) source?

Does the information provided contradict or confirm information from other sources?

Does the author provide references to confirm the accuracy of the information?

Does the author provide verifiable statistics to support conclusions?

Do you have the whole truth?

Are all sides of controversial issues presented, or is it necessary to seek alternative views?

If the document deals with controversial issues, is the bias of the author clearly identified?

Are there indications of careless or hasty preparation, such as spelling or grammatical errors?

Are you going around in circles?

Are links annotated?

Are links provided primarily to resources rather than "lists" of resources?

How reliable are the links (are there inactive links or references to sites that have been moved?)?

Try searching the Argus Clearinghouse for evaluated topical guides to Internet-based information resources. (http://www.clearinghouse.net/).

More Information:

Truth, Lies and the Internet by CNET.
(http://www.cnet.com/Content/Features/Dlife/Truth/index.html).
Includes net hoaxes, pseudoscience and urban myths, web advertising, truth-seeking on the Net, and (my favourite) the Internet Lie Detector Test.

How to Critically Analyze Information Sources, Cornell University Library, (http://www.library.cornell.edu/okuref/research/skill26.htm).

Evaluating Internet Research Sources by Robert Harris
(http://www.sccu.edu/faculty/R_Harris/evalu8it.htm).

Thinking Critically about World Wide Web Resources by Esther Grassian (http://www.library.ucla.edu/libraries/college/instruct/critical.htm).

Evaluating Web Resources, Widener University Wolgram Memorial Library (http://www.science.widener.edu/~withers/webeval.htm).

Evaluation Criteria and Indicators of Quality for Internet Resources by Gene L. Wilkinson, Lisa T. Bennett and Kevin M. Oliver, Educational Technology, May–June 1997, pp. 52-59.

Lifelong Learning Through the Libraries, Office of Information Literacy, University of Louisville
(http://www.louisville.edu/infoliteracy/evaltips.htm).

How can I develop my children's interest in books and reading?

Lorraine Douglas, Coordinator of Youth Services at the Winnipeg Centennial Library describes the series of programs and services offered by the Winnipeg Public Library System to help parents develop their children's interest in reading. The following description of these services will give parents an idea of what public libraries in general can provide by way of support.

Winnipeg Public Library provides a wide range of collections and services for young people and their families.

Jamie Ybarra of the Winnipeg Goldeyes Baseball Club leading a story hour at the Winnipeg Centennial Library

Our collections begin with board books for babies, picture books for preschoolers, and fiction and non-fiction materials in book, magazine, video, CD-ROM and recorded formats. Our special collections include Braille, large-print, talking books and tactile kits for the visually and physically impaired; books in a variety of languages; Native Studies collections; toy and game collections at four libraries; and young adult fiction collections.

All of our libraries provide programs and services especially aimed encouraging reading and the life-long use of the library. These include:

Books for Your Baby
This program is for children under the age of two and the special people in their lives—parents, grandparents, and caregivers. It provides an introduction to the kinds of materials which the library has to offer new parents and babies and everyone shares in the enjoyment of rhymes and stories. This program is sponsored through the Frances M. Pishker Memorial Library Fund.

Times for Twos
This parent-child program is an interactive introduction to rhymes, songs and stories just right for children two years of age.

Story Times for Preschoolers
Story time programs are offered at all library branches. Imaginative presentations of stories and activities enhance the enjoyment of the library and its materials. Activities include music, songs, felt board stories, puppet shows, rhymes and video presentations. Each program is based upon a theme which would appeal to the interests of children aged three to five. French language story times are also held at the St. Boniface Library and in the Riel district on a regular basis.

Story Time for Deaf Preschoolers
The Centennial Library offers a regular monthly story time program for deaf preschoolers. This session is filled with fun! Highly visual, tactile and interactive materials are specially chosen to be shared and library staff are assisted by a preschool teacher who signs for the children.

School and Day Care Visits
Classroom teachers and day care leaders are invited to come to the library to enjoy a tour or story program. Appointments can be made by contacting your nearest library.

Visits by Authors, Illustrators and Special Celebrity Guests
The library hosts visits by guest authors and illustrators who make presentations on their work. Sheree Fitch, Sheldon Oberman and Tim Wynne-Jones have appeared at the library. The Canadian Children's Book Centre sponsors an annual tour during Canadian Children's Book Week in November and the Winnipeg Public Library is often a stop on the tour.

The library has also had guest appearances by players from the Winnipeg Goldeyes and the Winnipeg Cyclone.

Summer Reading Programs
Each summer the library focuses on a summer reading reading program for children who read on their own. Each child who registers receives a bookllet with a reading log and activities. A reading club for families with preschool children is also offered.

Parent Pack Services
Several libraries offer the Parent Pack service to new parents. The Parent Pack is filled with materials specially chosen for the very young child. This program is available at the Cornish and Monroe libraries and is sponsored by community donations. In 1999, the service will be available at the West End and St. John's libraries.

Suggestions for Sharing Books with your Family
Parents are a child's best friend when it comes to learning to read.

Read together as often as you can. Try to set aside a time just for reading.

Take books and magazines to places or appointments where you have a long wait. Enjoying a story together can help make the time go faster. Take books, magazines and recordings on trips.

Ask the library staff to help you find items which are just right for your child's age and interests. Preview the books and make sure that you as a parent will enjoy sharing them with your child.

Picture books can easily be shared in a family that includes children of various ages. Even older children like a good picture book. Talk about the pictures as well as the story.

When you are reading a long story aloud, be sure to stop at a suspenseful point.

If your child is not interested in the book, just put it away. Try it again another day.

Reading is fun!

With contributions from Ruth Reedman, Louise Shah, Karen Hunt and Lorraine Douglas.

Contributors

Ralph Abramson is Director, The Treaty and Aboriginal Rights Research Centre of Manitoba, Inc.

Vera Andrysiak is Administrative Coordinator of Central Branch Services at Winnipeg Public Library.

Sandra Armstrong is the Librarian at the Assiniboine Community College Library.

Phyllis Barich is a librarian at the Instructional Resources Unit, Manitoba Department of Education and Training.

Norman Beattie is Coordinator, Reference Services, Red River College Library.

Morag Belliveau is at the William Potoroka Memorial Library of the Addictions Foundation of Manitoba.

Sue Bishop is the Legislative Librarian for the Province of Manitoba.

Jim Blanchard is Head, Reference Services, Elizabeth Dafoe Library, University of Manitoba.

David Borowski is at the Selkirk and St. Andrews Regional Library, Selkirk, Manitoba.

Marcel Boulet is Head Librarian, Alfred-Monnin Library, Collège universitaire de Saint-Boniface

Pat Bozyk is the Library Director, Red River College Library.

Jo Ann Brewster teaches in the Library and Information Technology program at Red River College.

Gerald R. Brown is a Library and Information Services Consultant in Winnipeg.

Violet Chalmers is the Librarian at the Peoples' Library, Manitoba Indian Cultural Education Centre.

Karen Clay is Librarian at the William R. Newman Library, University of Manitoba.

David Colborne was the Information Specialist at the NRC Information Centre, Winnipeg from 1993 to 1998.

Kenlyn Collins is the Librarian at the Clara Lander Library, Winnipeg Art Gallery.

Carol Cooke is the Resource Development Librarian at the Neil John Maclean Health Sciences Library, University of Manitoba.

Thora Cooke is a Researcher/Historian at the Western Canada Pictorial Index Inc.

Bob Cooney is the Communications Officer at Brandon University.

Ganga Dakshinamurti is a librarian at the Albert D. Cohen Management Library, University of Manitoba.

Betty Dearth is the Librarian at the Industrial Technology Centre Library.

Linwood DeLong is a librarian at the University of Winnipeg Library.

A Guide to Libraries in Manitoba

Gail Doherty is Coordinator of Library Information Services and New Initiatives at the Winnipeg Public Library.

Lorraine Douglas is Administrative Coordinator of Youth Services at the Winnipeg Public Library.

Abe Dueck is the Director of The Centre for Mennonite Brethren Studies.

Diane Dwarka is the Multicultural Resources Specialist at the Instructional Resources Unit, Manitoba Department of Education and Training.

Dennis Felbel is Librarian at the Albert D. Cohen Management Library.

Leslie Fitch is a member of the Canadian Library Association and co-authored *Dividends: The Value of Public Libraries in Canada* published by the Book and Periodical Council (1997).

Lorraine Freeman is the Chairperson of the Métis Resource Centre.

Hazel Fry is the Executive Director of the Council of Prairie and Pacific University Libraries.

Pat Gagné is a teacher at Sun Valley School, Winnipeg.

John Giesbrecht is the Client Services Specialist at the Canada/Manitoba Business Service Centre.

Norma Godavari is the Librarian at the Engineering Library, University of Manitoba.

Faye Goranson has worked as a staff reporter for the *Interlake Spectator* and has been a columnist for the *Stonewall Argus* and *Teulon Times*.

Phyllis Hallett is the Librarian at the Boissevain and Morton Regional Library in Boissevain, Manitoba.

Don Hamilton is the Education Librarian at the University of Victoria.

Pat Hebert is in charge of the MFL Occupational Health Centre Library.

Eric Hunt is Head of Adult Services at the Winnipeg Centennial Library.

Karen Hunt is Coordinator, Access Services, Red River College Library.

Judy Inglis is the Librarian at the J.W. Crane Memorial Library, Deer Lodge Centre.

Sigrid Johnson is Head, Icelandic Collection, University of Manitoba.

Nancy Klos is a Research Associate at the Institute of Urban Studies.

Nevia Koscevic is Head of the Slavic Collection, Elizabeth Dafoe Library, University of Manitoba.

Michelle Larose-Kuzenko is the teacher-librarian at Sun Valley School, Winnipeg.

Carolyn Ledwell is a certified teacher and has recently completed the diploma program in teacher-librarianship at the University of Prince Edward Island.

Bruno LeGal is Coordinator of French Language Services, Winnipeg Public Library.

Doris Lemoine is the Director of (DREF) Direction des ressources éducatives françaises of the Manitoba Department of Education and Training.

Bob Lincoln is the bibliographer for the Shastri Indo-Canadian Institute Collection at the University of Manitoba.

Naomi Lloyd is the Librarian at the Centre for Indigenous Environmental Resources Library.

Mary Lockhead is the Librarian at the Fine Arts/Architecture Library, University of Manitoba.

Rick MacLowick is Head, Reference Services, Legislative Library of Manitoba.

Michael Mooseberger is Archivist at the Department of Archives and Special Collections, University of Manitoba.

Anne Morton is Head, Research and Reference, Hudson's Bay Company Archives, Provincial Archives of Manitoba.

Shelley Penziwol is the Librarian at the Environment Library/Bibliothèque de l'Environnement.

Liz Price is the Coordinator, Children's Hospital Family Information Libraries.

Thomas Quigley is Head of the Joe Fortes Branch of the Vancouver Public Library and convenor of the Canadian Library Association's Action for Literacy Interest Group.

Gretta Redahl is Library Administrator at the Flin Flon Public Library.

Ruth Reedman is the Librarian at the Canadian Wheat Board Library.

Pat Routledge teaches in the Library and Information Technology program at Red River College.

Marlene Roy is the Information Specialist at the International Institute for Sustainable Development.

Elena Ruivivar is the Librarian at Keewatin Community College Library.

Claudia Schmidt is the secretary-treasurer of the Valley Library Foundation, Morris, Manitoba.

Louise Shah was a Consultant with Public Library Services, Brandon, until July 1998.

Catherine Shields was the Librarian at the Clara Lander Library, Winnipeg Art Gallery until July 1998.

Cindi Steffan is the Librarian at the Manitoba Museum of Man and Nature Library.

Bonnie Tregobov is the Archivist, The Jewish Historical Society of Western Canada.

Larissa Tulchinsky is the Librarian at the Ukrainian Cultural and Education Centre Library.

Rick Walker is the Manager of Library Services, Winnipeg Public Library.

Jody Warner was the researcher and co-author of *Dividends: The Value of Public Libraries in Canada*, published by the Book and Periodical Council (1997).

Darlene Wusaty is a librarian at the Winnipeg Centennial Library.

Theresa Yauk is Branch Head, Sir William Stephenson Library, Winnipeg Public Library.

APPENDIX 1

Professional Library Associations

Canadian Library Association

The mission of the Canadian Library Association is to provide leadership in the promotion, development and support of library and information services in Canada for the benefit of Association members, the profession and Canadian society. In the spirit of this mission CLA aims:

> to engage the active, creative participation of library staff, trustees and governing bodies in the development and management of high quality Canadian library service; to assert and support the right of Canadians to the freedom to read and to free universal access to a wide variety of library materials and services; to promote librarianship and to enlighten all levels of government as to the significant role that libraries play in educating and socializing the Canadian people; and to link libraries, librarians, trustees, and others across the country for the purpose of providing a united nationwide voice in matters of critical concern.

The Canadian Library Association was founded in Hamilton, Ontario in 1946, and was incorporated under the Companies Act on November 26, 1947. CLA is a non-profit voluntary organization, governed by an elected Executive Council, which is advised by over thirty interest groups and committees. The Association's five constituent divisions are:

> The Canadian Association of College and University Libraries (CACUL), including the Community and Technical College (CTCL) section.
>
> The Canadian Association of Public Libraries (CAPL), including the Canadian Association of Childrens' Librarians (CACL) section.
>
> The Canadian Association of Special Libraries and Information Services (CASLIS), with chapters in Calgary, Edmonton, Manitoba, Ottawa, Toronto and Atlantic Canada.
>
> The Canadian Library Trustees' Association.
>
> The Canadian School Library Association, including the School Library Administrators (SLA) section.

Canadian Library Association Position Statements

The Executive Council of the Canadian Library Association has approved position statements on the following topics: Actional for Literacy, Intellectual Freedom, Information and Telecommunication Access Principles, and the CLA Statement on Internet Access. The full text of these documents can be viewed at the CLA Web site: (http://www.cla.amlibs.ca/)

Contact information:
Vicki Whitmell, Executive Director
Canadian Library Association
200 Elgin Street, Suite 602
Ottawa, Ontario K2P 1L5
Telephone: (613) 232-9625 Fax: (613) 563-9895
CLA Web site: (http://www.cla.amlibs.ca/)

Manitoba Library Association

Founded in 1936, the Manitoba Library Association is a provincial, voluntary, non-incorporated association with over 350 personal and institutional members. MLA is a registered charity, and has a strictly non-profit, educational orientation.

The Manitoba Library Association provides leadership in the promotion, development and support of library and information services in Manitoba for the benefit of Association members, the library community and the citizens of Manitoba. MLA publishes a monthly Newsline and offers access to a variety of library resources, including a directory of libraries in Manitoba through its Web site.

Contact Information:
Jo Anne Brewster, President, 1998–1999
Manitoba Library Association
606–100 Arthur St. Winnipeg, MB R3B 1H3
Telephone: (204) 943-4567 Fax: (204) 942-1555
e-mail: jbrewste@rrc.mb.ca
MLA Web Site: (www.mla.mb.ca)

Canadian Association of Special Libraries and Information Services (CASLIS) Manitoba Chapter

CASLIS Manitoba is the Manitoba Chapter of the Canadian Association of Special Libraries and Information Services, a division of the Canadian Library Association. As such its mandate is two-fold: (1) to support the objectives and activities of the Canadian Library Association and (2) to represent the concerns and serve the needs of the special library community, as well as independent information consultants in Manitoba. To that end, the Chapter strives to provide a means of communication among its members; to promote co-operation among special librarians, information specialists, and others offering information services; to promote special libraries and information centres as essential avenues of access to information; and to encourage and provide a continuing educational programs to enhance the capabilities of special library and information centre personnel. CASLIS Manitoba publishes a quarterly newsletter "Special Delivery".

Membership in CASLIS Manitoba is open to all CLA members interested in the work of special libraries and information services, either as the result of choosing CASLIS as their one free division with their basic CLA membership fees, or as an extra, costed division. Membership fees in CLA itself vary according to category of membership and income.

Contact Information:
Marlene Roy, Chair, 1998–1999
CASLIS Manitoba
Tel: (204) 958-7724 Fax: (204) 958-7710
e-mail: mroy@iisdpost.iisd.ca
Mailing Address:
P.O. Box 2646
Winnipeg, MB R0C 4B3

The Manitoba Association of Library Technicians

The Manitoba Association of Library Technicians was established in 1971 as a nonprofit organization to promote and advance the role of library technicians and to respond to issues that relate to the entire library community. These objectives are embodied in a constitution and are carried out by an elected executive committee.

Monthly meetings are held by the executive and are open to all members. Membership in MALT is open to any interested person. MALT produces a quarterly newsletter, is involved in sponsoring various programs and workshops and maintains a job bank which advertises library positions for technicians. A representative of MALT participates on the Library Education Advisory Committee of Red River College.

Mailing Address:
Manitoba Association of Library Technicians
P.O. Box 1872
Winnipeg, MB
R3C 3R1
MALT Web site: (http://home.cc.umanitoba.ca/~jhollosy)
Job Bank number (204) 256-8633

Manitoba School Library Association

The Manitoba School Library Association is one of twenty-nine special area groups affiliated with the Manitoba Teachers' Society. Members include teachers and teacher-librarians (as well as a few non-teaching library staff) who seek support, information, and activities pertaining to their professional duties. The association publishes the MSLA Journal.

Contact Information:
Margaret Stimson, President, MSLA, 1998–1999
Coordinator Media Services/Gifted Education
Assiniboine South School Division #3
6691 Rannock Ave., Winnipeg, MB R3R OZ3
Telephone: (204) 897-1027 Fax: (204) 897-1006
e-mail: mstimson@minet.gov.mb.ca
MSLA Web Site: (http://www.mbnet.mb.ca/~msla)

Manitoba Health Libraries Association

The Manitoba Health libraries Association's objective is to promote the provision of quality library service to the health community in Manitoba by communication and mutual assistance. The MHLA was formally accepted as chapter of the Canadian Health Libraries Association on June 14, 1979. The Association publishes a quarterly newsletter, *MHLA News*, for its members.

Contact Information:
Tania Gottschalk, President, MHLA, 1998–1999
Neil John Maclean Health Sciences Library
University of Manitoba
Winnipeg, MB R3T 2N2
Tel: 789-3464 Fax: 789-3922
e-mail: Tania_Gottschalk@umanitoba.ca
MHLA Web Site: (http://home.cc.umanitoba.ca/~ccooke/mhla/)

ALARM (Alliance of Libraries, Archives and Records Management)

ALARM Educational Opportunities is an ongoing compilation (marketplace/directory) and discussion (open forum/personal interaction) of formal and informal education and training opportunities in the Information Resources Sector composed of libraries, archives, and records management.
    ALARM Web Site: (http://www.mbnet.mb.ca/~alarm/)

APPENDIX 2

Directory of Libraries in Manitoba

The Directory includes the following types of libraries: public, academic, government and special libraries and information centres. The Manitoba Library Association would like to thank Public Library Services for providing access to its database of library information that was used to create the 1993 *Directory of Libraries in Manitoba*. The PLS database was also used to create the online version of the Directory of Libraries in Manitoba located at the Manitoba Library Association's Web site: (www.mla.mb.ca). These two databases were used as the starting point for obtaining up-to-date directory information from Manitoba's libraries. Our thanks to all libraries that responded to our questionnaire.

The Directory is indexed by type of library and by subject.

The information contained in this directory will be up-dated regularly at the Manitoba Library Association's Web site (www.mla.mb.ca).

Note: Because of space constraints, we were not able to include Manitoba's more than 900 school libraries. For further information about Manitoba's school libraries, please visit the Manitoba School Library Association's Web site: (http://www.mbnet.mb.ca/~msla/).

The following page contains a sample entry from the Directory together with explanatory notes.

Sample Entry

Federal Laboratories Library/Bibliothèque de laboratoires fédéraux
1015 Arlington St., Winnipeg R3E 3P6
Mailing Address: P.O. Box 1000, Winnipeg R3E 3PG
Inquiries: 789-6001 **Toll Free**: 1-800-888-8888
Library Hours: 789-9000 **Fax**: 789-5300
Electronic Access: http://www.flb.ca
e-mail: Lisa_Demchuk@hc-sc.gc.ca
Listserv: What's New at FL
NL Symbol: MWFLL
Mandate: To provide support to the staff of the research and diagnostic programs by collecting & providing access to the scientific literature & providing reference, literature searching, training & document delivery.
Primary Clientele: Staff of Federal Laboratories
Programs & Services: Copying; ILL offered; Languages: French
Collection: Subjects: Microbiology; virology; veterinary medicine; biosafety; laboratory methods & procedures; infectious diseases. **Special Collections**: The Infectious Disease Collection. **Languages**: French, German, Russian
External Users: Appointments required; must provide identification to security personnel; access permitted only to library.
Publications: *The Diagnostic Review*

Explanation of Entry

Name: Where the library offers bilingual service, the translated name of the library follows the slash /
Street Address:
Mailing Address: Shown, if different from street address.
Inquiries: This is generally the number for the information & reference service. **Toll Free**: Listed only for libraries that have this service. **Library Hours**: This is a dedicated line for library hours. **Fax**: This is the fax number for library administration, unless otherwise noted.
Electronic Access: The library's URL—uniform resource locator is listed. e-mail address: this is generally the electronic mail address for library administration, unless otherwise noted. **Listservs**: The names of listservs moderated by the host library are included.
NL Symbol: This 3-5 letter code has been assigned by the National Library of Canada to facilitate interlibrary loans.
Mandate: Information generally given only for special, government and academic libraries.
Primary Clientele: Information included only for special and government libraries.
Programs & Services: Copying, indicates presence of a public photocopying machine. ILL offered indicates that the library does participate in interlibrary lending. Languages: indicates languages in which reference & information service is provided. English is assumed unless otherwise noted.
Collection: Subjects: The main subject areas collected by the library are listed. **Special Collections**: The library's special collections are llistedby their official name, with an indication of subject area. Examples of listings here include: Canadian or ethnic collections; archival & manuscript collections; maps; photographs; extensive newspaper collections. **Language**: Indicates languages the library is ollecting. English is assumed unless otherwise noted. **Level**: Special and government libraries collect specialized material. Therefore, the following three categories may be listed to show the suitability of the collection for external users:
1. researchers/specialists 2. graduate students 3. undergraduates/public.
External Users: This information will facilitate use of the library by members of the public. The following types of information are listed: appointment required to use the library; hours of access; whether or not loans/interlibrary loans can be arranged for external users; costs for membership.
Fee-Based Information Services: A brief description of the types of services offered to external users is offered. Libraries should be contacted individually to determine the cost of these services.
Publications: The following types of publications are not included: monthly acquisition lists; annual reports and public relations materials

Directory of Libraries in Manitoba

17 Wing Recreational Library
Westwin Community Centre, Winnipeg R3J 3Y5
Mailing Address: 17 Wing Winnipeg, P.O. Box 17000 Stn. Forces, Winnipeg R3J 3Y5
Inquiries: 833-2500 ext. 2490 **Fax**: 833-2755
Mandate: To serve the military and civilian personnel and families associated with the Department of National Defense.
Programs & Services: Copying; Internet access
Collection: Languages: French. **Level**: Undergraduate/public
External Users: Materials may be used on site; no borrowing privileges

The Addictions Foundation of Manitoba. William Potoroka Memorial Library
1031 Portage Ave., Winnipeg R3G 0R8
Inquiries: 944-6233 **Fax**: 772-0225
Electronic Access: http://www.afm.mb.ca
e-mail: library@afm.mb.ca
NL Symbol: MWAF
Mandate: To provide up-to-date information and resources for the research, prevention and treatment programs related to addictions in individuals and communities.
Programs & Services: Copying; ILL offered
Collection: Subjects: Alcohol and drug use and abuse; compulsive gambling; self help; FAS/E; workplace-EAP issues; violence; anger management; driving while impaired; solvent abuse; smoking. **Special Collections**: Fetal Alcohol Syndrome/Fetal Alcohol Effects (FAS/FAE); "Be a Prevention Player" Solvent Abuse Prevention Program. **Languages**: French. **Level**: Specialist/researcher; graduate student; undergraduate/public
External Users: Materials may be used on-site; register to borrow materials
Publications: *Directions*

Aikins, Macaulay and Thorvaldson Management Services Library
30th Floor, 360 Main St., Winnipeg R3C 4G1
Inquiries: 957-4785 **Fax**: 957-0840
Mandate: To provide legal information resources and research facilities for lawyers and articling students with the firm.
Primary Clientele: Lawyers; staff
Programs & Services: ILL not offered
Collection: Subjects: Law in Canada. **Special Collections**: Comprehensive collection of Canadian case law; repository library for judgments in Manitoba. **Level**: Specialist/researcher
External Users: No public access
Fee-based Information Services: Offered

Albert D. Cohen Management Library
[See: University of Manitoba Libraries]

Altona Branch Library
[See: South Central Regional Library]

Appraisal Institute of Canada
1111 Portage Ave., Winnipeg R3G 0S8
Inquiries: 783-2224 **Fax**: 783-5575
Primary Clientele: Members
Programs & Services: ILL not offered

Arborg Branch Library
[See: Evergreen Regional Library, Arborg Branch]

Archdiocese of Winnipeg Catholic Centre Resource Library
1495 Pembina Hwy., Winnipeg R3T 2C6
Inquiries: 452-2227 **Fax**: 475-4409
Electronic Access:
e-mail: rcwpgresource@mb.sympatico.ca
Mandate: To provide access to books, periodicals and audiovisual resources in support of ministries in the Archdiocese of Winnipeg.
Primary Clientele: Religious Education instructors for young to adult; lay ministers in parishes; priests; religious groups and organizations
Programs & Services: Copying
Collection: Subjects: Catholicism; scripture; study and resource; religious education programs. **Level**: Specialist/researcher; graduate students; undergraduate/public
External Users: Yearly fee charged for library membership

Architecture/Fine Arts Library
[See: University of Manitoba Libraries]

The Arthritis Society (Manitoba Division) Resource Library
105-386 Broadway, Winnipeg R3C 3R6
Inquiries: 942-4892 **Fax**: 942-4794
Electronic Access: http://www.arthritis.ca
e-mail: info@mb.arthritis.ca
Programs & Services: Copying; ILL offered
Collection: Subjects: Arthritis & rheumatic diseases—treatment, self-management and exercise programs.
Level: Undergraduate/public
External Users: Books & videos available to the general public on loan at no charge for 2-4 weeks; items can be mailed to rural locations

Assiniboine Community College Library
1430 Victoria Ave. E., Brandon R7A 2A9
Inquiries: 726-6636 **Fax**: 726-7014

Electronic Access:
http://www.assiniboinec.mb.ca/library
e-mail: library@assiniboinec.mb.ca
NL Symbol: MBAC
Primary Clientele: Staff; students
Programs & Services: Copying; ILL offered
Collection: Subjects: Business; hospitality & tourism; office administration; nursing; child development; First Nations; plumbing; agriculture; carpentry; automotive
External Users: No appointment necessary; no loans provided for reference materials, audio-visual materials or serials

Associated Manitoba Arts Festival Resource Library
424–100 Arthur St., Winnipeg R3B 1H3
Inquiries: 945-4578 **Fax:** 948-2073
Electronic Access: http://www.amaf.mb.ca
e-mail: amaf@pangea.ca
Mandate: To provide music scores and copies of poetry and prose for selections found in the Provincial Syllabus.
Programs & Services: Copying. **Languages:** French
Collection: Subjects: Music; poetry; prose. **Languages:** French
External Users: Please contact A.M.A.F. office
Publications: *Sowing the Seeds of Culture; Favourite Festival Foods; Provincial Syllabus*

Ayamiscikewikamik Norway House Public Library
Norway House R0B 1B0
Inquiries: 359-6047 **Fax:** 359-6262
NL Symbol: MNHA
Programs & Services: ILL offered

***The Beaver* Magazine Research Library**
478–167 Lombard Ave., Winnipeg R3B 0T6
Inquiries: 988-9300 **Fax:** 988-9309
Mandate: To provide research resources for editorial staff of *The Beaver* Magazine.
Collection: Subjects: Canadian history; Canadian fur trade history. **Special Collections:** Exploration journals; 18th and 19th century history books
External Users: No public access or service

Benito Branch Library
[See: North-West Regional Library]

Bethania Mennonite Personal Care Home Library
1045 Concordia Ave., Winnipeg R2K 3S7
Primary Clientele: Staff
Collection: Subjects: Aging
External Users: No public access

Bette Winner Public Library
240 Mattonnabee Ave., Gillam R0B 0L0
Mailing Address: P.O. Box 718, Gillam R0B 0L0
Inquiries: 652-2617 **Fax:** 652-2261
Electronic Access: e-mail: libraryl@cancom.net
NL Symbol: MGI
Programs & Services: Copying; ILL offered; laminating

Bibliothèque Alfred-Monnin
[See: Collège universitaire de Saint-Boniface. Bibliothèque Alfred-Monnin]

Bibliothèque Allard Library
14 Baie Caron, St. Georges R0E 1V0
Mailing Address: P.O. Box 157, St. Georges R0E 1V0
Inquiries: 367-8443
Electronic Access: e-mail: allard@granite.mb.ca
NL Symbol: MSTGA
Programs & Services: ILL offered
Collection: Languages: French

Bibliothèque Montcalm Library
2nd Ave., St. Jean-Baptiste R0G 2B0
Mailing Address: P.O. Box 345, St. Jean-Baptiste R0G 2B0
Inquiries: 758-3137 **Fax:** 758-3117
Electronic Access:
e-mail: dmtberard@hotmail.com
NL Symbol: MSJB
Programs & Services: Copying; ILL offered; public Internet access; laminating. **Languages:** French
Collection: Languages: French

Bibliothèque Père-Champagne
Mailing Address: P.O. Box 399, Notre-Dame-de-Lourdes R0G 1M0
Inquiries: 248-2386
NL Symbol: MNDP
Programs & Services: ILL offered. **Languages:** French
Collection: Special Collections: Centennial books. **Languages:** French

Bibliothèque Régionale Jolys
[See: Jolys Regional Library]

Bibliothèque Ritchot Library
Mailing Address: C.P. 581, Ile des Chenes R0A 0T0
Inquiries: 878-2147 **Fax:** 878-3495
Electronic Access: e-mail: brlib@minet.gov.mb.ca
NL Symbol: MIBR
Programs & Services: ILL offered; Internet access.
Languages: French
Collection: Languages: French; Spanish
Branches:
Ste. Agathe Branch
Mailing Address: P.O. Box 40, Ste. Agathe R0G 1Y0
Inquiries: 882-2275

Bibliothèque Régionale Ste. Rose
[See: Ste. Rose Regional Library]

Bibliothèque Somerset
[See: Somerset Library/Bibliothèque Somerset]

Bibliothèque Saint Claude Library
50–1st St., Saint Claude R0G 1Z0
Mailing Address: P.O. Box 203, Saint Claude R0G 1Z0
Inquiries: 379-2524 **Fax:** 379-2014
Electronic Access: e-mail: stclib@portage.net
NL Symbol: MSCL
Programs & Services: ILL offered. **Languages:** French
Collection: Languages: French

Bibliothèque Ste. Anne Library
Mailing Address: C.P. 220, Ste. Anne R0A 1R0
Inquiries: 422-9958
NL Symbol: MSA

A Guide to Libraries in Manitoba

Bibliothèque Saint-Joachim Library
Mailing Address: P.O. Box 10, La Broquerie R0A 0W0
Inquiries: 424-5287 **Fax**: 424-5610
NL Symbol: MLB

Binscarth Library
[See: Russell & District Regional Library]

Birch River & District Branch Library
[See: Parkland Regional Library]

Birtle Branch Library
[See: Parkland Regional Library]

Boissevain & Morton Regional Library
436 South Railway, Boissevain R0K 0E0
Mailing Address: P.O. Box 340, Boissevain R0K 0E0
Inquiries: 534-6478 **Fax**: 534-3710
Electronic Access:
http://www.town.boissevain.mb.ca/library
e-mail: mbom@mail.techplus.com
NL Symbol: MBOM
Programs & Services: Copying; ILL offered; public Internet access
Collection: **Special Collections**: Joe McDonald North American Native Heritage Resource Collection; local history archives
Fee-based Information Services: Archival research
Publications: *Library Links*

Border Regional Library
312 Seventh Ave. S., Virden R0M 2C0
Mailing Address: P.O. Box 970, Virden R0M 2C0
Inquiries: 748-3862 **Fax**: 748-3862
Electronic Access:
e-mail: borderlibraryvirden@yahoo.com
NL Symbol: MVE
Programs & Services: ILL offered
Collection: **Special Collections**: Archival collection.
Languages: French; Spanish
Branches:
Elkhorn Branch Library
110 Richhill Ave. E., Elkhorn R0M 0N0
Mailing Address: P.O. Box 370, Elkhorn R0M 0N0
Inquirers: 845-2292 **Fax**: 845-2292
NL Symbol: MVEE

McAuley Branch Library
Mailing Address: P.O. Box 234, McAuley R0M 1H0
Inquiries: 722-2221 **Fax**: 722-2221
NL Symbol: MVEM

Bowsman Branch Library
[See: Parkland Regional Library]

Boyne Regional Library
15–1st Ave. S.W., Carman R0G 0J0
Mailing Address: P.O. Box 788, Carman R0G 0J0
Inquiries: 745-3504
NL Symbol: MCB
Programs & Services: Copying; ILL offered
Collection: **Languages**: French; Dutch

Brandon General Hospital Library Services
150 McTavish Ave. E., Brandon R7A 2B3
Inquiries: 726-2257 **Fax**: 727-0317
Mandate: To provide and facilitate access to health and related information resources for all customers in the Brandon community and regional referral area.
Programs & Services: Copying; ILL offered
Collection: **Subjects**: Medical; nursing; allied health; consumer health. **Level**: Specialist/researcher, graduate students, undergraduate/public
External Users: Library may be used during regular business hours

Brandon University. John E. Robbins Library
270–18th St., Brandon University, Brandon R7A 6A9
Inquiries: 727-9646 **Fax**: 726-1072
Library Hours: 727-9645
Electronic Access:
http://www.brandonu.ca/Library/
e-mail: Reference@brandonu.ca
NL Symbol: MBC
Mandate: To meet the research needs of students, faculty and staff at Brandon University.
Programs & Services: Copying; ILL offered
Collection: **Subjects**: Humanities; social sciences; science; music; education; nursing. **Special Collections**: Native Literature Collection; Great Plains Collection.
Level: Undergraduate/public
External Users: Brandon residents and researchers with a COPPUL Borrowing Card have access to the collection; reserve items and periodicals may not be borrowed; ILL not offered to Brandon residents.

Bren Del Win Centennial Library
211 North Railway W., Deloraine R0M 0M0
Mailing Address: P.O. Box 584, Deloraine R0M 0M0
Inquiries: 747-2415 **Fax**: 747-3446
Electronic Access:
e-mail: bdwlib@mail.techplus.com
NL Symbol: MDB
Programs & Services: Copying; ILL offered; Internet access
Collection: **Special Collections**: Complete holdings of the *Deloraine Times & Star* newspaper collection on microfilm.

Bristol Aerospace Engineering Reference Library
660 Berry St., P.O. Box 874, Winnipeg R3C 2S4
Inquiries: 775-8331 **Fax**: 783-2168
Collection: **Subjects**: Engineering; technology; manufacturing; physical sciences
External Users: No public access

Brokenhead River Regional Library
427 Park Ave., Beausejour R0E 0C0
Mailing Address: P.O. Box 1087, Beausejour R0E 0C0
Inquiries: 268-3588 **Fax**: 268-3588
Electronic Access:
http://www.granite.mb.ca/brrlibr
e-mail: brrlibr@granite.mb.ca
NL Symbol: MBBR
Programs & Services: Copying; ILL offered; public Internet access
Collection: **Languages**: French

C.A.C. Manitoba Info-Centre
[See: Consumers' Association of Canada (Manitoba) Consumer Resource Centre]

DIRECTIONS

**Canada. Agriculture & Agri-Food Canada.
Brandon Research Centre Library & Information Centre**
Mailing Address: P.O. Box 1000A, R.R. # 3, Brandon R7A 5Y3
Inquiries: 726-7650 ext. 247 **Fax**: 728-3858
Electronic Access: e-mail: libbrandon@em.agr.ca
NL Symbol: MBAG
Mandate: To meet the information needs of our scientists and researchers.
Programs & Services: Copying; ILL offered
Collection: Subjects: Land resource management; barley breeding; beef production systems. **Special Collections**: Scientists' Scientific Manuscript Archives; Technology Transfer Archives. **Level**: Specialist/researcher
External Users: Library may be used during regular business hours
Fee-based Information Services: Offered

**Canada. Agriculture & Agri-Food Canada.
Winnipeg Research Station**
195 Dafoe Rd., Winnipeg R3T 2M9
Inquiries: 983-0721 **Fax**: 983-4604

Canada. Fisheries & Oceans Canada. Freshwater Institute Library. The Eric Marshall Aquatic Research Library
501 University Cres., Winnipeg R3T 2N6
Inquiries: 983-5169 **Fax**: 261-7646
Electronic Access:
e-mail: library-fwi@dfo-mpo.gc.ca
NL Symbol: MWFW
Programs & Services: ILL offered
Collection: Subjects: Fisheries; aquatic sciences. **Special Collections**: Fritsch Collection of Illustrations of Freshwater Algae, on microfiche. **Languages**: French; Russian. **Level**: Specialist/researcher; graduate student; undergraduate/public
External Users: Library may be used during regular office hours

Canada. Health Canada. Federal Laboratories Library/Bibliothèque de laboratoires fédéraux
1015 Arlington St., Winnipeg R3E 3P6
Inquiries: 789-6001 **Fax**: 789-5003
NL Symbol: MWFLL
Mandate: To provide support to the research and diagnostic programs undertaken by the staff of the Federal Laboratories.
Programs & Services: Copying; ILL offered. **Languages**: French
Collection: Subjects: Microbiology; virology; veterinary medicine; biosafety; laboratory methods and procedures; infectious diseases. **Languages**: French. **Level**: Specialist/researcher
External Users: Appointment required; identification must be provided to security; access to library only

Canada. Indian & Northern Affairs. Regional Library
8th Floor, 275 Portage Ave., Winnipeg R3B 3A3
Inquiries: 983-4928 **Fax**: 983-7821
Programs & Services: ILL offered

Canada. Industry Canada. Canada/Manitoba Business Service Centre
[See: Canada/Manitoba Business Service Centre]

Canada. Labour Canada. Central Region Resource Centre
201–301 York Ave., Winnipeg R3C 0P4
Inquiries: 983-6375 **Fax**: 983-1248
Primary Clientele: Public
Programs & Services: ILL not offered
Collection: Subjects: Federal labour law; regulation; safety; equal opportunity. **Languages**: French
External Users: No public access

Canada. Justice Canada. Library
301-310 Broadway, Winnipeg R3C 0S6
Inquiries: 984-1348 **Fax**: 983-3636
Collection: Subjects: Law. **Languages**: French
External Users: No public access; no interlibrary loans provided

**Canada/Manitoba Business Service Centre/
Centre de services aux entreprises du Canada/Manitoba**
250-240 Graham Ave., Winnipeg R3C 4B3
Mailing Address: P.O. Box 2609, Winnipeg R3C 4B3
Inquiries: 984-2272 **Fax**: 983-3852
Electronic Access: http://www.cbsc.org/manitoba
e-mail: manitoba@cbsc.ic.gc.ca
NL Symbol: MWCMB
Mandate: To support the development of small business in Manitoba through a one-stop business centre that provides accurate, speedy, user-friendly information and programs and services required for small business decision making.
Programs & Services: Copying; ILL offered; Internet access; Business Start financial program; Aboriginal economic development. **Languages**: French
Collection: Subjects: Demographics; entrepreneurship; business management; marketing; business reference; finance; industry sector development; trade government documents; company annual reports. **Special Collections**: French language business collection; the only records management collection in Manitoba; Pro-Quest CD ROM system covering 3000 North American periodicals. **Languages**: French. **Level**: Specialist/researcher; graduate student; undergraduate/public
External Users: Materials may be used on site; video collection may be borrowed for seven day loan periods

Canada. Revenue Canada. Winnipeg District Office Research & Library Services
325 Broadway, Winnipeg R3C 4T4
Inquiries: 983-1013 **Fax**: 983-1015
Collection: Subjects: Accounting; customs; employee resources; GST; taxation

Canadian Authors Association Library
208–63 Albert St., Winnipeg R3B 1G3
Inquiries: 974-0512 **Fax**: 948-2073
Programs & Services: ILL not offered

Canadian Bison Association Library
Mailing Address: P.O. Box 1387, Morden R0G 1J0
Inquiries: 822-3219 **Fax**: 822-4328

Canadian Broadcasting Corporation Record Library
541 Portage Ave., Winnipeg R3C 2H1
Mandate: To provide recorded music to radio programmers and background music for television productions.

A Guide to Libraries in Manitoba

Primary Clientele: Broadcasters at C.B.C.
Collection: Subjects: Commercial recorded music
External Users: No public access or service

Canadian Centre for Philanthropy
3rd Floor, 5 Donald St. S., Winnipeg R3L 2T4
Inquiries: 477-5180 **Fax**: 453-6198
Programs & Services: ILL offered
Collection: Subjects: Fundraising; philanthropy; marketing

Canadian Forces School of Aerospace Studies
[See: LGen K. E. Lewis Memorial Library]

Canadian Grain Commission Library/ Bibliothèque commission canadienne des grains
300–303 Main St., Winnipeg R3C 3G8
Inquiries: 983-0878 **Fax**: 983-6098
Electronic Access: http://www.cgc.ca
e-mail: library@cgc.ca
NL Symbol: MWGR
Mandate: To support the organization's role in the Canadian grain quality assurance system.
Programs & Services: Copying; ILL offered
Collection: Subjects: Cereal and oilseed chemistry; plant biochemistry; food science; post-harvest technology; brewing; milling; baking; Canadian grain trade economics; grain statistics. **Special Collections**: Complete lecture series of the Canadian International Grains Institute; Grain Elevators in Canada, a complete list from 1912; C.G.C. Archives. **Languages**: French; German; Italian; Japanese. **Level**: Specialist/researcher; graduate student; undergraduate/public
External Users: Library may be used during regular business hours; check in with security officers on main floor
Fee-based Information Services: Offered

Canadian Mennonite Bible College Library
600 Shaftesbury Blvd., Winnipeg R3P 0M4
Inquiries: 888-6781 **Fax**: 831-5675
Electronic Access:
http://www.mbnet.mb.ca/~cmbc
e-mail: pfriesen@confmenno.ca
NL Symbol: MWCM
Programs & Services: Copying; ILL offered
Collection: Subjects: Biblical Studies; theology; music; Mennonite history. **Special Collections**: Mennonite Historical Library. **Languages**: German

Canadian Paraplegic Association (MB) Inc. Library
[See: Tony Mann Library]

Canadian Parents for French Library
411 Moroz St., Winnipeg R2C 2X4
Inquiries: 222-6537 **Fax**: 222-8180

Canadian Red Cross Society
200–360 Broadway, Winnipeg R3C 0T6
Inquiries: 982-7300 **Fax**: 942-8367
Programs & Services: ILL not offered

Canadian Wheat Board Library
423 Main St., Winnipeg R3C 2P5
Mailing Address: P.O. Box 816, Station Main, Winnipeg R3C 2P5

Inquiries: 983-3437 **Fax**: 983-4031
Electronic Access: http://www.cwb.ca
e-mail: library@cwb.ca
NL Symbol: MWCWB
Mandate: To provide information resources for the CWB staff concentrating on agriculture and economic information with the emphasis on marketing and transporting grain.
Programs & Services: Copying; ILL offered
Collection: Subjects: Grain trade; agricultural economics; international agriculture, economic and financial statistics. **Languages**: French; Spanish; Portuguese; German; Russian; Chinese; Italian
External Users: Appointment preferred
Fee-based Information Services: Offered

Carberry/North Cypress Branch Library
[See: Western Manitoba Regional Library]

Carolyn Sifton-Helene Fuld Library
[See: University of Manitoba Libraries Neil John Maclean Health Sciences Library]

Cartwright Branch Library
[See: Lakeland Regional Library]

Centennial Library
[See: Winnipeg Public Library Centennial Library]

Centre for Indigenous Environmental Resources (C.I.E.R.)
310 Johnston Terminal, 25 Forks Market Rd., Winnipeg R3C 4S8
Inquiries: 956-0660 **Fax**: 956-1895
Electronic Access: http://www.cier.mb.ca
e-mail: cierlib@mb.sympatico.ca
Programs & Services: ILL not offered
Collection: Subjects: Indigenous environmental
External Users: Appointment required; no loans provided

Centre for Mennonite Brethren Studies
169 Riverton Ave., Winnipeg R2L 2E5
Inquiries: 669-6575 **Fax**: 654-1865
Electronic Access: e-mail: adueck@cdnmbconf.ca
Programs & Services: Copying. **Languages**: German
Collection: Subjects: Theology; Mennonite history, theology, culture and genealogy; Hutterites. **Special Collections**: John A. Toews Historical Collection; The Ben and Esther Horch Music Collection. **Languages**: German
External Users: No appointment necessary; limited lending
Publications: *Mennonite Historian*

Certified General Accountants Association of Manitoba
4 Donald St. S., Winnipeg R3L 2T7
Inquiries: 477-1256 **Fax**: 453-7176
Primary Clientele: Members
Programs & Services: ILL not offered
Collection: Subjects: Accounting; finance; auditing; taxation; management information systems

Charleswood Public Library
[See: Winnipeg Public Library]

Children's Hospital Family Information Library
CK204-840 Sherbrook St., Winnipeg R3A 1S1
Inquiries: 787-1012 **Fax**: 787-2265
Electronic Access: e-mail: LPrice@hsc.mb.ca
Mandate: To provide information about the health care of children to families in hospital and to the public.
Programs & Services: Copying; ILL offered. **Languages**: French
Collection: Subjects: Disease specific information; psycho-social issues; parenting. **Languages**: French.
Level: Specialist/researcher; undergraduate/public
External Users: Patrons complete a request for information form

Children's Hospital Patient Library
CH253-840 Sherbrook St., Winnipeg R3A 1S1
Inquiries: 787-4340 **Fax**: 787-2265
Electronic Access: e-mail: LPrice@hsc.mb.ca
Mandate: To meet the recreational, educational and cultural needs of the in-patients of Children's Hospital and their families.
Collection: Books, audiotapes, videotapes and magazines suitable for children and adolescents. **Languages**: French, Aboriginal languages, Braille.

Churchill Public Library
Mailing Address: P.O. Box 730, Churchill R0B 0E0
Inquiries: 675-2731 **Fax**: 675-2934
NL Symbol: MCH

Churchill Research Centre Library
Launch Rd., Churchill R0B 0E0
Mailing Address: P.O. Box 610, Churchill R0B 0E0
Inquiries: 675-2307 **Fax**: 675-2139
External Users: Materials may be used on-site

C.I.S.T.I. Biodiagnostics Branch
[See: N.R.C. Information Centre Winnipeg]

Clara Lander Library. Winnipeg Art Gallery
300 Memorial Blvd., Winnipeg R3C 1V1
Inquiries: 786-6641 **Fax**: 788-4998
Electronic Access: http://www.wag.mb.ca
Mandate: To promote public access to information about the visual arts created by Canadians, and particularly by Manitobans, for the citizens of Manitoba
Programs & Services: Copying
Collection: Subjects: Fine arts; art history; Inuit art; Canadian art. **Special Collections**: Winnipeg Art Gallery publications. **Languages**: French

Collège universitaire de Saint-Boniface. Bibliothèque Alfred-Monnin
200 av. de la Cathédrale, Winnipeg R2H 0H7
Inquiries: 235-4403 **Fax**: 233-9472
Electronic Access: http://www.ustboniface.mb.ca
e-mail: biblio@ustboniface.mb.ca
NL Symbol: MSC
Mandate: To provide students and faculty members with the information resources and services required for the study programmes of the Collège.
Programs & Services: Copying; ILL offered. **Languages**: French
Collection: Subjects: General arts and science; education; business; computer science; translations; French literature and language. **Languages**: French; Spanish.

Level: Graduate student; undergraduate/public
External Users: Deposit required for those who are not students or faculty members
Fee-based Information Services: Offered

Community Therapy Services Inc.
5th Floor, 35 King St., Winnipeg R3B 1H4
Inquiries: 949-0533 **Fax**: 942-1428
Electronic Access: e-mail: ctsinc@mb.sympatico.ca
Programs & Services: Copying
Collection: Subjects: Medical rehabilitation; physiotherapy; occupational therapy; mental health; orthopedics; geriatrics. **Level**: Specialist/researcher
External Users: Appointment required

Concord College Library
169 Riverton Ave., Winnipeg R2L 2E5
Inquiries: 669-6583 **Fax**: 663-2468
Electronic Access:
http://www.concordcollege.mb.ca/concord/library.htm
e-mail: rthiessen@concordcollege.mb.ca
NL Symbol: MWMBC
Mandate: To serve the college community members of the public.
Programs & Services: Copying; ILL offered
Collection: Subjects: Biblical studies; theology; Anabaptist-Mennonite studies; church history; music; sacred music; humanities; social sciences. **Special Collections**: Anabaptist-Mennonite writings. **Languages**: German. **Level**: Specialist/researcher; graduate student; undergraduate/public
External Users: May use the library; must register at the circulation desk to borrow items

Concordia Hospital Library
1095 Concordia Ave., Winnipeg R2K 3S8
Inquiries: 661-7163 **Fax**: 663-7301
Electronic Access: e-mail: chlibrary@mb.imag.net
Primary Clientele: Staff; doctors
Programs & Services: Copying; ILL offered
Collection: Subjects: General medicine. **Level**: Specialist/researcher

Conference of Manitoba & Northwestern Ontario Resource Centre
170 St. Mary's Rd., Winnipeg R2H 1H9
Inquiries: 233-8911 **Fax**: 233-3289
Electronic Access:
http://www3.mb.sympatico.ca /~confmnwo/
e-mail: confmnwo@mb.sympatico.ca
Mandate: To serve the Christian community at large by providing leadership resources and learning tools to enable people to discover, accept, express and respond to the gospel of Jesus Christ.
Primary Clientele: Christian educators; study group learners; clergy
Programs & Services: Copying; ILL offered
Collection: Subjects: Bible studies; theology; Christian education; worship; Christian life; devotional literature; pastoral works. **Level**: Undergraduate/public
External Users: Open to anyone who lives in Manitoba or Northwestern Ontario; new users are asked to fill in an information form

Consumers' Association of Canada (Manitoba), Consumer Resource Centre

21–222 Osborne St. S., Winnipeg R3L 1Z3
Inquiries: 452-2572 **Fax**: 284-1876
Electronic Access:
http://www.mbnet.mb.ca/crm/law/eac01.html
e-mail: cacmb@mts.net
Mandate: To offer consumer education and information to the public and to help empower Manitobans in the marketplace.
Primary Clientele: Consumers in Manitoba
Programs & Services: Copying; Info-Line; Product Info Network
Collection: Subjects: Consumer issues; product information; consumer legislation and guidelines; consumer rights. **Languages**: French
External Users: Materials may be used on site; no loans provided

Cornish Public Library
[See: Winnipeg Public Library]

Crane Library
[See: J.W. Crane Memorial Library of Gerontology and Geriatrics]

The Daily Graphic **Library**
Mailing Address: P.O. Box 130, Portage la Prairie R1N 3B4
Inquiries: 857-3427 **Fax**: 239-1270
Collection: Subjects: Communication; mass media; current events
External Users: No public access

D'Arcy & Deacon Law Library
12th Floor, 330 St. Mary Ave., Winnipeg R3C 4E1
Inquiries: 942-2271 **Fax**: 943-4242
Collection: Subjects: Law; law enforcement

D.P.I.'s Resource Centre
101–7 Evergreen Pl., Winnipeg R3L 2T3
Inquiries: 287-8010 **Fax**: 453-1367
Electronic Access: e-mail: dpi@dpi.org
Collection: Subjects: Disabled persons; advocacy; human rights. **Languages**: French; Spanish. **Level**: Specialist/researcher; graduate student; undergraduate/public
External Users: Resource centre may be used during regular business hours; special loan requests by the general public will be assessed individually by administration

Dauphin Branch Library
[See: Parkland Regional Library]

David Winton Bell Memorial Library
Delta Waterfowl & Wetlands Research Station, R.R. #1, P.O. Box 1, Portage la Prairie R1N 3A1
Inquiries: 239-1900 **Fax**: 239-5950
Electronic Access:
e-mail: delta@deltawaterfowl.com
NL Symbol: MDW
Mandate: A resource for graduate students and researchers studying at the Delta Waterfowl & Wetlands Research Station.
Programs & Service: Copying; ILL offered
Collection: Subjects: Ornithology; wetland biology; ecology; animal behavior; natural history. **Level**:

A Guide to Libraries in Manitoba 143

Specialist/researcher; graduate student
External Users: Appointment required

Deer Lodge Centre Library
[See: J.W. Crane Memorial Library of Gerontology and Geriatrics]

Deloitte & Touche Chartered Accountants Research Centre
2200–360 Main St., Winnipeg R3C 3Z3
Inquiries: 942-0051 **Fax**: 947-9390
Programs & Services: ILL offered
Collection: Subjects: Economics
External Users: No public access

Disabled Peoples International's Resource Centre
[See: D.P.I.'s Resource Centre]

Donald W. Craik Engineering Library
[See: University of Manitoba Libraries]

D.S. Woods Education Library
[See: University of Manitoba Libraries]

Ducks Unlimited Institute for Wetland & Waterfowl Research Library
Mailing Address: Stonewall P.O. Box 1160, Oak Hammock Marsh R0C 2Z0
Inquiries: 467-3276 **Fax**: 467-9028
Electronic Access: http://www.ducks.ca/library/
Mandate: To locate and store information on waterfowl and wetlands that supports premier programs of research, the education of professionals in wetland and waterfowl biology and conservation and the conservation efforts of Ducks Unlimited.
Primary Clientele: Staff; employees
Programs & Services: ILL offered
Collection: Subjects: Wetlands; waterfowl; conservation; biology

Eckhardt-Grammatté Music Library
[See: University of Manitoba Libraries]

Economic Innovation and Technology Council Industrial Technology Centre
[See: Manitoba Industry, Trade & Tourism Industrial Technology Centre Library & Information Services]

E.K. Williams Law Library
[See: University of Manitoba Libraries]

Elizabeth Dafoe Library
[See: University of Manitoba Libraries]

Elkhorn Branch Library
[See: Border Regional Library]

Emerson Library
104 Church Street, Emerson R0A 0L0
Mailing Address: P.O. Box 340, Emerson R0A 0L0
Inquiries: 373-2002 **Fax**: 373-2486
Electronic Access: e-mail: emlibrary@hotmail.com
NL Symbol: MELP
Programs and Services: Copying; ILL offered; Internet access

Environment Canada Central Regional Library
[See: Environment Library/Bibliothèque de l'Environnement]

Environment Library/Bibliothèque de l'Environnement
160–123 Main St., Winnipeg R3C 1A5
Inquiries: 945-7126 **Fax**: 948-2357
Electronic Access:
http://www.gov.mb.ca/environ/pages/library.html
e-mail: spenziwol@env.gov.mb.ca
NL Symbol: MWEM
Mandate: To provide a full range of library services to staff of Manitoba Environment, Environment Canada and the Canadian Council of Ministers of the Environment.
Programs & Services: Copying; ILL offered
Collection: Subjects: Environmental protection; environmental quality; environmental conservation; pollution prevention; environmental legislation; climatology; meteorology; hydrology; wildlife management.
Special Collections: Manitoba Public Registry (Environment Act); Manitoba Contaminated Sites Registry (Contaminated Sites Remediation Act). **Languages**: French. **Level**: Specialist/researcher; graduate student; undergraduate/public
External Users: Materials may be used on-site

Energy & Mines Library
[See: Manitoba Energy & Mines Library]

The Eric Marshall Aquatic Research Library
[See: Canada Fisheries & Oceans Freshwater Institute Library The Eric Marshall Aquatic Research Library]

Erickson District Library
[See: Parkland Regional Library]

Eriksdale Public Library
Mailing Address: P.O. Box 219, Eriksdale R0C 0W0
Inquiries: 739-2668
NL Symbol: MEL

Evergreen Regional Library
63 First Ave., Gimli R0C 1B0
Mailing Address: P.O. Box 1140, Gimli R0C 1B0
Inquiries: 642-7912
Electronic Access: chk549@freenet.mb.ca
NL Symbol: MGE
Programs & Services: Copying; ILL offered
Collection: Languages: Icelandic; French; Ukrainian; German; Italian; Polish; Norwegian. **Special Collections**: Icelandic collection
Branches:
Arborg Branch Library
202 Main St., Arborg R0C 0A0
Mailing Address: P.O. Box 4053, Arborg R0C 0A0
Inquiries: 376-5238
Electronic Access: e-mail: lhegg@en.mb.ca
NL Symbol: MAB
Programs & Services: ILL offered
Collection: Special Collections: Icelandic Collection.
Languages: Icelandic

Riverton Branch Library
Mailing Address: P.O. Box 310, Riverton R0C 2R0

Inquiries: 378-2988
Electronic Access: e-mail: dhk550@ecn.mb.ca
NL Symbol: MRB
Programs & Services: ILL offered
Collection: Special Collections: Icelandic Collection

Father Harold Drake, S.J. Library
[See: University of Manitoba Libraries St. Paul's College]

Federal Laboratories Library/Bibliothèque de laboratoires fédéraux
[See: Canada Health Canada Federal Laboratories Library / Bibliothèque de laboratoires fédéraux]

Fillmore Riley Library
1700–360 Main St., Winnipeg R3M 0N3
Inquiries: 956-2970 **Fax**: 957-0516
Electronic Access: http://frinfo@fillmoreriley.com
e-mail: cstewart@fillmoreriley.com
Mandate: To provide library and legal research services to lawyers and articling students at Fillmore Riley.
Collection: Subjects: Law; intellectual property; insurance law
External Users: Appointments required; restrictions on use

Fire Fighters Historical Society of Winnipeg
56 Maple St., Winnipeg R3B 0Y8
Inquiries: 942-4817 **Fax**: 885-1306
Electronic Access: e-mail: kuryluk@gatewest.net
Mandate: To promote and encourage public interest in the Fire Service history.
Programs & Services: Copying; genealogical research
Collection: Subjects: Fire history; fire prevention; fire reports; fire records; fire losses. **Special Collections**: Newspaper clippings, 1882 to present; Photo library of approximately 7500 photographs. **Level**: Specialist/researcher; graduate student; undergraduate/public
External Users: Please contact library; materials may be used on site; photocopying of most documents is allowed; on-site study periods can be arranged
Publications: *Alarm of Fire*

Flin Flon Public Library
58 Main St., Flin Flon R8A 1J8
Inquiries: 687-3397 **Fax**: 687-4233
Electronic Access: e-mail: ffpl@hotmail.com
NL Symbol: MFF
Programs & Services: Copying; ILL offered; fax service; Internet access
Collection: Languages: French
Friends Group

Food Development Centre Library
[See: Manitoba Rural Development Food Development Centre]

Fort Garry Public Library
[See: Winnipeg Public Library]

Fort Whyte Centre Library
1961 McCreary Rd., Winnipeg R3P 2K9
Inquiries: 989-8355 **Fax**: 895-4700
Electronic Access:
http://www.mbnet.mb.ca/fortwhyte

e-mail: fwc@fortwhyte.mb.ca
Programs & Services: Copying; ILL not offered
External Users: Non-members may use collection on site but cannot borrow materials; fee charged for membership

Foxwarren Branch Library
[See: Parkland Regional Library]

Gilbert Plains Branch Library
[See: Parkland Regional Library]

Gillam Public Library
[See: Bette Winner Public Library]

Gladstone & District Library
[See: Parkland Regional Library]

Glenboro/South Cypress Branch Library
[See: Western Manitoba Regional Library]

Glenwood & Souris Regional Library
18–114 2nd St. S., Souris R0K 2C0
Mailing Address: P.O. Box 760, Souris R0K 2C0
Inquiries: 483-2757
Electronic Access: e-mail: gsrl@techplus.com
NL Symbol: MSOG
Programs & Services: Copying; ILL offered
Collection: **Special Collections**: Local area histories

Grace General Hospital Library
300 Booth Dr., Winnipeg R3J 3M7
Inquiries: 837-0127 **Fax**: 885-7909
Electronic Access: e-mail: gracelib@escape.ca
Mandate: To provide easy and effective access to information and resources to all levels of staff, students, physicians, patients, families and the community.
Programs & Services: Copying; ILL offered
Collection: **Subjects**: Medical; nursing; allied health; consumer health. **Level**: Specialist/researcher; graduate student; undergraduate/public
External Users: Required to register with library

Grand Library Grand Lodge of Manitoba
420 Corydon Ave., Winnipeg R3L 3M7
Inquiries: 453-7410
Primary Clientele: Masonic Lodges
Programs & Services: ILL offered
Collection: **Subjects**: Freemasonry

Grandview Branch Library
[See: Parkland Regional Library]

Great Library
331–408 York Ave., Winnipeg R3C 0P9
Inquiries: 945-1958 **Fax**: 948-2138
Mandate: To serve the legal profession, judges, Department of Justice staff, other government departments and the general public.
Programs & Services: Copying; ILL offered
Collection: **Subjects**: Law. **Special Collections**: Collection of Manitoba judgments, 1970 to present

Guertin Brothers Coatings & Sealants Ltd. Library
50 Panet Rd., Winnipeg R2J 0R9
Inquiries: 237-0241 **Fax**: 233-5051

Collection: **Subjects**: Paint; Material Safety Data sheets; Product Safety Data sheets. **Languages**: French
External Users: No public access; paint users may request Product and Material Safety Data sheets

Guild of Canadian Weavers
c/o 11 Shakespeare Bay, Winnipeg R3K 0M5
Mandate: To provide resources for weavers
Primary Clientele: Members
Collections: **Subjects**: Weaving. **Languages**: Swedish. **Level**: Specialist/researcher
External Users: No public access

Hamiota Centennial Library
[See: Parkland Regional Library]

Hamiota District Health Centre Library
177 Birch Ave. E., Hamiota R0M 0T0
Inquiries: 764-2412 **Fax**: 764-2325
Mandate: To provide current health resources to health care professionals and the general public.
Programs & Services: Copying; ILL offered
Collection: **Subjects**: Professional health references; consumer health information
External Users: No restrictions on use

Headingley Municipal Library
81 Alboro St., Headingley R4J 1A3
Inquiries: 888-5410
NL Symbol: MHH
Programs & Services: Copying; ILL offered

Henderson Public Library
[See: Winnipeg Public Library]

Heritage Winnipeg Corp. Resource Centre
509–63 Albert St., Winnipeg R3B 1G4
Inquiries: 942-2663 **Fax**: 942-2094
Electronic Access: e-mail: heritage@escape.ca
Mandate: To educate the public on history and heritage.
Programs & Services: Copying
Collection: **Subjects**: International history; architectural heritage; Canadian, Manitoban and Winnipeg history. **Languages**: French. **Level**: Specialist/researcher; graduate student; undergraduate/public
External Users: Appointments preferred; no borrowing privileges for non-members; fee charged for membership

Hudson's Bay Company Archives
[See: Manitoba Culture, Heritage & Citizenship. Hudson's Bay Company Archives Provincial Archives of Manitoba]

Industrial Technology Centre Library & Information Services
[See: Manitoba Industry, Tourism & Trade Industrial Technology Centre Library & Information Services]

Institut Joseph-Dubuc
2122–200 av. de la Cathédrale, Winnipeg R2H 0H7
Inquiries: 235-4405 **Fax**: 233-0245
Electronic Access:
e-mail: institut@ustboniface.mb.ca
Mandate: To provide French speaking lawyers with resource material in the field of Common Law.

Programs & Services: Languages: French
Collection: Subjects: Common law. **Languages:** collection is in French only. **Level:** Specialist/researcher
External Users: Materials may be used on site

Institute of Urban Studies Reference Library
346 Portage Ave., Winnipeg R3C 0C3
Inquiries: 982-1140 **Fax:** 943-4695
Electronic Access:
http://www.uwinnipeg.ca/ius/title.htm
e-mail: nancy.klos@coned.uwinnipeg.ca
Mandate: The I.U.S. Library has a dual function as a university research library and a community resource centre, specializing in the multi-disciplinary field of urban studies with a focus on Canada and Winnipeg.
Primary Clientele: University students; government research staff; private consultants
Programs & Services: Copying
Collection: Subjects: City planning; inner cities; urban transportation; municipal government; urban Aboriginal issues; housing; sustainable urban development; urban policy. **Special Collections:** Institute of Urban Studies Publication collection. **Languages:** French. **Level:** Specialist/researcher; graduate student; undergraduate/public
External Users: Appointment required; limited borrowing privileges restricted to University of Winnipeg staff and faculty

International Institute for Sustainable Development Information Centre
161 Portage Ave. E., 6th Floor, Winnipeg R3B 0Y4
Inquiries: 958-7724 **Fax:** 958-7710
Electronic Access: http://iisd.ca/ic/
e-mail: mroy@iisdpost.iisd.ca
Listservs: Weekly Journal Review; New & Notable for IISD
Mandate: The IC's role is to develop a highly focused collection and database on sustainable development; to provide international access to the collection; to respond to information and research inquiries; to inform decision-makers about the latest sustainable development information materials.
Primary Clientele: Staff of the Institute
Programs & Services: Copying; ILL not offered
Collection: Subjects: International relations; international organizations; ecological economics; population; climate change policy. **Level:** Specialist/researcher; graduate student; undergraduate/public
External Users: Appointment required; no loans provided
Fee-based Information Services: Offered
Publications: *Hot Topic*; *Developing Ideas*

Islamic Ahmadiyya Library
525 Kylemore Ave., Winnipeg R3L 1B5
Inquiries: 475-2642 **Fax:** 452-2455
Mandate: To make information on Islam easily accessible to all those who are seeking to increase their knowledge of Islam.
Primary Clientele: Members
Programs & Services: ILL offered
Collection: Subjects: Islam; Ahmadiyyat. **Languages:** French; Urdu, Arabic. various African, Asian and European languages. **Level:** Specialist/researcher; graduate students; undergraduate/public

External Users: Appointment required

J.W. Crane Memorial Library of Gerontology and Geriatrics
2109 Portage Ave., Winnipeg R3J 0L3
Inquiries: 831-2152 **Fax:** 888-1805
Electronic Access:
http://www.deerlodge.mb.ca
e-mail: jwclib@deerlodge.mb.ca
NL Symbol: MWDL
Mandate: To provide resources and services to the staff and clients of Deer Lodge Centre, the Riverview Health Centre and long term care facilities throughout the province.
Primary Clientele: Health care providers and consumers
Programs & Services: Copying; ILL offered
Collection: Subjects: Geriatrics; gerontology; long term care
External Users: Materials may be used on site during regular business hours
Fee-based Information Services: Fee charged to non-affiliates

Jake Epp Library
255 Elmdale St., Steinbach R0A 2A0
Mailing Address: P.O. Box 2050, Steinbach R0A 2A0
Inquiries: 326-6841 **Fax:** 623-6859
Electronic Access:
http://www.ccco.net/~cap_stb/stblib.html
e-mail: steinlib@rocketmail.com
NL Symbol: MSTE
Programs & Services: Copying; ILL offered
Collection: Special Collections: *Carillon* newspaper collection. **Languages:** German
Publications: *History of the Steinbach Public library, 1968–1997*
Friends Group

Jewish Historical Society of Western Canada
C116–123 Doncaster St., Winnipeg R3N 2B2
Inquiries: 477-7460 **Fax:** 477-7465
Electronic Access:
http://www.concentric.net/~lkessler/jhswc.shtml
Collection: Subjects: History of Jewish people in Western Canada; genealogy

Jewish Public Library
1725 Main St., Winnipeg R2V 1Z4
Inquiries: 338-4048
Primary Clientele: Jewish community; public
Programs & Services: ILL offered
Collection: Subjects: Judaica. **Languages:** Hebrew; Yiddish; Russian

John E. Robbins Library
[See: Brandon University John E. Robbins Library]

Jolys Regional Library
505 Hebert Ave. N., St-Pierre-Jolys R0A 1V0
Mailing Address: P.O. Box 118, St-Pierre-Jolys R0A 1V0
Inquiries: 433-7729
Electronic Access:
http://www.pli.mb.ca/jolyslibrary
e-mail: stplibrary@pli.mb.ca

Programs & Services: Copying; ILL offered. **Languages**: French
Collection: Languages: French
Branches:
St. Malo Branch Library
Room 84, Chalet Malouin, St. Malo R0A 1T0
Inquiries: 347-5606
Electronic Access: e-mail: stmlibrary@pli.mb.ca

Keewatin Community College Library
7th St. E., The Pas R9A 1M7
Mailing Address: P.O. Box 3000, The Pas R9A 1M7
Inquiries: 627-8561 **Fax**: 623-4597
NL Symbol: MTPK
Mandate: To meet the education, information and research needs of users and to support K.C.C.'s programs by offering quality service and a variety of resources in different formats and media.
Programs & Services: Copying; ILL offered
Collection: Subjects: Natural resources; nursing; dental assisting; Aboriginal studies; process engineering; business administration; recreational leadership; automotive; trade and technology. **Special Collections**: Aboriginal studies. **Level**: Undergraduate/public

Lac du Bonnet Regional Library
84–3rd St., Lac du Bonnet R0E 1A0
Mailing Address: P.O. Box 216, Lac du Bonnet R0E 1A0
Inquiries: 345-2653 **Fax**: 345-6287
Electronic Access:
http://www.granite.mb.ca/llibrary/
e-mail: mldb@granite.mb.ca
NL Symbol: MLDB
Programs & Services: Copying; ILL offered; Internet access

Lakeland Regional Library
318 Williams Ave., Killarney R0K 1G0
Mailing Address: P.O. Box 970, Killarney R0K 1G0
Inquiries: 523-4949 **Fax**: 523-7460
Electronic Access:
http://www.techplus.com/lrl/index.html
e-mail: lrl@mail.techplus.com
NL Symbol: MKL
Programs & Services: ILL offered
Collection: Special Collections: *Killarney Guide* newspaper collection on microfilm, 1896-1994
Branches:
Cartwright Branch Library
Railway Ave., Cartwright R0K 0L0
Inquiries: 529-2161

Pilot Mound Branch Library
219 Broadway Ave. W., Pilot Mound R0G 1P0
Mailing Address: P.O. Box 126, Pilot Mound R0G 1P0
Inquiries: 825-2035 **Fax**: 825-2116
Electronic Access:
http://www.mts.net/~afoidart/pmen.htm
e-mail: pmlibrary@mts.net
NL Symbol: MPM
Programs & Services: ILL offered
Collection: Special Collections: Archival books with photographs of all babies born in Pilot Mound Hospital; Burial records for Pilot Mound Cemetery, 1882–present

Langruth Library
[See: Parkland Regional Library]

Laura Delamater Resource Centre
[See: The Marquis Project – The Laura Delamater Resource Centre]

Leaf Rapids Public Library
Mailing Address: P.O. Box 190, Leaf Rapids R0B 1W0
Inquiries: 473-2742 **Fax**: 473-8828
Electronic Access: e-mail: mlr@cancom.net
NL Symbol: MLR
Programs & Services: Copying; ILL offered
Collection: Languages: French; Cree

League for Life in Manitoba Library
579 Des Meurons St., Winnipeg R2H 2P6
Inquiries: 233-8047 **Fax**: 233-0523
Mandate: To provide information on life issues to teachers, high school and university students.
Programs & Services: Copying
Collection: Subjects: Abortion; euthanasia/assisted suicide; reproductive technology; post abortion syndrome; teen sexuality. **Languages**: French. **Level**: Undergraduate/public
External Users: Library may be used during regular office hours

Legislative Assembly. Elections Manitoba Library
200 Vaughan St., Winnipeg R2K 0L7
Inquiries: 945-3225 **Fax**: 945-6011
Collection: Special Collections: Electoral Reform & Party Financing (Royal Commission Collection)

Legislative Library of Manitoba
[See: Manitoba Culture, Heritage & Citizenship Legislative Library]

Library Allard
[See: Bibliothèque Allard Library]

Library of the Fire Service Museum of Winnipeg
[See: Fire Fighters Historical Society of Winnipeg]

Lieutenant General K.E. Lewis Memorial Library
P.O. Box 17000, Stn. Forces, Winnipeg R3J 3Y5
Inquiries: 833-2500 ext. 5662 **Fax**: 833-2529
NL Symbol: MWCF
Mandate: To provide access to the information necessary to fulfill the mission of the Canadian Forces School of Aerospace Studies and secondarily, to Canadian Forces 17 Wing.
Programs & Services: Copying; ILL offered. **Languages**: French
Collection: Subjects: Aerospace operation; aerospace procurement; aerospace programme management; aerospace technologies; air warfare; history of air power; information warfare; joint warfare; leadership and officer development. **Languages**: French. **Level**: Specialist/researcher; graduate student; undergraduate/public
External Users: Appointment required
Fee-based Information Services: Offered

Literacy Partners of Manitoba Resource Centre
998–167 Lombard Ave., Winnipeg R3L 1S3
Inquiries: 947-5755 **Fax**: 944-9918
Electronic Access:
http://www.nald.ca/litpman.htm
e-mail: literacy@magic.mb.ca
Mandate: To provide adult literacy information and materials to members of Literacy Partners of Manitoba and to the public.
Primary Clientele: Members; employees
Collection: Subjects: Adult literacy
External Users: Non-members may use materials in-house only; outreach to adult literacy programs throughout Manitoba

L.M. Architectural Group Library
300–290 Vaughan St., Winnipeg R3B 2L9
Inquiries: 942-0681 **Fax**: 943-8676
Collection: Subjects: Architecture; engineering
External Users: No public access

Louis Riel Public Library
[See: Winnipeg Public Library]

Lynn Lake Centennial Library
Mailing Address: P.O. Box 1127, Lynn Lake R0B 0W0
Inquiries: 356-8222
NL Symbol: MLLC

M.F.L. Occupational Health Centre Library
102–275 Broadway, Winnipeg R3C 4M6
Inquiries: 949-0811 **Fax**: 956-0848
Electronic Access: e-mail: mflohc@mflohc.mb.ca
NL Symbol: MWMFL
Programs & Services: Copying
Collection: Subjects: Occupational medicine; safety; toxicology. **Special Collections**: Extensive collection of National Institute of Occupational Safety and Health (N.I.O.S.H.) publications. **Level**: Specialist/researcher; graduate student; undergraduate/public
External Users: Materials may be used on-site; no loans provided

Manitoba Archaeological Society
438–167 Lombard Ave., Winnipeg R3C 2Y4
Mailing Address: P.O. Box 1171, Winnipeg R3C 2Y4
Inquiries: 942-7243 **Fax**: 942-3749
Publications: *Manitoba Archaeological Journal*; *Manitoba Archaeological Newsletter*

Manitoba Association for Rights & Liberties
502–177 Lombard Ave., Winnipeg R3B 0W5
Inquiries: 947-0213 **Fax**: 946-0403
Electronic Access: e-mail: marl@pangea.ca
Programs & Services: Copying
External Users: Appointment required

Manitoba Association of Playwrights
503–100 Arthur St., Winnipeg R3B 1H3
Inquiries: 942-8941 **Fax**: 942-1555
Mandate: To maintain an archive of Manitoba plays and a library of Canadian plays
Collection: Subjects: Canadian & Manitoban plays
External Users: Appointment preferred

Manitoba Association of School Trustees (M.A.S.T.)
191 Provencher Blvd., Winnipeg R2H 0G4
Inquiries: 233-1595 **Fax**: 231-1356
Electronic Access: http://www.mast.mb.ca
e-mail: aplant@mast.mb.ca
Mandate: To maintain a collection of resources on education-specific topics and issues for members and the public.
Programs & Services: Copying
Collection: Subjects: Education
External Users: Appointment required

Manitoba Cancer Treatment and Research Education Library
100 Olivia St., Winnipeg R3E 0V9
Inquiries: 787-2136 **Fax**: 787-1184
Electronic Access: e-mail: donnac@mctrf.mb.ca
Primary Clientele: Staff
Programs & Services: Copying; ILL offered
Collection: Subjects: Oncology; cellular biology
External Users: No public access

Manitoba Child Care Association Resource Library
364 McGregor St., Winnipeg R2W 4X3
Inquiries: 586-8587 **Fax**: 589-5613
Programs & Services: ILL not offered
Collection: Subjects: Child day care; early childhood education

Manitoba Crafts Museum and Library
392 Academy Rd., Winnipeg R3N 0B8
Primary Clientele: Members
Collection: Level: Specialist/researcher; graduate student; undergraduate/public
External Users: Materials may be used on-site

Manitoba Culture, Heritage & Citizenship. Legislative Library
200 Vaughan St., Winnipeg R3C 1T5
Inquiries: 945-4330 **Fax**: 948-2008
Electronic Access: http://www.gov.mb.ca/leg-lib/
e-mail: legislative_library@chc.gov.mb.ca
NL Symbol: MWP
Mandate: To support the conduct of public affairs and the development of a well-informed society by providing efficient, effective and impartial access to specialized information resources for the Legislature, government and people of Manitoba and ensure future access to Manitoba's published heritage.
Programs & Services: Copying; ILL offered. **Languages**: French
Collection: Subjects: Law and legislation; politics and government; economic and social issues; public administration; management; Manitoba history; western Canadian history. **Special Collections**: Most complete collection of historical newspapers in Manitoba dating back to 1859; depository collection of books, periodicals and documents published in Manitoba; depository and exchange collections of Federal government documents, provincial government publications, U.N. and other international organizations; political, historical and biographical newspaper clippings; Rare Book Collection. **Languages**: French; German; Icelandic; Polish; Swedish; Ukrainian; Yiddish. **Level**: Specialist/researcher
External Users: Materials may be used on site

Publications: *Manitoba Government Publications Monthly Checklist*
Branches:
Legislative Reading Room
Room 260, Legislative Building, 450 Broadway, Winnipeg R3C 0V8
Inquiries: 945-4243 **Fax**: 948-2167
Electronic Access: e-mail: reading@leg.gov.mb.ca

Manitoba Culture, Heritage & Citizenship. Hudson's Bay Company Archives Provincial Archives of Manitoba
200 Vaughan St., Winnipeg R3L 0H4
Inquiries: 945-4949 **Fax**: 948-3236
Electronic Access:
http://www.gov.mb.ca/chc/archives/hbca/index.html
e-mail: hbca@chc.gov.mb.ca
Mandate: To serve as an information resource for staff and clientele of the Hudson's Bay Company Archives.
Programs & Services: Copying; ILL offered
Collection: **Subjects**: Hudson's Bay Company; fur trade; North West Company; Western Canada; Western United States; Arctic Canada; Arctic exploration; Aboriginal peoples of North America. **Special Collections**: Rare Book Collection; 18th and 19th century holdings of travel and exploration literature. **Level**: Specialist/researcher; graduate students; undergraduate/public
External Users: Materials may be used on-site Hudson's Bay Company Trust Fund; Hudson's Bay History Foundation

Manitoba Culture, Heritage & Citizenship. Public Library Services
200-1525 1st St., Brandon R7A 7A1
Inquiries: 726-6590 **Toll Free**: 1-800-252-9998
Fax: 726-6868
Electronic Access: http://pls.chc.gov.mb.ca:80801
e-mail: pls@chc.gov.mb.ca
NL Symbol: MWPL
Primary Clientele: Rural libraries and open shelf patrons of Manitoba
Programs & Services: Copying; ILL offered; traveling libraries; open shelf
Collection: **Languages**: French; Chinese; Dutch; Finnish; German; Hungarian; Italian; Japanese; Norwegian; Polish; Portuguese; Russian; Spanish; Swedish; Ukrainian; Vietnamese; some Native languages; Braille
External Users: Traveling libraries and open shelf restricted to those without library services; talking books restricted to visually handicapped
Publications: *PLS Newsletter*

Manitoba Development Centre Library
Mailing Address: P.O. Box 1190, Portage la Prairie R1N 3C6
Inquiries: 856-4205 **Fax**: 856-4258
Collection: **Subjects**: Developmental handicaps

Manitoba Eco-Network Environmental Resource Centre
2-70 Albert St., Winnipeg R3B 1E7
Inquiries: 947-6511 **Fax**: 947-6514
Electronic Access: e-mail: men@web.net
Mandate: To be a resource for students and the general public on a wide range of environmental issues.
Programs & Services: Copying

Collection: **Subjects**: Sustainability; forests; toxins; waste reduction; health and the environment; nuclear energy; energy alternatives; climate change. **Languages**: French
External Users: Library may be used during business hours; appointments can be made to access the collection after hours

Manitoba Education & Training. Direction des ressources éducatives françaises (D.R.E.F.)
S208–200 av. de la Cathédrale, Winnipeg R2H 0H7
Inquiries: 945-8594 **Fax**: 945-0092
Electronic Access:
http://bibliotheque.edu.gov.mb.ca
e-mail: ldoucet@minet.gov.mb.ca
NL Symbol: MWDRE
Mandate: To provide instructional materials and library services to teachers of all grades in Franco-Manitoban and French Immersion schools and schools providing Basic French courses in Manitoba.
Primary Clientele: Educators
Programs & Services: ILL offered. **Languages**: French
Collection: **Subjects**: Science; math; French as a language; social studies; music; art; physical education; health; education. **Special Collections**: French-language CD-ROM collection supporting the K-S4 curriculum. **Languages**: French
External Users: Contact the library or access the collection on the Internet

Manitoba Education & Training. Instructional Resources Unit
Main Floor, 1181 Portage Ave., Winnipeg R3G 0T3
Inquiries: 945-7830 **Library Hours**: 945-5371
Toll Free: 1-800-282-8069
Toll Free (Media Booking only): 1-800-592-7330
Fax: 945-8756
Electronic Access: http://library.edu.gov.mb.ca
e-mail: iru@minet.gov.mb.ca
NL Symbol: MWE
Mandate: To provide Kindergarten through Senior 4 educators and teachers-in-training with curriculum implementation, educational research and professional development resources.
Programs & Services: Copying; ILL offered
Collection: **Subjects**: Education; approved textbooks; educational research, theory and practice. **Special Collections**: Multicultural Education Resource Centre; Old Textbook Collection
External Users: Materials may be used on-site

Manitoba Education & Training. Special Materials Services
215–1181 Portage Ave., Winnipeg R3G 0T3
Inquiries: 945-7842 **Fax**: 945-7914
NL Symbol: MWESM
Programs & Services: ILL not offered

Manitoba Energy & Mines Library
360–1395 Ellice Ave., Winnipeg R3G 3P2
Inquiries: 945-6569 **Fax**: 945-8427
Electronic Access:
http://www.gov.mb.ca/em/information/index.html
e-mail: library@em.gov.mb.ca
NL Symbol: MWEMM
Programs & Services: Copying; ILL offered; Internet

access; GSC link terminal to access the Geological Survey of Canada. **Languages**: French
Collection: Subjects: Manitoba geology; mining and petroleum resources; energy conservation; alternative energies. **Special Collections**: Geological Survey of Canada publications; comprehensive map collection on Manitoba geology; exchange publications for United States Geological Survey, Ontario, Saskatchewan, North Dakota and Minnesota geological surveys. **Level**: Specialist/researcher; graduate student; undergraduate/public
External Users: Materials may be used on site; no borrowing privileges

Manitoba Environment Resource Centre
[See: Environment Library/Bibliothèque de l'Environnement]

Manitoba Federation of Labour. Occupational Health Centre Library
[See: M.F.L. Occupational Health Centre Library]

Manitoba Finance. Federal-Provincial Relations & Research Library
910–386 Broadway, Winnipeg R3C 3R6
Inquiries: 945-3757 **Fax**: 945-5051
Electronic Access: e-mail: bemiller@gov.mb.ca
NL Symbol: MWFI
Programs & Services: Copying; ILL offered
Collection: Subjects: Taxation; finance; economics.
Level: Specialist/researcher
External Users: No public access; phone requests and photocopying services only

Manitoba Genealogical Society
Unit E, 1045 St. James St., Winnipeg R3H 1B1
Inquiries: 783-9139 **Fax**: 783-0190
Programs & Services: ILL not offered
Collection: Subjects: Genealogy; family history

Manitoba Health. Library Services
P.O. Box 925, 599 Empress St., Winnipeg R3C 2T6
Inquiries: 786-7124 **Fax**: 945-5063
Electronic Access:
http://www.gov.mb.ca/health/library
e-mail: library@health.gov.mb.ca
NL Symbol: MWHP
Mandate: To provide library and information services to departmental staff and the public to support corporate research and planning and to increase the public's knowledge and awareness of health issues.
Programs & Services: Copying; ILL offered
Collection: Subjects: Health; health administration.
Special Collections: Health care reform; Health Department reports. **Language**: French. **Level**: Specialist/researcher
External Users: Walk-in clients must register; limit of 4 books; reference books and journals restricted to library use; AV materials restricted to departmental staff, schools, libraries and associations

Manitoba Historical Society Library
470–167 Lombard Ave., Winnipeg R3B 0T6
Inquiries: 947-0559 **Fax**: 943-1093
Primary Clientele: Members; students
Programs & Services: Copying; ILL not offered

Collection: Subjects: Manitoba history
External Users: Materials do not circulate

Manitoba Hydro Library
820 Taylor Ave., Winnipeg R3M 3T1
Mailing Address: P.O. Box 815, Winnipeg R3C 2P4
Inquiries: 474-3614 **Fax**: 453-1838
Electronic Access:
http://www.ils.ca/mbl/index.htm
e-mail: rlapierre@hydro.mb.ca
NL Symbol: MWH
Mandate: To serve the work-related information needs of Manitoba Hydro employees
Programs & Services: Copying; ILL offered
Collection: Subjects: Engineering; electrical; utilities; business. **Special Collection**: Manitoba Hydro technical reports. **Level**: Specialist/researcher
External Users: Appointment preferred
Fee-based Information Services: Offered

Manitoba Indian Cultural Education Centre. Peoples Library
119 Sutherland Ave., Winnipeg R2W 3C9
Inquiries: 942-0228 **Fax**: 947-6564
Publications: *Education Kit List, Children's Materials, VHS Tapes for Circulation*

Manitoba Industry, Tourism & Trade Canada/ Manitoba Business Service Centre
[See: Canada/Manitoba Business Service Centre]

Manitoba Industry, Tourism & Trade. Industrial Technology Centre Library & Information Services
1329 Niakwa Rd. E., Winnipeg R2J 3T4
Inquiries: 945-1413 **Fax**: 945-1784
Electronic Access: www.itc.mb.ca
e-mail: library@itc.mb.ca
NL Symbol: MWMRC
Mandate: To provide the best source of technical information to Manitoba industry, business, entrepreneurs and innovators.
Primary Clientele: Manitoba industry and business
Programs & Services: ILL offered
Collection: Subjects: Applied technical information and sourcing in: industrial engineering; mechanical engineering; manufacturing; product design; testing; metals; plastics; innovation and patents; electronics. **Special Collections**: Worldwide Standards Index; Industry Standards and Specifications; Patent Information; Industrial Directories; Buyer's Guides.
External users: Appointments not necessary, but please call ahead of visit
Fee-based Information Services: Offered

Manitoba Justice. Attorney General's Library
6th Floor, 405 Broadway, Winnipeg R3C 3L5
Inquiries: 945-2895 **Fax**: 948-2150
Primary Clientele: Staff
Collection: Subjects: Law
External Users: No public access

Manitoba Justice. Community & Youth Correctional Services Library
8th Floor, 405 Broadway, Winnipeg R3C 3L6
Inquiries: 945-2574 **Fax**: 948-2166

A Guide to Libraries in Manitoba

External Users: Please contact library

Manitoba Labour Board Library
404–428 Portage Ave., Winnipeg R3C 0E2
Inquiries: 945-3783 **Fax**: 945-1296
Collection: Subjects: Labour relations

Manitoba Labour. Education Centre
206–275 Broadway, Winnipeg R3C 4M6
Inquiries: 942-6532
Collection: Subjects: Labour movement

Manitoba Labour. Research Branch
409–401 York Ave., Winnipeg R3C 0P8
Inquiries: 945-3412 **Fax**: 948-2085
Programs & Services: ILL not offered

Manitoba Labour. Workplace Safety & Health Library
200–401 York Ave., Winnipeg R3C 0P8
Inquiries: 945-0580 **Fax**: 945-4556
Library Hours: 945-3446
Electronic Access:
http://www.gov.mb.ca/labour/safety/library
NL Symbol: MWLW
Mandate: To provide library and information services to departmental staff and the public in support of the Workplace Safety and Health Division whose mandate is to administer the act and regulations related to the protection of health and safety of workers in the Province of Manitoba.
Programs & Services: Copying; ILL offered
Collection: Subjects: Industrial safety; industrial hygiene; occupational health; toxicology; legislation. **Special Collections**: N.I.O.S.H. (National Institute for Occupational Safety & Health – U.S.) publications; Canadian Standards Association (C.S.A.) publications.
Level: Specialist/researcher; graduate student; undergraduate/public
External Users: Appointment required; no borrowing privileges

Manitoba Métis Federation Library
412 McGregor Ave., Winnipeg R2W 4X5
Inquiries: 586-8474 **Fax**: 586-4235
Programs & Services: ILL not offered
Collection: Subjects: Métis culture and history. **Languages**: French; Michif; Cree
External Users: Appointment preferred; materials may be used on-site

Manitoba Museum of Man and Nature Library
190 Rupert Ave., Winnipeg R3B 0N2
Inquiries: 988-0692 / 988-0662 **Fax**: 942-3679
Electronic Access:
http://www.manitobamuseum.mb.ca
e-mail: library@mbnet.mb.ca
NL Symbol: MWMM
Mandate: To support the work of the Museum.
Primary Clientele: Staff and volunteers of the Museum
Programs & Services: Copying; ILL offered
Collection: Subjects: Archaeology; astronomy; botany; Native ethnology; geology; Manitoba history; museology; science and technology; zoology; multicultural studies. **Special Collections**: Oral history tapes; photograph collection; Eaton's catalogues.
Languages: French. **Level**: Specialist/researcher; graduate student; undergraduate/public
External Users: Appointment preferred; no borrowing privileges; ILL offered
Fee-based Information Services: Offered

Manitoba Natural Resources. Air Photo Library
1007 Century St., Winnipeg R3H 0W4
Inquiries: 945-6669 **Fax**: 945-1365
Library Hours: 945-6666
Electronic Access: e-mail: mapsales@nr.gov.mb.ca
Programs & Services: Reproductions of aerial photographs
Collection: Special Collections: Aerial photographs of Manitoba dating back to 1928. **Level**: Specialist/researcher; graduate student; undergraduate/public
External Users: Library may be used during business hours

Manitoba Natural Resources Library
26–200 Saulteaux Cres., Winnipeg R3J 3W3
Inquiries: 945-6610
Electronic Access: e-mail: mnr_lib@nr.gov.mb.ca
NL Symbol: MWDRR
Mandate: To provide services in support of the research needs of the Department of Natural Resources.
Programs & Services: Copying; ILL offered
Collection: Subjects: Wildlife; fisheries; parks; water resources; lands; forestry. **Special Collections**: Historical collection of journals; comprehensive collection of departmental manuscripts on fisheries and wildlife studies since 1930. **Level**: Specialist/researcher; graduate student; undergraduate/public
External Users: Appointment required

Manitoba Naturalists Society
401–63 Albert St., Winnipeg R3B 1G4
Inquiries: 943-9029 **Fax**: 943-9029
Electronic Access: http://www.mbnet.mb.ca/mns/
e-mail: mns@escape.ca
Primary Clientele: Members
Programs & Services: Copying
Collection: Subjects: Natural history; birds; plants
External Users: Appointment required; no loans provided

The Manitoba Pharmaceutical Association Library
187 St. Mary's Rd., Winnipeg R2H 1J2
Inquiries: 233-1411 **Fax**: 237-3468
Electronic Access: e-mail: info@mpha.mb.ca
Primary Clientele: Association members; pharmacy students
Programs & Services: Copying
Collection: Subjects: Contemporary pharmacy practice; history of pharmacy; pharmacology; clinical pharmacy and therapeutics; drug information resources; pharmaceutical care; business management. **Level**: Specialist/researcher; graduate student; undergraduate/public
External Users: Access to the library during office hours

Manitoba Rural Development
600–800 Portage Ave., Winnipeg R3G 0N4
Inquiries: 945-4129 **Fax**: 945-3769
Programs & Services: ILL offered

Collection: Subjects: Rural economic development; municipal government; building standards; land use planning and resources

Manitoba Rural Development. Food Development Centre Library
810 Phillips St., Portage la Prairie R1N 3J9
Mailing Address: P.O. Box 1240 Portage la Prairie R1N 3J9
Inquiries: 239-3162 **Toll Free**: 1-800-870-1044
Fax: 239-3180
Electronic Access: http://www.fdc.mb.ca
e-mail: Lpetriuk@fdc.mb.ca
NL Symbol: MPCFP
Mandate: To support the research and industrial interests of staff, students, academics, professionals and entrepreneurs in the field of food sciences and technology and the agri-food industry.
Programs & Services: Copying; ILL offered
Collection: Subjects: Food science; agri-food processing; food analysis; food labeling; food service; animal feeds; pet foods; nutraceuticals. **Level**: Specialist/researcher; graduate student; undergraduate/public
External Users: Appointment required
Fee-based Information Services: Offered; fee exemptions for students and entrepreneurs

Manitoba Telecom Services. Corporate Library
489 Empress St., Box 6666, Winnipeg R3C 3V6
Inquiries: 941-6344 **Fax**: 772-2155
NL Symbol: MWTS
Programs & Services: ILL offered
Collection: Subjects: Telecommunications
Publications: *Corporate Library News*

Manitoba Trucking Association
25 Bunting St., Winnipeg R2X 2P5
Inquiries: 632-6600 **Fax**: 694-7134
Primary Clientele: Members
Programs & Services: ILL not offered
Collection: Subjects: Transportation; dangerous goods; deregulation
External Users: No public access

Manitoba Women's Directorate Resource Centre
100–175 Carlton St., Winnipeg R3C 3H9
Inquiries: 945-3476 **Fax**: 945-0013
Mandate: To carry out research regarding women's issues and to report to the Minister Responsible for the Status of Women.
Collection: Subjects: Aboriginal women; women in non-traditional careers; violence against women; social trends; educational issues; statistical data. **Level**: Specialist/researcher
External Users: No public access

Manitoba Writers' Guild, Writers' Resource Centre
206–100 Arthur St., Winnipeg R3B 1H3
Inquiries: 942-6134 **Fax**: 942-5754
Electronic Access: http://www.mbwriter.mb.ca
e-mail: mbwriter@escape.ca
Mandate: To help meet the information needs of new and established writers.
Programs & Services: Copying; ILL not offered

Collections: Subjects: Writing and publishing; markets; copyright; contracts; fiction and non-fiction by local authors. **Level**: undergraduate/public
External Users: No loans, on-site use of materials only. Library may be used during regular business hours

Manitou Public Library
418 Main St., Manitou R0G 1G0
Mailing Address: P.O. Box 432, Manitou R0G 1G0
Inquiries: 242-3134
Electronic Access: e-mail: manitlib@cici.mb.ca
NL Symbol: MMA
Programs & Services: Copying; ILL offered; Internet access for members

The Marquis Project Laura Delamater Resource Centre
711 Rosser Ave., Brandon R7A 0K8
Inquiries: 727-5675 **Fax**: 727-5683
Electronic Access:
e-mail: marquis@mb.sympatico.ca
Collection: Subjects: International development education; United Nations

McCauley Branch Library
[See: Border Regional Library]

McCreary District Library
[See: Parkland Regional Library]

Meadowood Manor Personal Care Home
577 St. Anne's Rd., Winnipeg R2M 5B2
Inquiries: 257-2394 **Fax**: 254-5402
Primary Clientele: Staff
Collection: Subjects: Nursing; gerontology
External Users: No public access or service

Mennonite Brethren Bible College
[See: Concord College Library]

Mennonite Heritage Village Library
Hwy. 12 N., Steinbach R0A 2A0
Mailing Address: P.O. Box 1136, Steinbach R0A 2A0
Inquiries: 326-9661 **Fax**: 326-5046
Mandate: To provide Mennonite history and religious books and papers to the public.
Programs & Services: Copying
Collection: Subjects: Mennonite history and religion.
Languages: High German; Low German. **Level**: Specialist/researcher; graduate; undergraduate/public
External Users: Appointment required

The Métis Resource Centre Inc.
506–63 Albert St., Winnipeg R3B 1G4
Inquiries: 956-7767 **Fax**: 956-7765
Electronic Access:
http://www.metisresourcecentre.mb.ca
e-mail: metisrc@mb.sympatico.ca
Programs & Services: Copying
Collection: Subjects: Métis land, Métis people
External Users: Access to collection during business hours; no loans provided
Publications: *Buffalo Trails & Tales*

Minitonas Library
[See: Parkland Regional Library]

A Guide to Libraries in Manitoba

Minnedosa Regional Library
Mailing Address: Box 1226, Minnedosa R0J 1E0
Inquiries: 867-2585 **Fax**: 867-5204
Electronic Access: e-mail: mmr@techplus.com
NL Symbol: MMR

Misericordia Health Centre Library
99 Cornish Ave., Winnipeg R3C 1A2
Inquiries: 788-8109
Electronic Access:
e-mail: mghlib@mb.sympatico.ca
Primary Clientele: Physicians; nurses; health care personnel; students
Programs & Services: Copying; ILL offered
Collection: Subjects: Medicine; nursing; health care administration. **Level**: Specialist/researcher
External Users: Library may be used during business hours; no borrowing privileges
Misericordia Health Centre Foundation

Morden Branch Library
[See: South Central Regional Library]

Morris Library
[See: Valley Regional Library]

Munroe Public Library
[See: Winnipeg Public Library]

Myers, Weinberg, Kussin, Weinstein, Bryk
724–240 Graham Ave., Winnipeg R3C 0J7
Inquiries: 942-0501 ext. 230 **Fax**: 956-0625
Primary Clientele: Lawyers; staff

Napinka Branch Library
[See: Southwestern Manitoba Regional Library]

National Research Council Information Centre Winnipeg
435 Ellice Ave., Winnipeg R3B 1Y6
Inquiries: 984-5621 **Fax**: 984-2434
Electronic Access: http://www.ibd.nrc.ca/~cisti/
e-mail: ibd.library@nrc.ca
NL Symbol: MWBI
Mandate: To serve the information needs of staff of the N.R.C.'s Institute for Biodiagnostics and to serve as a regional branch for the Canadian Institute for Scientific and Technical Information.
Programs & Services: Copying; ILL offered. **Languages**: French
Collection: Subjects: Biomedicine; computer science; medical devices; biomedical engineering; magnetic resonance; diagnostic imaging. **Special Collections**: Magnetic resonance. **Level**: Specialist/researcher
External Users: Appointment preferred; must sign in at the security desk

Natural Resources Library
[See: Manitoba Natural Resources Library]

Neepawa Branch Library
[See: Western Manitoba Regional Library]

Neil John MacLean Health Sciences Library
[See: University of Manitoba Libraries]

North Norfolk MacGregor Regional Library
Mailing Address: P.O. Box 622, MacGregor R0H 0R0
Inquiries: 685-2796
Electronic Access: e-mail: maclib@portage.net
NL Symbol: MMNN

North-West Regional Library
200–6th Ave. N., Swan River R0L 1Z0
Mailing Address: P.O. Box 999, Swan River R0L 1Z0
Inquiries: 734-3880 **Fax**: 734-3880
Electronic Access:
e-mail: nwrl@swanvalley.freenet.mb.ca
NL Symbol: MSRN
Programs & Services: Copying; ILL offered
Collection: Special Collections: Local history collection; sheet music collection
Branches:
Benito Branch Library
Benito R0L 0C0
Inquiries: 539-2446
Electronic Access:
e-mail: benlib@swanvalley.freenet.mb.ca
NL Symbol: MBB
Programs & Services: Copying; ILL offered; public Internet access
Collection: Special Collections: Collection of history books from the Swan Valley Area

Norway House Public Library
[See: Ayamiscikewikamik Norway House Public Library]

Ochre River Library
[See: Parkland Regional Library]

Osborne Public Library
[See: Winnipeg Public Library]

Oseredok's Library
[See: Ukrainian Cultural & Educational Centre Library]

Parkland Regional Library
504 Main St. N., Dauphin R7N 1C9
Inquiries: 638-6410 **Fax**: 638-9483
Electronic Access: e-mail: parklibr@mb.sympatico.ca
NL Symbol: MDP
Branches:
Birch River & District Branch Library
Mailing Address: P.O. Box 245, 3rd St., Birch River R0L 0E0
Inquiries: 236-4419
Electronic Access: e-mail: birchlib@mb.sympatico.ca

Birtle Branch Library
1161 St. Clare St., Birtle R0M 0C0
Mailing Address: P.O. Box 207, Birtle R0M 0C0
Inquiries: 842-3418
Electronic Access: e-mail: birtlib@mb.sympatico.ca
Programs & Services: ILL offered

Bowsman Branch Library
Mailing Address: P.O. Box 209, Bowsman R0L 0H0
Inquiries: 238-4615
Electronic Access: e-mail: bowslib@mb.sympatico.ca
Programs & Services: ILL offered

Dauphin Branch Library
504 Main St. N., Dauphin R7N 1C9
Inquiries: 638-3055
Electronic Access: e-mail: daulibr@mb.sympatico.ca
Programs & Services: Copying; ILL offered
Collection: Special Collections: Local area histories; Dauphin newspapers on microfilm from 1899 Dauphin Public Library Book Endowment Fund

Erickson District Library
Mailing Address: P.O. Box 385, Erickson R0J 0P0
Inquiries: 636-2325
Electronic Access: e-mail: ericlib@mb.sympatico.ca

Foxwarren Branch Library
Mailing Address: P.O. Box 204, Foxwarren R0J 0R0
Inquiries: 847-2080
Programs & Services: ILL offered

Gilbert Plains Branch Library
Mailing Address: P.O. Box 303, Gilbert Plains R0L 0X0
Inquiries: 548-2733
Electronic Access: e-mail: gilblib@mb.sympatico.ca

Gladstone & District Library
42 Morris Ave. N., Gladstone R0J 0T0
Mailing Address: P.O. Box 720, Gladstone R0J 0T0
Inquiries: 385-2641
Electronic Access: e-mail: gladlib@mb.sympatico.ca
Programs & Services: ILL offered

Grandview Branch Library
Grandview R0L 0Y0
Inquiries: 546-2398
Electronic Access: e-mail: grandlib@mb.sympatico.ca

Hamiota Centennial Library
Mailing Address: P.O. Box 610, Hamiota R0M 0T0
Inquiries: 764-2680
Electronic Access: e-mail: hamlib@mb.sympatico.ca

Langruth Library
Mailing Address: P.O. Box 154, Langruth R0H 0N0
Inquiries: 445-2030

McCreary District Library
Mailing Address: P.O. Box 297, Burrows Rd., McCreary R0J 1B0
Inquiries: 835-2629
Electronic Access: e-mail: mccrlib@mb.sympatico.ca
Programs & Services: Copying; ILL offered
Collection: Languages: French
Publications: *McCreary Milestones & Memories*; *Rainbows End*

Minitonas Library
Minitonas R0L 1G0
Inquiries: 525-4910
Electronic Access:
e-mail: minitlib@mb.sympatico.ca

Ochre River Library
Ochre River R0L 1K0
Inquiries: 733-2293
Electronic Access: e-mail: ochrelib@mb.sympatico.ca

Roblin & District Library
123–1st Ave. N.W., Roblin R0L 1P0
Mailing Address: P.O. Box 1342, Roblin R0L 1P0
Inquiries: 937-2443
Electronic Access: e-mail: roblib@mb.sympatico.ca
Programs & Services: ILL offered

Shoal Lake Community Library
418 The Drive, Shoal Lake R0J 1Z0
Mailing Address: P.O. Box 428, Shoal Lake R0J 1Z0
Inquiries: 759-2242
Electronic Access: e-mail: shoallib@mb.sympatico.ca
Programs & Services: ILL offered

Siglunes District Library
Mailing Address: P.O. Box 368, Ashern R0C 0E0
Inquiries: 768-2048
Electronic Access: e-mail: ashlib@mb.sympatico.ca

Winnipegosis Branch Library
Mailing Address: P.O. Box 370, Winnipegosis R0L 2G0
Inquiries: 656-4876
Electronic Access: e-mail: wpglib@mb.sympatico.ca

Pauline Johnson Library
23 Main St., Lundar R0C 1Y0
Mailing Address: P.O. Box 698, Lundar R0C 1Y0
Inquiries: 762-5367 **Fax**: 762-5177
Electronic Access: e-mail: mlpj@escape.ca
NL Symbol: MLPJ
Programs & Services: ILL offered
Collection: Special Collections: *The Complete Sagas of Icelanders*; local area histories. **Languages**: French; Icelandic

Pembina Trail Public Library
[See: Winnipeg Public Library]

Peoples Library
[See: Manitoba Indian Culture-Education Centre – Peoples Library]

Pharmacy House Library
[See: The Manitoba Pharmaceutical Association Library]

Pierson Branch Library
[See: Southwestern Manitoba Regional Library]

Pilot Mound Branch Library
[See: Lakeland Regional Library]

Pinawa Public Library
Vanier Ave., Pinawa R0E 1L0
Mailing Address: General Delivery, Pinawa R0E 1L0
Inquiries: 753-2496 **Fax**: 753-8201
Electronic Access: e-mail: plibrary@granite.mb.ca
Programs & Services: ILL offered; Internet access

Pitbaldo Buchwald Asper Law Library
2500–360 Main St., Winnipeg R3C 4H6
Fax: 957-0227
Electronic Access: e-mail: bagh1@escape.ca
Mandate: To serve the lawyers and staff of the firm.
Collection: Subjects: Criminal law; family law; corporate law; labour law; commercial law; tax law; estate

planning; constitutional law; Aboriginal law; business law; bankruptcy
External Users: No public access or service

Portage la Prairie City Library
170 Saskatchewan Ave. W., Portage la Prairie R1N 0M1
Inquiries: 857-4271 **Fax**: 239-4387
Electronic Access: e-mail: portlib@mb.sympatico.ca
NL Symbol: MPLP
Programs & Services: Copying; ILL offered; Internet access
Collection: Special Collections: Local history collection; Aboriginal collection
External Users: No restrictions on in-house use; appointment may be required to use special collections

Prairie Crocus Regional Library
670 Second Ave., Rivers R0K 1X0
Mailing Address: P.O. Box 609, Rivers R0K 1X0
Inquiries: 328-7613
Electronic Access: mrip@mb.sympatico.ca
NL Symbol: MRIP
Programs & Services: Copying; ILL offered; public Internet access

Providence College & Seminary Library
Otterburne R0A 1G0
Inquiries: 433-7488 **Fax**: 433-7158
Mandate: To provide for the curricular, reference, research and informational needs of Providence College & Seminary students, faculty and staff; secondarily, to serve as an informational resource for alumni, pastors and members of the community.
Programs & Services: Copying; ILL offered; Internet access
Collection: Subjects: Theology; Bible studies; church history; counseling; psychology; pastoral studies; sociology
External Users: Library card required to check out materials; annual fee charged for library card

Public Library Services
[See: Manitoba Culture, Heritage & Citizenship. Public Library Services]

Rapid City Regional Library
114–3rd Ave., Rapid City R0K 1W0
Mailing Address: P.O. Box 8, Rapid City R0K 1W0
Inquiries: 826-2732
Electronic Access: e-mail: jaimoe@mb.sympatico.ca
Programs & Services: Copying; ILL offered
Collection: Languages: Dutch, French

R.C.A. Museum Library & Archives
[See: Royal Canadian Artillery Museum Library & Archives]

R.C.M.P. Forensic Laboratory Services, Scientific Information Centre
621 Academy Rd., Winnipeg R3N 0E3
Inquiries: 983-7352 **Fax**: 983-6399
Mandate: To provide up-to-date information for forensic specialists.
Primary Clientele: Staff
Programs & Services: ILL not offered
Collection: Subjects: Forensic science

Red River Apiarists Association
Mailing Address: P.O. Box 1448, Steinbach R0A 2A0
Inquiries: 326-3763
Primary Clientele: Members
Programs & Services: ILL not offered

Red River College Library
2055 Notre Dame Ave., Winnipeg R3H 0J9
Inquiries: 632-2233 **Fax**: 697-4791
Library Hours: 632-2322
Electronic Access: http://www.rrc.mb.ca/~library
e-mail: library@rrc.mb.ca
NL Symbol: MWRR
Programs & Services: Copying; ILL offered
Mandate: To provide educational resources and information services that support student success.
Primary Clientele: Students, faculty and staff of the College
Collection: Subjects: Aboriginal topics/issues; business; computers; hospitality; nursing and allied health; technologies (civil, mechanical, electrical, electronic); trades; communication (journalism & writing); animal health technology; library science
External Users: Citizen's borrowers cards are available upon completion of application form, presentation of two pieces of identification, and payment of $10 fee. Some restrictions on items that may be borrowed. Students enrolled in day programs at the University of Manitoba or the University of Winnipeg are issued borrowing cards free of charge
Publications: From the Library
Library Advisory Committee

Reimer Library
[See: Providence College & Seminary Library]

Reston District Library
220–4th St., Reston R0M 1X0
Mailing Address: P.O. Box 340, Reston R0M 1X0
Inquiries: 877-3673
Electronic Access: e-mail: restonlb@mb.sympatico.ca
NL Symbol: MRP
Programs & Services: ILL offered

Ritchot Library
[See: Bibliothèque Ritchot Library]

River Heights Public Library
[See: Winnipeg Public Library]

Riverton Branch Library
[See: Evergreen Regional Library]

Roblin & District Library
[See: Parkland Regional Library]

Rossburn Regional Library
53 Main St. N., Rossburn R0J 1V0
Mailing Address: P.O. Box 87, Rossburn R0J 1V0
Inquiries: 859-2687
NL Symbol: MRO
Programs & Services: Copying; ILL offered

Royal Canadian Artillery Museum Library & Archives
Mailing Address: P.O. Box 5000, Stn. Main, Canadian Forces Base Shilo R0K 2A0

Inquiries: 765-3000 ext. 3534 **Fax**: 765-5031
Electronic Access: http://www.artillery.net
e-mail: rcamuseum@techplus.com
Mandate: To collect and preserve documents, both primary and secondary, relating to the history and development of the Royal Regiment of Artillery; development of artillery, guns, ordnance and military equipment; and the military history of Canada.
Programs & Services: Copying. **Languages**: French
Collection: **Subjects**: Military history; unit histories of R.C.A.; equipment manuals. **Special Collections**: War diaries of RCA units from WWII; military maps; photograph collection. **Languages**: French. **Level**: Specialist/researcher; undergraduate/public
External Users: Appointment required; photocopying and research services available

R.M. of Argyle Public Library
Mailing Address: P.O. Box 10, Baldur R0K 0B0
Inquiries: 535-2314 **Fax**: 535-2242
Electronic Access: e-mail: baldur@mbnet.mb.ca
NL Symbol: MBA

Russell & District Regional Library
339 Main St., Russell R0J 1W0
Mailing Address: P.O. Box 340, Russell R0J 1W0
Inquiries: 773-3127 **Fax**: 773-3759
Electronic Access: e-mail: rdrl@techplus.com
NL Symbol: MRD
Programs & Services: Copying; ILL offered
Collection: **Special Collections**: Women's Institute history and records
Branches:
Binscarth Branch
106 Russell St., Binscarth R0J 0G0
Mailing Address: P.O. Box 204, Binscarth R0J 0G0
Inquiries: 532-2447
NL Symbol: MBI
Programs & Services: ILL offered

Sainte Claude Library
[See: Bibliothèque Sainte Claude Library]

Sam Waller Museum
306 Fischer Ave., The Pas R9A 1K4
Mailing Address: P.O. Box 185, The Pas R9A 1K4
Inquiries: 623-3802 **Fax**: 623-3951
Programs & Services: ILL not offered
Collection: **Subjects**: Northern Manitoba; natural history; local history; religious texts. **Languages**: Cree
External Users: Materials may be used on-site

Sciences & Technology Library
[See: University of Manitoba Libraries]

Selkirk & St. Andrews Regional Library
303 Main St., Selkirk R0E 0C0
Inquiries: 482-3522 **Fax**: 482-6166
Electronic Access:
http://www3.mb.sympatico.ca/~slklib
e-mail: slklib@mb.sympatico.ca
Programs & Services: Copying; ILL offered
Friends Group

Selkirk Mental Health Centre Central Library
825 Manitoba Ave., Selkirk R1A 2B5

Inquiries: 482-1650 **Fax**: 785-8936
Electronic Access: e-mail: smhc@gov.mb.ca
NL Symbol: MSEMH
Mandate: To meet the mental health/illness information needs of Selkirk Mental Health Centre, staff, volunteers, students, patients and their families and the community.
Primary Clientele: Staff; patients
Programs & Services: Copying; ILL offered
Collection: **Subjects**: Psychiatry; mental illness; mental health; administration of a mental health centre. **Level**: Specialist/researcher
External Users: Please phone ahead to ensure library is open and materials needed are available

Seven Oaks General Hospital Library
2300 McPhillips St., Winnipeg R2V 3M3
Inquiries: 632-3124 / 632-3107 **Fax**: 684-8240
Electronic Access: e-mail: analynb@sogh.winnipeg.ca
NL Symbol: MWSOGH
Mandate: To provide current relevant health information to hospital staff and affiliated physicians.
Programs & Services: Copying; ILL offered
Collection: **Subjects**: Nursing; medicine; health management. **Level**: Specialist/researcher
External Users: Materials may be used on-site during business hours; circulation is restricted to hospital staff and affiliated physicians

Sexuality Education Resource Centre
731B Princess Ave., Brandon R7A 0P4
Inquiries: 727-0417 **Fax**: 729-8364
Electronic Access:
e-mail: Serc2mb@mb.sympatico.ca
Mandate: To provide information on all aspects of human sexuality to the general public, educators and those who work in the community.
Collection: **Subjects**: Sexuality; homosexuality; family planning; pregnancy; AIDS/HIV; sexually transmitted infections (STIs); sexual education

Sexuality Education Resource Centre
2nd Floor, 555 Broadway, Winnipeg R3C 0W4
Inquiries: 982-7800 **Fax**: 982-7819
Electronic Access: http://www.serc.mb.ca
e-mail: serc_mb@escape.ca
Programs & Services: Limited resources in Winnipeg; see Brandon office for main collection

Shilo Community Library
Community Center, Shilo R0K 2A0
Mailing Address: P.O. Box 545, Shilo R0K 2A0
Inquiries: 765-2590
NL Symbol: MSSC
Programs & Services: Copying
Collection: **Languages**: French, German

Shoal Lake Community Library
[See: Parkland Regional Library]

Siglunes District Library
[See: Parkland Regional Library]

Sir William Stephenson Library
[See: Winnipeg Public Library]

Snow Lake Community Library
Joseph H. Kerr School, Snow Lake R0B 1M0
Mailing Address: P.O. Box 760, Snow Lake R0B 1M0
Inquiries: 358-2322
NL Symbol: MSL
Programs & Services: Copying; ILL offered

Société Historique de Saint-Boniface
340 Provencher Ave., Winnipeg R2H 0G7
Inquiries: 233-4888 **Fax**: 231-2562
Collection: **Subjects**: Genealogy; French Canadians; Métis history. **Languages**: French

Society for Manitobans with Disabilities Inc.
Stephen Sparling Library
825 Sherbrook St., Winnipeg R3A 1M5
Inquiries: 786-5601 ext. 319 **Fax**: 783-2919
Electronic Access: e-mail: smdlib@cyberspc.mb.ca
NL Symbol: MWSC
Mandate: To provide library services and information on disabilities, rehabilitation and related topics to staff, clients, and board members.
Programs & Services: Copying; ILL offered
Collection: **Subjects**: Physical disabilities; rehabilitation therapy; learning disabilities; housing; advocacy; special education; other disability issues. **Special Collections**: Software Lending Library. The Library also houses the collections of the Manitoba Head Injury Association and the Winnipeg League for the Hard of Hearing.
External Users: Membership required
Fee-based Information Services: Offered

Somerset Library/Bibliothèque Somerset
289 Carlton Ave., Somerset R0G 2L0
Mailing Address: P.O. Box 279, Somerset R0G 2L0
Inquiries: 744-2170
Electronic Access: e-mail: somerlib@portage.net
NL Symbol: MS
Programs & Services: Copying; ILL offered. **Languages**: French
Collection: **Languages**: French

South Central Regional Library
185 Main St., Civic Centre, Winkler R6W 1B4
Inquiries: 325-5864 **Fax**: 325-5915
Electronic Access: e-mail: iloewen@hotmail.com
Programs & Services: Copying; ILL offered; free Internet access
Collection: **Special Collections**: Mennonite history.
Languages: German
Branches:
Altona Branch
Mailing Address: P.O. Box 650, Altona R0G 0B0
Inquiries: 324-1503
Electronic Access: e-mail: scrla@hotmail.com

Morden Branch
514 Stephen St., Morden R6M 1T7
Inquiries: 822-4092
Electronic Access: e-mail: scrlm@hotmail.com
NL Symbol: MMOW
Programs & Services: ILL offered

South Interlake Regional Library
385 Main St., Stonewall R0C 2Z0

Inquiries: 467-8415 **Fax**: 467-9809
Electronic Access: e-mail: sirl@minet.gov.mb.ca
NL Symbol: MSTOS
Programs & Services: Copying; ILL offered; bookmobile
Branches:
Teulon Branch Library
70 Main St., Teulon R0C 3B0
Mailing Address: P.O. Box 68, Teulon R0C 3B0
Inquiries: 886-3648
NL Symbol: MTSIR
Programs & Services: Copying; ILL offered

Southwestern Manitoba Regional Library
149 Main St., Melita R0M 1L0
Mailing Address: P.O. Box 670, Melita R0M 1L0
Inquiries: 522-3923 **Fax**: 522-3721
Electronic Access:
e-mail: swmblib@mail.techplus.com
NL Symbol: MESM
Programs & Services: Copying; ILL offered; Internet access
Collection: **Special Collections**: Local area history; palliative care collection to support Palliative Care Program
Branches:
Napinka Library
Mailing Address: P.O. Box 58, Souris St., Napinka R0M 1N0
Inquiries: 665-2282
Programs & Services: ILL offered

Pierson Library
Railway Ave., Pierson R0M 1S0
Mailing Address: P.O. Box 39, Pierson R0M 1S0
Inquiries: 634-2215 **Fax**: 634-2479
Electronic Access:
http://www.techplus.com/pierson/index.htm
e-mail: pcilibrary@mail.techplus.com
NL Symbol: MESP
Programs & Services: ILL offered

Spina Bifida & Hydrocephalus Association of Canada Resource Library
220–388 Donald St., Winnipeg R3B 2J4
Inquiries: 925-3650 **Fax**: 925-3654
Electronic Access: http://www.sbhac.ca
e-mail: spinab@pop.mts.net
Mandate: To supply information and resources to people with spina bifida and/or hydrocephalus and to their families, friends and allies.
Programs & Services: Copying
Collection: **Subjects**: Spina bifida; hydrocephalus.
Level: Specialist/researcher; graduate student; undergraduate/public
External Users: Materials may be used on site; public can request a catalogue of articles available to order; fee charged for photocopying
Fee-based Information Services: Offered

St. Andrew's College Library
29 Dysart Rd., Winnipeg R3T 2M7
Inquiries: 474-8901 **Fax**: 474-7624
NL Symbol: MWSA
Mandate: The Library serves the Theology and the Ukrainian Studies faculties of the college.

Programs & Services: Copying; ILL not offered. **Languages**: Ukrainian; Russian; German; Polish
Collection: **Subjects**: Eastern Christianity; Ukrainian studies; iconography. **Special Collections**: Rare Book Collection; Ukrainian Canadiana. **Languages**: Ukrainian; Russian; Polish. **Level**: Specialist/researcher; graduate students; undergraduate/public
External Users: University student numbers or references are required

St. Boniface General Hospital Research Centre. Carolyn Sifton-Helen Fuld Library
[See University of Manitoba. Neil John Maclean Health Sciences Library. Carolyn Sifton-Helen Fuld Library]

St. Boniface Public Library
[See: Winnipeg Public Library]

St. James-Assiniboia Public Library
[See: Winnipeg Public Library]

St. John's College Library
[See: University of Manitoba Libraries]

St. John's Public Library
[See: Winnipeg Public Library]

St. Malo Branch Library
[See: Jolys Regional Library]

St. Paul's College Library
[See: University of Manitoba Libraries]

St. Vital Public Library
[See: Winnipeg Public Library]

Ste. Agathe Branch Library
[See: Bibliothèque Ritchot Library]

Ste. Rose Regional Library
580 Central Ave., Ste. Rose Du Lac R0L 1S0
Mailing Address: General Delivery, Ste. Rose Du Lac R0L 1S0
Inquiries: 447-2527 **Fax**: 447-2374
Electronic Access: e-mail: sroselib@mb.sympatico.ca
NL Symbol: MSTR
Programs & Services: ILL offered. **Languages**: French
Collection: **Languages**: French

Steinbach Bible College Library
Hwy. 12 N., Steinbach R0A 2A0
Mailing Address: P.O. Box 1420, Steinbach R0A 2A0
Inquiries: 326-6451 ext. 238 **Fax**: 326-6908
Electronic Access:
http://www.sbcollege.mb.ca/Library/index.htm
e-mail: Vic_Froese@SBC.mb.ca
NL Symbol: MSBC
Programs & Services: Copying; ILL offered. **Languages**: German
Collection: **Subjects**: Biblical studies; theology; Christian missions; Mennonite history. **Languages**: French, German

Steinbach Public Library
[See: Jake Epp Library]

Swan River Public Library
[See: North-West Regional Library]

Take Pride Winnipeg Inc.
604–167 Lombard Ave., Winnipeg R3B 0V3
Inquiries: 956-7590 **Fax**: 956-7628
Primary Clientele: Staff; volunteers
Programs & Services: Copying
Collection: **Subjects**: Graffiti removal and control; solid waste management; recycling; litter control; community clean-ups. **Special Collections**: Collection of photographs of all Take Pride Winnipeg murals. **Level**: Undergraduate/public
External Users: Please phone ahead; resources must be used on site; no borrowing privileges

T.A.R.R. Centre
[See: Treaty & Aboriginal Rights Research Centre]

Taylor McCaffrey Library
11th Floor, 400 St. Mary Ave., Winnipeg R3C 4K5
Mailing Address: 9th Floor, 400 St. Mary Ave., Winnipeg R3C 4K5
Inquiries: 988-0463 **Fax**: 957-0945
Electronic Access:
e-mail: dsikorsky@tmlawyers.com
Mandate: To provide a range of specialized materials which support the goals and objectives of the Taylor McCaffrey Law Firm.
Primary Users: Lawyers, students and support staff at Taylor McCaffrey
Programs & Services: Copying; ILL not offered
Collection: **Subjects**: Law; taxation. **Level**: Specialist/researcher
External Users: No public access or service

Teshmont Consultants Inc.
1190 Waverly St., Winnipeg R3T 0P4
Inquiries: 284-8100 **Fax**: 475-4601
Electronic Access: e-mail: sgarvin@teshmont.mb.ca
Programs & Services: ILL not offered
Collection: **Subjects**: HVDC transmission systems
External Users: No public access or service

Teulon Branch Library
[See: South Interlake Regional Library]

The Pas Public Library
53 Edwards Ave., The Pas R9A 1R2
Mailing Address: P.O. Box 4100, The Pas R9A 1R2
Inquiries: 623-2023 **Fax**: 623-4594
Electronic Access: http://www.mbnet.mb.ca/~paslibra
e-mail: the_pas_library@mbnet.mb.ca
NL Symbol: MTP
Programs & Services: Copying; ILL offered; faxing; Internet access

Thompson Dorfman Sweatman Library
201–2200 Portage Ave., Winnipeg R3B 3L3
Inquiries: 934-2449 **Fax**: 943-6445
Electronic Access: e-mail: patb@tds.mb.ca
Mandate: To provide library resources for the in-house population of lawyers and staff.
Collection: Subjects: Law. **Languages**: French. **Level**: Specialist/researcher
External Users: No public access or service

A Guide to Libraries in Manitoba

Thompson Public Library
81 Thompson Dr. N., Thompson R8N 0C3
Inquiries: 677-3717 **Fax**: 778-5844
Electronic Access:
http://204.112.107.5/library/index.html
e-mail: libweb@mysterynet.ca
NL Symbol: MTH
Programs & Services: Copying; ILL offered; faxing; Internet access; computers available for word processing and printing
Collection: **Languages**: French

Tiger Hills Arts Association
116 Broadway St., Holland R0G 0X0
Mailing Address: P.O. Box 58, Holland R0G 0X0
Inquiries: 526-2063 **Fax**: 526-2105
Mandate: To provide arts-related services to the local communities.
Primary Clientele: Teachers; students
Programs & Services: Copying
Collection: **Subjects**: Music; art. **Level**: Undergraduate/public
External Users: Members only

Tony Mann Library
825 Sherbrook St. Winnipeg R3A 1M5
Inquiries: 786-4753 **Fax**: 786-1140
Electronic Access: e-mail: cpa@awnet.com
Mandate: To provide information to Manitobans with spinal cord injuries and similar disabilities
Collection: **Subjects**: Spinal cord injury. **Level**: Specialist/researcher; graduate student; undergraduate/public
Publications: *Paratracks*
External Users: No appointment necessary; no restrictions on use

Transcona Public Library
[See: Winnipeg Public Library]

Treaty & Aboriginal Rights Research Centre
300–153 Lombard Ave., Winnipeg R3B 0T4
Inquiries: 943-6456 **Fax**: 942-3202
Mandate: The research and development of claims of our member First Nations, with an emphasis on Manitoba issues.
Programs & Services: Copying
Collections: **Subjects**: First Nation history; treaties. **Special Collections**: Morris Papers; Archibald Papers; Church Missionary Society records; mapping products; Canada Sessional Papers
External Users: Appointment preferred; internal reports done for First Nations, membership records and correspondence files restricted
Publications: *A Debt To Be Paid: Treaty Land Entitlement in Manitoba*

Ukrainian Cultural & Educational Centre Library
184 Alexander Ave. E., Winnipeg R3B 0L6
Inquiries: 942-0218 **Fax**: 943-2857
Electronic Access: e-mail: ucec@mb.sympatico.ca
Programs & Services: Copying. **Languages**: Ukrainian, Russian
Collection: **Subjects**: Ethnography; language; literature; Ukrainian history; Ukrainian art & music; Ukrainian settlement of Canada. **Special Collections**: Olexander Koshetz library; Pavlo Macenko library; rare book collection. **Languages**: Ukrainian; Russian; Old Slavonic, Polish. **Level**: Specialist/researcher; undergraduate/public
Publications: *A Comprehensive Guide to the Periodical Holdings of the Ukrainian Cultural & Educational Centre: On the Occasion of the 50th Anniversary of the U.C.E.C.*

UNICEF Manitoba
160 Stafford St., Winnipeg R3M 2V8
Inquiries: 477-4600 **Fax**: 477-4040
Collection: **Languages**: French. **Level**: Specialist/researcher; graduate student; undergraduate/public

United Church Resource Centre
[See: Conference of Manitoba & Northwestern Ontario Resource Centre]

University of Manitoba. Library Administration
156 Elizabeth Dafoe Library, Winnipeg R3T 2N2
Inquiries: 747-9881 **Fax**: 474-7583
Electronic Access:
http://www.umanitoba.ca/libraries

University of Manitoba. Albert D. Cohen Management Library
Room 206, Drake Centre for Management Studies, University of Manitoba, Winnipeg R3T 5V4
Mailing Address: 181 Freedman Cres., Drake Centre for Management Studies, University of Manitoba, Winnipeg R3T 5V4
Inquiries: 474-8440 **Fax**: 474-7542
Electronic Access:
http://www.umanitoba.ca/libraries/units/management
e-mail: Dennis_Felbel@UManitoba.CA
NL Symbol: MWU
Programs & Services: ILL offered
Collection: **Subjects**: Accounting and finance; business administration; marketing

University of Manitoba. Architecture/Fine Arts Library
84 Curry Pl., Winnipeg R3T 2N2
Mailing Address: 206 Russell Bldg., University of Manitoba, Winnipeg R3T 2N2
Inquiries: 474-9216 **Library Hours**: 474-9770
Fax: 474-7539
Electronic Access:
http://www.umanitoba.ca/academic support/libraries/units/archfa
e-mail: Mary_Lochhead@umanitoba.ca
NL Symbol: MWU
Programs & Services: Copying; ILL offered. **Languages**: Norwegian
Collection: **Subjects**: Architecture; art history; interior design; graphic design; environmental design; city planning; studio art. **Special Collections**: Architectural Drawings; Art Reproductions; Building File; Historic Urban Plans; Map Collection; Product Catalogue Collection; Slide Collection; Winnipeg Building Index; Winnipeg Photograph Collection. **Languages**: French. **Level**: Specialist/researcher; graduate student; undergraduate/public

University of Manitoba. D.S. Woods Education Library
100 Education Bldg., University of Manitoba, Winnipeg R3T 2N2

Inquiries: 474-9976 **Fax**: 474-7541
Electronic Access:
http://www.umanitoba.ca/libraries/units/education
e-mail: edref@cc.umanitoba.ca
NL Symbol: MWU
Programs & Services: Copying; ILL offered
Collection: Subjects: Education; higher education; child development; sport & recreation

University of Manitoba. Donald W. Craik Engineering Library
351 Engineering Bldg., University of Manitoba, Winnipeg R3T 2N2
Inquiries: 474-6360 **Fax**: 474-7520
Electronic Access:
http://www.umanitoba.ca/libraries/units/engineering
e-mail: ngodava@cc.umanitoba.ca
NL Symbol: MWU
Programs & Services: ILL offered
Collection: Subjects: Engineering; standards; patents

University of Manitoba. E.K. Williams Law Library
401 Robson Hall, 224 Dysart Rd., University of Manitoba, Winnipeg R3T 2N2
Inquiries: 474-9997 **Fax**: 474-7582
Electronic Access:
http://www.umanitoba.ca/faculties/law/library_pages/library.html
NL Symbol: MWUL
Programs & Services: Copying; ILL offered
Collection: Subjects: Law; Aboriginal justice. **Special Collections**:Aboriginal Justice Inquiry Collection.
Languages: French. **Level**: Specialist/researcher; graduate student; undergraduate/public
Fee-based Information Services: Offered

University of Manitoba. Eckhardt-Grammatté Music Library
Room 223-4, 65 Dafoe Rd., University of Manitoba, Winnipeg R3T 2N2
Inquiries: 474-9567 **Fax**: 474-9567
Electronic Access:
http://www.umanitoba.ca/libraries/units/music
e-mail: simosko@cc.umanitoba.ca
NL Symbol: MWU
Programs & Services: ILL offered

University of Manitoba. Elizabeth Dafoe Library
University of Manitoba, Winnipeg R3T 2N2
Inquiries: 474-9544 **Library Hours**: 474-9770
Fax: 474-7577
Electronic Access:
http://www.umanitoba.ca/academic_support/libraries/units/dafoe
e-mail: dafoe_ref@cc.umanitoba.ca
NL Symbol: MWU
Programs & Services: Copying; ILL offered. **Languages**: French; German; Icelandic; Ukrainian; Russian
Collection: Subjects: Humanities; social sciences; education; human ecology; nursing; physical education and recreation studies; social work. **Special Collection**: Canadiana Collection; Icelandic Collection; Slavic Collection; Archives and Special Collections; government publications; maps and atlases. **Languages**: French; Spanish; Italian; German; Greek; Latin; Cree; Ojibwa; Icelandic; Danish; Norwegian; Swedish; Russian; Ukrainian; Polish; Sanskrit; Hindi; Chinese. **Level**: Specialist/researcher; graduate student; undergraduate/public
External Users: Materials may be used on-site; borrowing privileges are extended to qualified citizens of Manitoba upon payment of a $50 fee (or $10 fee for members of the Alumni Association). Application forms must be filled out and signed; two references are required. There are some restrictions on use.
Publications: Selected Microform Collections, sets and newspapers in the Elizabeth Dafoe Library
Friends of the Libraries

University of Manitoba. Neil John Maclean Health Sciences Library
Brodie Centre, 200 Level, 727 McDermot Ave., Winnipeg
Mailing Address: 770 Bannatyne Ave., University of Manitoba, Winnipeg R3E 0W3
Inquiries: 789-3464 **Toll Free**: 1-800-432-1960
Fax: 789-3923
Electronic Access:
http://www.umanitoba.ca/libraries/units/njmhsl/
e-mail: njm_ref@umanitoba.ca
NL Symbol: MWM
Mandate:To support the teaching, research and patient care requirements of the staff and students of the University of Manitoba, Faculties of Dentistry, Medicine, Nursing and the Schools of Dental Hygiene and Medical Rehabilitation.
Programs & Services: Copying; ILL offered
Collection: Subjects: Clinical medicine; biomedical sciences; dentistry; dental hygiene; nursing; rehabilitation; Aboriginal health; consumer health. **Special Collections**:Antique Medical Instruments Collection; History of Medicine Collection; University of Manitoba, Faculty of Medicine Archives; Aboriginal Health Collection; Rare Book Collection; Manitoba Authors Collection. **Languages**: French. **Level**: Specialist/researcher; graduate student; undergraduate/public
External Users: Materials may be used on-site; fee charged for University of Manitoba External Borrowers card
Publications: NJMHSL Health Connections; NJMHSL Serials Holdings List
Fee-based Information Services: MHINET; INFO-Rx
Section: St. Boniface General Hospital Section. Carolyn Sifton-Helene Fuld Library
St. Boniface General Hospital Research Centre, 351 Taché Ave., Winnipeg R2H 2A6
Mailing Address: 409 Taché Ave., Winnipeg R2H 2A6
Inquiries: 237-2807 **Fax**: 235-3339
Electronic Access:
e-mail: library@sbrc.umanitoba.ca
NL Symbol: MWSBM
Mandate:To serve the education and information needs of staff and students at St. Boniface General Hospital by providing health sciences information, resources to support patient care, education, management, research and outreach services.
Programs & Services: Copying; ILL offered
Collection: Subjects: Medicine; nursing; health faculty

administration **Languages**: French. **Level**: Specialist/ researcher; graduate student; undergraduate/public

University of Manitoba. Sciences & Technology Library
211 Machray Hall, University of Manitoba, Winnipeg R3T 2N2
Inquiries: 474-9281 **Fax**: 474-7627
Electronic Access:
http://www.umanitoba.ca/libraries/units/science
e-mail: sci_ref@umanitoba.ca
Programs & Services: Copying; ILL offered; Internet access

University of Manitoba. St. John's College Library
92 Dysart Rd., University of Manitoba, Winnipeg R3T 2M5
Inquiries: 474-8542 **Fax**: 474-7614
Electronic Access:
http://www.umanitoba.ca/libraries/units/stjohns
e-mail: pat_wright@umanitoba.ca
Programs & Services: ILL offered
Collection: **Subjects**: Canadian history; political studies; English and French Canadian literature; Old and New Testament studies; pastoral studies; Anglicanism.
Languages: French

University of Manitoba. St. Paul's College. Father Harold Drake, S.J. Library
430 Dysart Rd., University of Manitoba, Winnipeg R3T 2M6
Inquiries: 474-8585 **Fax**: 474-7615
Electronic Access:
http://www.umanitoba.ca/colleges/st_pauls/library/lib.htm
e-mail: umstonge@cc.umanitoba.ca
NL Symbol: MWU
Programs & Services: ILL offered
Collection: **Subjects**: Roman Catholic theology; women in religion; Catholic studies; medieval studies; philosophy. **Special Collections**: Index Thomisticus.
Languages: French; Latin

University of Manitoba. William R. Newman Agriculture Library
236E Agriculture Bldg., University of Manitoba, Winnipeg R3T 2N2
Inquiries: 474-8382 **Fax**: 474-7527
Electronic Access:
http://www.umanitoba.ca/libraries/units/agriculture
e-mail: karen_clay@umanitoba.ca
NL Symbol: MWU
Programs & Services: ILL offered
Collection: **Subjects**: Agriculture economics; animal science; entomology; farm management; food science; plant science; soil science

University of Winnipeg Library
515 Portage Ave., Winnipeg R3B 2E9
Inquiries: 786-9815 **Fax**: 783-8910
Library Hours: 786-9808
Electronic Access:
http://www.mercury.uwinnipeg.ca
e-mail: libadmin@uwinnipeg.ca
e-mail address for ILL: ill@c-h.uwinnipeg.ca

NL Symbol: MWUC
Programs & Services: Copying; ILL offered
Collection: **Subjects**: Liberal arts; science. **Special Collections**: The Ashdown Collection of Canadiana; Dr. Charles Newcombe Collection of Old Testament Literature; The Mamie Pickering Thompson Collection; Mary Iris Atchison Film Collection; The Nodelman Little Red Riding Hood Collection; The Rare Book Room Library; The Samuel J. Drache, Q.C. and Arthur B.C. Drache, Q.C. Legal Collection; Science Fiction Collection; East European Genealogical Society Inc. Collection; Asian Development Bank Depository Collection; Reavis Reading Area. **Languages**: French; German.
Level: Undergraduate/public
Fee-based Information Services: offered

Valley Regional Library
141 Main St. S., Morris R0G 1K0
Mailing Address: P.O. Box 397, Morris R0G 1K0
Inquiries: 746-2136 **Fax**: 746-6953
Electronic Access: http://town.morris.mb.ca
e-mail: valleylib@techplus.com
NL Symbol: MMVR
Programs & Services: Copying; ILL offered; Internet access
Collection: **Special Collections**: Complete collection of *Scratching River Post* newspaper, 1978-1996. **Languages**: French
Library Foundation

Victoria Municipal Library
102 Steward Ave., Holland R0G 0X0
Mailing Address: P.O. Box 371, Holland R0G 0X0
Inquiries: 526-2011
Electronic Access: e-mail: victlib@treherne.com
NL Symbol: MHP
Programs & Services: ILL offered; Internet access
Collection: **Languages**: French

Volunteer Centre of Winnipeg Library
410-5 Donald St. S., Winnipeg R3L 2T4
Inquiries: 477-5180 **Fax**: 284-5200
Mandate: To promote the concept of volunteerism in Manitoba.
Primary Clientele: Volunteer coordinators; non-profit organizations; government; students
Programs & Services: Copying
Collection: **Subjects**: Volunteer management; boardmanship; fundraising
External Users: Fee charged for yearly membership, except for students; appointment preferred

Waterworks Library
[See: Winnipeg Water & Waste Department Resource Centre]

West End Public Library
[See: Winnipeg Public Library]

West Kildonan Public Library
[See: Winnipeg Public Library]

Western Canada Aviation Museum Library
958 Ferry Rd., Winnipeg R3H 0Y8
Inquiries: 786-5503 **Fax**: 775-4761
Electronic Access: http://www.wcam.mb.ca

e-mail: info@wcam.mb.ca
Programs & Services: Copying. **Languages**: French
Collection: Subjects: Aviation. **Languages**: French.
Level: Specialist/researcher; undergraduate/public
External Users: Appointment required
Publications: *Aviation Review*

Western Canada Pictorial Index Inc.
404–63 Albert St., Winnipeg R3B 1G4
Inquiries: 949-1620 **Fax**: 949-0333
Electronic Access: http://www.telenium.ca/canpix
e-mail: westpics@escape.ca
Mandate: To copy and catalogue images relating to the history of Western Canada from the Lakehead to the Rockies and from the Arctic to the Missouri Basin.
Primary Clientele: Historians; teachers; authors; film makers; students
Programs & Services: Copying
Collection: Subjects: Agriculture; aviation; buildings; costumes; events; entertainment; fur trade; military; transportation; weather. **Special Collections**: James A. Richardson Aviation Collection; Canadian National Railway Collection; Oblates Fathers' Collection; Winnipeg Firefighters Collection; Institute of Arctic Research Collection; *Winnipeg Free Press* collection
Fee-based Information Services: Offered
Eric Wells Foundation

Western Christian College Library
220 Whitmore Ave., Dauphin R7N 2V5
Mailing Address: P.O. Box 5000, Dauphin R7N 2V5
Inquiries: 638-8801 **Fax**: 638-7054
Friends Group

Western Manitoba Regional Library
638 Princess Ave., Brandon R7A 0P3
Inquiries: 727-6648 **Fax**: 727-4447
Electronic Access:
e-mail: wmrlibrary@aplha.tkm.mb.ca
NL Symbol: MBW
Branches:
Carberry/North Cypress Branch Library
Mailing Address: P.O. Box 382, Carberry R0K 0H0
Inquiries: 834-3043
Electronic Access: e-mail: cnc@mb.sympatico.ca

Glenboro/South Cypress Branch Library
105 Broadway St., Glenboro R0K 0X0
Mailing Address: P.O. Box 429, Glenboro R0K 0X0
Inquiries: 827-2874 **Fax**: 827-2127
Electronic Access: e-mail: cap@cpnet.net
Programs & Services: ILL offered

Neepawa Branch Library
Mailing Address: P.O. Box 759, Neepawa R0J 1H0
Inquiries: 476-5648
Electronic Access:
e-mail: neepawalib@mail.techplus.com

Westwood Public Library
[See: Winnipeg Public Library]

William & Catherine Booth College Library
447 Webb Pl., Winnipeg R3B 2P2
Inquiries: 924-4858 **Fax**: 942-3856
NL Symbol: MWSACB

Mandate: To provide resources and services to meet the information needs of the college community.
Programs & Services: Copying; ILL offered
Collection: Subjects: Theology; biblical studies; Christian ministry; Salvation Army; social work and service; ethics. **Special Collections**: Salvation Army publications. **Level**: Undergraduate/public
External Users: Apply for a library card; no restrictions

William Molloy Library
19 Linacre Rd., Winnipeg R3T 3G5
Inquiries: 261-9366
Programs & Services: ILL offered
Collection: Subjects: Arctic; cooking; Canadiana; wines

William Potoroka Memorial Library
[See: The Addictions Foundation of Manitoba. William Potokoka Library]

William R. Newman Agriculture Library
[See: University of Manitoba Libraries]

Windsor Park Public Library
[See: Winnipeg Public Library]

Winkler Branch Library
[See: South Central Regional Library]

Winnipeg Art Gallery Library
[See: Clara Lander Library – Winnipeg Art Gallery]

Winnipeg Audit Department Library
3rd Floor, 185 King St., Winnipeg R3B 1J1
Inquiries: 986-2425

Winnipeg Clinic Library
425 St. Mary Ave., Winnipeg R3C 0N2
Inquiries: 957-1900 ext. 512 **Fax**: 943-2164
Programs & Services: Copying; ILL offered
Collection: Subjects: Medical. **Level**: Specialist/researcher
External Users: Please contact library for photocopies of journal articles

Winnipeg Free Press **Library**
1355 Mountain Ave., Winnipeg R2X 3B6
Inquiries: 697-7290
Programs & Services: ILL not offered
Collection: Subjects: Newspapers
External Users: No public access; staff use only

Winnipeg Gay/Lesbian Resource Centre (W.G.L.R.C.) Community Library
1–222 Osborne St., Winnipeg R3L 1Z3
Mailing Address: P.O. Box 1661, Winnipeg R3C 2Z6
Inquiries: 474-0212 **Toll Free**: 1-888-399-0005
Fax: 478-1160
Mandate: To educate and entertain the lesbian, gay and bisexual communities and to inform the community at large.
Primary Clientele: Members
Programs & Services: Copying; ILL offered. **Languages**: French
Collection: Subjects: Homosexuality; lesbianism;

A Guide to Libraries in Manitoba

bi-sexuality; human sexuality; gay rights; lesbian and gay history. **Special Collections**: Complete video collection of the locally produces series "Coming Out!". **Languages**: French; German. **Level**: Specialist/researcher; graduate student; undergraduate/public
External Users: Library membership is required to borrow materials; fee charged for membership

Winnipeg Public Library
Centennial Library
251 Donald St., Winnipeg R3C 3P5
Inquiries: 986-6450 **Library Hours**: 986-6432
Fax: 942-5671
Electronic Access: http://wpl.city.winnipeg.mb.ca
Mandate: To provide information services to enable the citizens of Winnipeg to achieve their individual goals and enhance their quality of life.
Programs & Services: Copying; ILL offered
Collection: Special Collections: National Film Board video collection in French & English; *Winnipeg Free Press* dating back to the 1870's; *Winnipeg Tribune* from 1890 to 1980; *New York Times*; telephone directories dating back to the early 1900's; *Henderson Directory* for Winnipeg from 1876 to present; *Henderson Directory* for Manitoba from 1876 to 1908; Children's Award-winning Book Collection. **Languages**: French; Arabic; Bengali; Chinese; Czech; Danish; Dutch; Farsi; Finnish; Gaelic; German; Greek; Hindi; Hungarian; Icelandic; Italian; Japanese; Korean; Norwegian; Polish; Portuguese; Punjabi; Russian; Slovac; Spanish; Swedish; Tagalog; Ukrainian; Urdu; Vietnamese
Publications: *Parent Handbook: Bookmates: Reading Partners Inc.*; *Forward Thinking: Winnipeg Public Library Plan 1996-2000*; *Memories of Manitoba/Souvenirs du Manitoba*; *Tracing Your Roots*; *Aboriginal Culture*
Friends of the Winnipeg Public Library; Winnipeg Public Library Foundation; Library Advisory Committee
Branches:
Charleswood Library
5044 Roblin Blvd., Winnipeg R3G 0G7
Inquiries: 986-3069 **Fax**: 986-3545

Cornish Library
20 West gate, Winnipeg R3C 2E1
Inquiries: 986-4679 **Fax**: 986-7126

Extension Services
Lower Level, 1910 Portage Ave., Winnipeg R3J 0J2
Inquiries: 986-5580

Fort Garry Library
1360 Pembina Hwy., Winnipeg R3T 2B4
Inquiries: 986-4910 **Fax**: 986-3399

Henderson Library
1-1050 Henderson Hwy., Winnipeg R2K 2M5
Inquiries: 986-4314 **Fax**: 986-3065

Louis Riel Library
1168 Dakota St., Winnipeg R2N 3T8
Inquiries: 986-4568 **Fax**: 986-3274

Munroe Library
489 London St., Winnipeg R2K 2Z4
Inquiries: 986-3736 **Fax**: 986-7125

Osborne Library
625 Osborne St., Winnipeg R3L 2B3
Inquiries: 986-4775 **Fax**: 986-7124

Pembina Trail Library
2724 Pembina Hwy., Winnipeg R3T 2H7
Inquiries: 986-4370 **Fax**: 986-3290

River Heights Library
1520 Corydon Ave., Winnipeg R3N 0J6
Inquiries: 986-4934 **Fax**: 986-3544

St. Boniface Library
100-131 Provencher Blvd., Winnipeg R2H 0G2
Inquiries: 986-4330 **Fax**: 986-6827

St. James-Assiniboia Library
1910 Portage Ave., Winnipeg R3J 0J2
Inquiries: 986-5583 **Fax**: 986-3798

St. John's Library
500 Salter St., Winnipeg R2W 4M5
Inquiries: 986-4689 **Fax**: 986-7123

St. Vital Library
6 Fermor Ave., Winnipeg R2M 0Y2
Inquiries: 986-5625 **Fax**: 986-3173

Sir William Stephenson Library
765 Keewatin St., Winnipeg R2X 3B9
Inquiries: 986-7070 **Fax**: 986-7201

Transcona Library
111 Victoria Ave. W., Winnipeg R2C 1S6
Inquiries: 986-3950 **Fax**: 986-3172

West End Library
823 Ellice Ave., Winnipeg R3G 0C3
Inquiries: 986-4677 **Fax**: 986-7129

West Kildonan Library
365 Jefferson Ave., Winnipeg R2V 0N3
Inquiries: 986-4384 **Fax**: 986-3373

Westwood Library
66 Allard Ave., Winnipeg R3K 0T3
Inquiries: 986-4742 **Fax**: 986-3799

Windsor Park Library
955 Cottonwood Rd., Winnipeg R2J 1G3
Inquiries: 986-4945 **Fax**: 986-7122

***Winnipeg Sun* Library**
1700 Church Ave., Winnipeg R2X 3A2
Inquiries: 694-2022
Collection: Subjects: Current events; news clippings; photographs

Winnipeg Symphony Orchestra Music Library
101-555 Main St., Winnipeg R3B 1C3
Inquiries: 949-3954 **Fax**: 942-2082
Electronic Access:
http://www.aroundmanitoba.com/wso
e-mail: wso@mb.sympatico.ca
Mandate: To provide music for performances of the Winnipeg Symphony Orchestra

Collection: Non-copyright music as used by the W.S.O.
External Users: No outside access or service

Winnipeg Water & Waste Department Resource Centre
1500 Plessis Rd., Winnipeg R2C 5G6
Inquiries: 986-3250 **Fax**: 244-0032
Electronic Access:
e-mail: jdasilva@city.winnipeg.mb.ca
NL Symbol: MWWW
Mandate: To provide library and information services in support of the work of the City of Winnipeg's Water and Waste Department to departmental staff and consultants, other city departments and the general public.
Programs & Services: Copying; ILL offered
Collection: Subjects: Water supply, treatment and distribution; wastewater collection, treatment and disposal; land drainage and flood protection; solid waste collection and disposal; waste minimization and recycling.
Special Collections: Manufacturer's catalogues; office copies of departmental specifications; design notes; standards/specifications. **Languages**: French. **Level**: Specialist/researcher; graduate student; undergraduate/public
External Users: Appointment required; materials may be used on-site

Winnipegosis Branch Library
[See: Parkland Regional Library]

Wolch, Pinx, Tapper, Scurfield
1000–330 St. Mary's Ave., Winnipeg R3G 0N6
Inquiries: 949-1700 **Fax**: 947-2593
Primary Clientele: Lawyers; staff

Workplace Safety & Health Library
[See: Manitoba Labour Workplace Safety & Health Library]

YM-YWCA Women's Resource Centre Library
301 Vaughan St., 2nd Floor, Winnipeg R3B 2N7
Inquiries: 947-3110 ext. 140 **Fax**: 943-6159
Programs & Services: Copying
Collection: Subjects: Physical health; mental health; psychology; feminism; violence against women; family violence; sexism. **Level**: Undergraduate/public
External Users: Library may be used during office hours; books may be borrowed if user has a permanent address

Index by Type

ACADEMIC
Assiniboine Community College Library
Brandon University. John E. Robbins Library
Canadian Mennonite Bible College Library
College universitaire de Saint-Boniface. Bibliothèque Alfred-Monnin
Concord College Library
Keewatin Community College Library
Providence College & Seminary Library
Red River College Library
St. Andrew's College Library
Steinbach Bible College Library
University of Manitoba. Albert D. Cohen Management Library
University of Manitoba. Architecture/Fine Arts Library
University of Manitoba. D.S. Woods Education Library
University of Manitoba. Donald W. Craik Engineering Library
University of Manitoba. E.K. Williams Law Library
University of Manitoba. Eckhardt-Grammatte Music Library
University of Manitoba. Elizabeth Dafoe Library
University of Manitoba. Neil John MacLean Health Sciences Library
University of Manitoba. Neil John MacLean Health Sciences Library. St. Boniface General Hospital Section. Carolyn Sifton-Helene Fuld Library
University of Manitoba. Sciences & Technology Library
University of Manitoba. St. John's College Library
University of Manitoba. St. Paul's College. Father Harold Drake S.J. Library
University of Manitoba. William R. Newman Agriculture Library
University of Winnipeg Library
Western Christian College Library
William & Catherine Booth College Library

GOVERNMENT - FEDERAL
Canada. Agriculture & Agri-Food Canada. Brandon Research Centre Library and Information Centre
Canada. Agriculture & Agri-Food Canada. Winnipeg Research Library
Canada. Fisheries & Oceans Canada. Freshwater Institute. The Eric Marshall Aquatic Research Library
Canada. Health Canada. Federal Laboratories Library Bibliothèque de laboratoires féderaux
Canada. Indian & Northern Affairs. Regional Library
Canada. Justice Canada. Library
Canada. Labour Canada. Central Region Resource Centre
Canada. Revenue Canada. Winnipeg District Office Research & Library Services
Canadian Grain Commission Library/Bibliothèque commission canadienne des grains

GOVERNMENT - FEDERAL/PROVINCIAL
Canada/Manitoba Business Service Centre
Environment Library/Bibliothèque de l'Environnement

GOVERNMENT - MUNICIPAL
Winnipeg Audit Department Library

Winnipeg Water & Waste Department Resource Centre

GOVERNMENT - PROVINCIAL
Legislative Assembly. Elections Manitoba Library
Manitoba Culture, Heritage & Citizenship. Legislative Library
Manitoba Culture, Heritage & Citizenship. Public Library Services
Manitoba Education & Training. Direction des ressources Educatives françaises (D.R.E.F.)
Manitoba Education & Training. Instructional Resources Unit
Manitoba Education & Training. Special Materials Services
Manitoba Energy & Mines Library
Manitoba Finance. Federal-Provincial Relations & Research Library
Manitoba Health. Library Services
Manitoba Industry Tourism & Trade. Industrial Technology Centre Library & Information Services
Manitoba Justice. Attorney General's Library
Manitoba Justice. Community & Youth Correctional Services
Manitoba Labour. Education Centre
Manitoba Labour. Research Branch
Manitoba Labour. Workplace Safety & Health Library
Manitoba Natural Resources. Air Photo Library
Manitoba Natural Resources Library
Manitoba Rural Development
Manitoba Rural Development. Food Development Centre Library

HOSPITAL & HEALTH
The Arthritis Society (Manitoba Division) Resource Library
Brandon General Hospital Library Services
Children's Hospital Family Information Library
Concordia Hospital Library
Grace General Hospital Library
Hamiota District Health Centre Library
J.W. Crane Memorial Library of Gerontology and Geriatrics
Manitoba Cancer Treatment and Research Education Library
Misericordia Health Centre Library
Selkirk Mental Health Centre Central Library
Seven Oaks General Hospital Library
Winnipeg Clinic Library

PUBLIC
Altona Branch Library
Arborg Branch Library
Ayamiscikewikamik Norway House Public Library
Benito Branch Library
Bette Winner Public Library
Bibliothèque Allard Library -
Bibliothèque Montcalm Library
Bibliothèque Pere-Champagne
Bibliothèque Regionale Jolys
Bibliothèque Ritchot Library
Bibliothèque Saint-Claude Library
Bibliothèque Saint-Joachim Library
Bibliothèque Ste. Anne Library
Binscarth Branch Library

Birch River & District Branch Library
Birtle Branch Library
Boissevain & Morton Regional Library
Border Regional Library
Bowsman Branch Library
Boyne Regional Library
Bren Del Win Centennial Library
Brokenhead River Regional Library
Carberry/North Cypress Branch Library
Cartwright Branch Library
Centennial Library
Charleswood Library
Churchill Public Library
Cornish Library
Dauphin Branch Library
Elkhorn Branch Library
Emerson Library
Erickson District Library
Eriksdale Public Library
Evergreen Regional Library
Flin Flon Public Library
Fort Garry Library
Foxwarren Branch Library
Gilbert Plains Branch Library
Gladstone & District Library
Glenboro/South Cypress Branch Library
Glenwood & Souris Regional Library
Grandview Branch Library
Hamiota Centennial Library
Headingley Municipal Library
Henderson Library
Jake Epp Library
Jewish Public Library
Jolys Regional Library
Lac du Bonnet Regional Library
Lakeland Regional Library
Langruth Library
Leaf Rapids Public Library
Louis Riel Library
Lynn Lake Centennial Library
Manitou Public Library
McAuley Branch Library
McCreary District Library
Minitonas Library
Minnedosa Regional Library
Morden Branch Library
Munroe Library
Napinka Library
Neepawa Branch Library
North Norfolk MacGregor Regional Library
North-West Regional Library
Ochre River Library
Osborne Library
Parkland Regional Library
The Pas Public Library
Pauline Johnson Library
Pembina Trail Library
Pierson Branch Library
Pierson Library
Pilot Mound Branch Library
Pinawa Public Library
Portage la Prairie City Library
Prairie Crocus Regional Library
R.M. of Argyle Public Library
Rapid City Regional Library
Reston District Library
River Heights Library
Riverton Branch Library
Roblin & District Library
Rossburn Regional Library
Russell & District Regional Library

Selkirk & St. Andrews Regional Library
Shilo Community Library
Shoal Lake Community Library
Siglunes District Library
Sir William Stephenson Library
Snow Lake Community Library
Somerset Library/Bibliothèque Somerset
South Central Regional Library
South Interlake Regional Library
Southwestern Manitoba Regional Library
St. Boniface Library
St. James-Assiniboia Library
St. John's Library
St. Malo Branch Library
St. Vital Library
Ste. Agathe Branch Library
Ste. Rose Regional Library
Teulon Branch Library
Thompson Public Library
Transcona Library
Valley Regional Library
Victoria Municipal Library
West End Library
West Kildonan Library
Western Manitoba Regional Library
Westwood Library
Windsor Park Library
Winnipeg Public Library
Winnipegosis Branch Library

SPECIAL
17 Wing Recreational Library
The Addictions Foundation of Manitoba. William Potoroka Memorial Library
Aikins, Macaulay and Thorvaldson Management Services Library
Appraisal Institute of Canada
Archdiocese of Winnipeg Catholic Centre Resource Library
Associated Manitoba Arts Festival Resource Library
The Beaver Magazine Research Library
Bethania Mennonite Personal Care Home Library
Bristol Aerospace Engineering Reference Library
Canadian Authors Association Library
Canadian Bison Association Library
Canadian Broadcasting Corporation Record Library
Canadian Centre for Philanthropy
Canadian Parents for French Library
Canadian Red Cross Society
Canadian Wheat Board Library
Centre for Indigenous Environmental Resources (C.I.E.R.)
Centre for Mennonite Brethren Studies
Certified General Accountants Association of Manitoba
Children's Hospital Patient Library
Churchill Research Centre Library
Clara Lander Library. Winnipeg Art Gallery
Community Therapy Services Inc.
Conference of Manitoba & Northwestern Ontario Resource Centre
Consumers' Association of Canada (Manitoba), Consumer Resource Library
D'Arcy & Deacon Law Library
D.P.I.'s Resource Centre Library
The Daily Graphic Library
David Winton Bell Memorial Library. Delta Waterfowl & Wetlands Research Station
Deloitte & Touche Chartered Accountants Research Centre
Ducks Unlimited Institute for Wetland & Waterfowl Research
Fillmore Riley Library
Fire Fighters Historical Society of Winnipeg
Fort Whyte Centre Library
Grand Library Grand Lodge of Manitoba

A Guide to Libraries in Manitoba

Great Library
Guertin Brothers Coatings & Sealants Ltd. Library
Guild of Canadian Weavers
Heritage Winnipeg Corp. Resource Centre
Institut Joseph-Dubuc
Institute of Urban Studies Reference Library
International Institute for Sustainable Development Information Centre
Islamic Ahmadiyya Library
L.M. Architectural Group Library
League for Life in Manitoba Library
Lieutenant General K.E. Lewis Memorial Library
Literacy Partners of Manitoba Resource Centre
M.F.L. Occupational Health Centre Library
Manitoba Archaeological Society
Manitoba Association for Rights & Liberties
Manitoba Association of Playwrights
Manitoba Association of School Trustees (M.A.S.T.)
Manitoba Child Care Association Resource Library
Manitoba Crafts Museum and Library
Manitoba Culture, Heritage & Citizenship. Hudson's Bay Company Archives, Provincial Archives of Manitoba
Manitoba Development Centre Library
Manitoba Eco-Network Environmental Resource Centre
Manitoba Genealogical Society
Manitoba Historical Society Library
Manitoba Hydro Library
Manitoba Indian Cultural Education Centre. Peoples Library
Manitoba Labour Board Library
Manitoba Métis Federation Library
Manitoba Museum of Man and Nature Library
Manitoba Naturalists Society
The Manitoba Pharmaceutical Association Library
Manitoba Telecom Services. Corporate Library
Manitoba Trucking Association
Manitoba Women's Directorate Resource Centre
Manitoba Writers' Guild. Writers' Resource Centre
The Marquis Project Laura Delamater Resource Centre
Meadowood Manor Personal Care Home
Mennonite Heritage Village Library
The Métis Resource Centre Inc.
Myers, Weinberg, Kussin, Weinstein, Bryk
National Research Council Information Centre Winnipeg
Pitbaldo Buchwald Asper Law Library
R.C.M.P. Forensic Laboratory Scientific Information Centre
Red River Apiarists Association
Royal Canadian Artillery Museum Library & Archives
Sam Waller Museum
Sexuality Education Resource Centre, Brandon
Sexuality Education Resource Centre, Winnipeg
Societe Historique de Saint-Boniface
Society for Manitobans with Disabilities Inc. Stephen Sparling Library
Spina Bifida & Hydrocephalus Association of Canada Resource
Take Pride Winnipeg Inc.
Taylor McCaffrey Library
Teshmont Consultants Inc.
Thompson Dorfman Sweatman Library
Tiger Hills Arts Association
Tony Mann Library
Treaty & Aboriginal Rights Research Centre
Ukrainian Cultural & Educational Centre Library
UNICEF Manitoba
Volunteer Centre of Winnipeg Library
Western Canada Aviation Museum Library
Western Canada Pictorial Index Inc.
William Molloy Library
Winnipeg Free Press Library
Winnipeg Gay/Lesbian Resource Centre (W.G.L.R.C.) Community Library
Winnipeg Sun Library
Winnipeg Symphony Orchestra Music Library
Wolch, Pinx, Tapper, Scurfield
YM-YWCA Women's Resource Centre Library

Index by Subject

ABORTION
League for Life in Manitoba Library

ACCOUNTING
Canada. Revenue Canada. Winnipeg District Office Research & Library Services
Certified General Accountants Association of Manitoba
Deloitte & Touche Chartered Accountants Research Centre
University of Manitoba. Albert D. Cohen Management Library

ADDICTIONS
The Addictions Foundation of Manitoba. William Potoroka Memorial Library

ADVOCACY
D.P.I.'s Resource Centre

AERIAL PHOTOGRAPHY
Manitoba Natural Resources. Air Photo Library

AERONAUTICS
Western Canada Aviation Museum Library

AEROSPACE TECHNOLOGY
Bristol Aerospace Engineering Reference Library
Lieutenant General K.E. Lewis Memorial Library

AGING
Bethania Mennonite Personal Care Home Library
J.W. Crane Memorial Library of Gerontology and Geriatrics
Meadowood Manor Personal Care Home

AGRI-FOOD INDUSTRY
Manitoba Rural Development. Food Development Centre Library

AGRICULTURAL ECONOMICS
Canadian Wheat Board Library
University of Manitoba. William R. Newman Agriculture Library

AGRICULTURE
Assiniboine Community College Library
Canada. Agriculture & Agri-Food Canada. Brandon Research Centre Library And Information Centre
Canada. Agriculture & Agri-Food Canada. Winnipeg Research Library

AGRICULTURE - HISTORY
Western Canada Pictorial Index Inc.

ALCOHOL & DRUGS
The Addictions Foundation of Manitoba. William Potoroka Memorial Library

ANIMAL FEEDSTUFFS
Manitoba Rural Development. Food Development Centre Library

ANIMAL SCIENCE
Canada. Agriculture & Agri-Food Canada. Brandon Research Centre Library and Information Centre
Canadian Bison Association Library
University of Manitoba. William R. Newman Agriculture Library

APPRAISALS
Appraisal Institute of Canada

AQUATIC SCIENCES
Canada. Fisheries & Oceans Canada. Freshwater Institute. The Eric Marshall Aquatic Research Library

ARCHAEOLOGY
Manitoba Archaeological Society
Manitoba Museum of Man and Nature Library

ARCHITECTURE
L.M. Architectural Group Library

ARCHITECTURE, HISTORICAL
Heritage Winnipeg Corp. Resource Centre

ARCTIC & NORTHWEST
Manitoba Culture, Heritage & Citizenship. Hudson's Bay Company Archives, Provincial Archives of Manitoba
William Molloy Library

ARCTIC & NORTHWEST - HISTORY
Western Canada Pictorial Index Inc.

ARMED FORCES
17 Wing Recreational Library
Lieutenant General K.E. Lewis Memorial Library

ART
Clara Lander Library. Winnipeg Art Gallery

ART & ARCHITECTURE
Tiger Hills Arts Association
University of Manitoba. Architecture/Fine Arts Library

ARTHRITIS
The Arthritis Society (Manitoba Division) Resource Library

AUDITING
Certified General Accountants Association of Manitoba
Winnipeg Audit Department Library

AVIATION
Lieutenant General K.E. Lewis Memorial Library
Western Canada Aviation Museum Library

AVIATION - HISTORY
Western Canada Pictorial Index Inc.

BEEKEEPING
Red River Apiarists Association

A Guide to Libraries in Manitoba

BIODIAGNOSTICS
National Research Council Information Centre Winnipeg

BIOLOGY
Churchill Research Centre Library
Manitoba Naturalists Society

BIOMEDICAL ENGINEERING
National Research Council Information Centre Winnipeg

BIOMEDICINE
University of Manitoba. Neil John MacLean Health Sciences Library

BISON
Canadian Bison Association Library

BOTANY
Manitoba Museum of Man and Nature Library
Manitoba Naturalists Society

BREWING
Canadian Grain Commission Library/Bibliothèque commission canadienne des grains

BUSINESS ADMINISTRATION
Assiniboine Community College Library
Canada/Manitoba Business Service Centre
Keewatin Community College Library
Red River College Library
University of Manitoba. Albert D. Cohen Management Library

CANADIAN LITERATURE
Canadian Authors Association Library
Collège universitaire de Saint-Boniface. Bibliothèque Alfred-Monnin
University of Manitoba. St. John's College Library
University of Winnipeg Library
Winnipeg Public Library

CANADIANA
University of Manitoba. St. John's College Library
University of Winnipeg Library
William Molloy Library
Winnipeg Public Library

CANCER
Manitoba Cancer Treatment and Research Education Library

CELL BIOLOGY
Manitoba Cancer Treatment and Research Education Library

CEREAL CHEMISTRY
Canadian Grain Commission Library/Bibliothèque commission canadienne des grains

CEREAL RESEARCH
Canada. Agriculture & Agri-Food Canada. Brandon Research Centre Library and Information Centre
Canada. Agriculture & Agri-Food Canada. Winnipeg Research Library

CHILD CARE
Children's Hospital Family Information Library
Manitoba Child Care Association Resource Library

CHILD DEVELOPMENT
Assiniboine Community College Library
University of Manitoba. D.S. Woods Education Library

CHILDREN'S MATERIAL
Children's Hospital Patient Library

CHRISTIAN LIFE
Conference of Manitoba & Northwestern Ontario Resource Centre

CITY PLANNING
Institute of Urban Studies Reference Library
University of Manitoba. Architecture/Fine Arts Library

CLIMATOLOGY
Churchill Research Centre Library
Environment Library/Bibliothèque de l'Environnement

COMMUNITY SERVICES
Take Pride Winnipeg Inc.

COMPUTER SCIENCE
National Research Council Information Centre Winnipeg

CONSERVATION
Ducks Unlimited Institute for Wetland & Waterfowl Research
Environment Library/Bibliothèque de l'Environnement

CONSUMER RIGHTS AND LEGISLATION
Consumers' Association of Canada (Manitoba). Consumer Resource Library

COOKING
William Molloy Library

COPYRIGHT
Manitoba Writers' Guild. Writers' Resource Centre

CRAFTS
Manitoba Crafts Museum and Library

DANGEROUS GOODS
Manitoba Trucking Association

DENTISTRY
University of Manitoba. Neil John MacLean Health Sciences Library

DEVELOPMENTAL HANDICAPS
Manitoba Development Centre Library

DISABILITY ISSUES
D.P.I.'s Resource Centre

DRAMA
Manitoba Association of Playwrights

DRUG ABUSE
The Addictions Foundation of Manitoba. William Potoroka Memorial Library

ECOLOGY
David Winton Bell Memorial Library. Delta Waterfowl & Wetlands Research Station
Ducks Unlimited Institute for Wetland & Waterfowl Research
Fort Whyte Centre Library

ECONOMICS
Canada/Manitoba Business Service Centre
Deloitte & Touche Chartered Accountants Research Centre
Manitoba Finance. Federal-Provincial Relations & Research Library

EDUCATION
Brandon University. John E. Robbins Library

College universitaire de Saint-Boniface. Bibliothèque Alfred-Monnin
Manitoba Association of School Trustees (M.A.S.T.)
Manitoba Education & Training. Direction des ressources Educatives françaises (D.R.E.F.)
Manitoba Education & Training. Instructional Resources Unit
Manitoba Education & Training. Special Materials Services
University of Manitoba. D.S. Woods Education Library
University of Manitoba. Elizabeth Dafoe Library

EDUCATION, EARLY CHILDHOOD
Manitoba Child Care Association Resource Library

ELECTIONS
Legislative Assembly. Elections Manitoba Library

ELECTORAL REFORM
Legislative Assembly. Elections Manitoba Library

ELECTRICITY
Manitoba Hydro Library

ENERGY CONSERVATION
Manitoba Energy & Mines Library

ENGINEERING
Bristol Aerospace Engineering Reference Library
Keewatin Community College Library
L.M. Architectural Group Library
Manitoba Hydro Library
Manitoba Industry Tourism & Trade. Industrial Technology Centre Library & Information Services
Red River College Library
Teshmont Consultants Inc.
University of Manitoba. Donald W. Craik Engineering Library

ENTOMOLOGY
Manitoba Museum of Man and Nature Library
University of Manitoba. William R. Newman Agriculture Library

ENTREPRENEURSHIP
Canada/Manitoba Business Service Centre
Manitoba Industry Tourism & Trade. Industrial Technology Centre Library & Information Services

ENVIRONMENT
Environment Library/Bibliothèque de l'Environnement
Fort Whyte Centre Library

ENVIRONMENTAL DESIGN
University of Manitoba. Architecture/Fine Arts Library

ENVIRONMENTAL HEALTH
Manitoba Eco-Network Environmental Resource Centre

ETHICS
William & Catherine Booth College Library

ETHNIC & CULTURAL COLLECTIONS
Manitoba Museum of Man and Nature Library
Mennonite Heritage Village Library
Ukrainian Cultural & Educational Centre Library

ETHNIC CULTURE & HERITAGE
University of Manitoba. Elizabeth Dafoe Library

EUTHANASIA
League for Life in Manitoba Library

FAMILY PLANNING
Sexuality Education Resource Centre, Brandon
Sexuality Education Resource Centre, Winnipeg

FAMILY VIOLENCE
Ym-Ywca Women's Resource Centre Library

FARM MANAGEMENT
University of Manitoba. William R. Newman Agriculture Library

FETAL ALCOHOL SYNDROME
The Addictions Foundation of Manitoba. William Potoroka Memorial Library

FINANCE
Manitoba Finance. Federal-Provincial Relations & Research Library
University of Manitoba. Albert D. Cohen Management Library

FIRE FIGHTING – HISTORY
Western Canada Pictorial Index Inc.

FIRE PREVENTION
Fire Fighters Historical Society of Winnipeg

FIRST NATIONS ISSUES
Assiniboine Community College Library
Canada. Indian & Northern Affairs. Regional Library
Keewatin Community College Library
Manitoba Indian Cultural Education Centre. Peoples Library
Sam Waller Museum
Treaty & Aboriginal Rights Research Centre

FISHERIES & OCEANS
Canada. Fisheries & Oceans Canada. Freshwater Institute. The Eric Marshall Aquatic Research Library

FITNESS
Ym-Ywca Women's Resource Centre Library

FLOOD PROTECTION
Winnipeg Water & Waste Department Resource Centre

FOOD SCIENCE
Canadian Grain Commission Library/Bibliothèque commission canadienne des grains
Manitoba Rural Development. Food Development Centre Library
University of Manitoba. William R. Newman Agriculture Library

FOREIGN TRADE
Canadian Wheat Board Library

FORENSIC SCIENCE
R.C.M.P. Forensic Laboratory Scientific Information Centre

FORESTRY
Manitoba Natural Resources Library

FREEMASONRY
Grand Library Grand Lodge of Manitoba

FRENCH CANADIAN STUDIES
College universitaire de Saint-Boniface. Bibliothèque Alfred-Monnin
Societe Historique de Saint-Boniface

FRENCH LANGUAGE & CULTURE
Canadian Parents for French Library

FRENCH LANGUAGE & LITERATURE
College universitaire de Saint-Boniface. Bibliothèque Alfred-Monnin

FUNDRAISING
Canadian Centre for Philanthropy
Volunteer Centre of Winnipeg Library

FUR TRADE – HISTORY
The Beaver Magazine Research Library
Manitoba Culture, Heritage & Citizenship. Hudson's Bay Company Archives, Provincial Archives of Manitoba
Western Canada Pictorial Index Inc.

GAMBLING, COMPULSIVE
The Addictions Foundation of Manitoba. William Potoroka Memorial Library

GAY RIGHTS
Winnipeg Gay/Lesbian Resource Centre (W.G.L.R.C.) Community Library

GENEALOGY
Manitoba Genealogical Society
Societe Historique de Saint-Boniface

GEOLOGY
Manitoba Energy & Mines Library
Manitoba Museum of Man and Nature Library

GERONTOLOGY
Bethania Mennonite Personal Care Home Library
J.W. Crane Memorial Library of Gerontology and Geriatrics
Meadowood Manor Personal Care Home

GRAIN TRADE
Canadian Grain Commission Library/Bibliothèque commission canadienne des grains
Canadian Wheat Board Library

HANDICAPPED AND DISABLED
D.P.I.'s Resource Centre

HEALTH ADMINISTRATION
Manitoba Health. Library Services

HEALTH CARE
Children's Hospital Family Information Library

HEALTH CARE ADMINISTRATION
Misericordia Health Centre Library

HISTORY – CANADA
The Beaver Magazine Research Library
College universitaire de Saint-Boniface. Bibliothèque Alfred-Monnin
Manitoba Culture, Heritage & Citizenship. Legislative Library
University of Manitoba. St. John's College Library
Western Canada Pictorial Index Inc.

HISTORY, JEWISH
Jewish Public Library

HISTORY – MANITOBA
Heritage Winnipeg Corp. Resource Centre
Manitoba Culture, Heritage & Citizenship. Hudson's Bay Company Archives, Provincial Archives of Manitoba
Manitoba Historical Society Library

Manitoba Museum of Man and Nature Library

HISTORY – WINNIPEG
Winnipeg Public Library

HOMOSEXUALITY
Sexuality Education Resource Centre, Brandon
Sexuality Education Resource Centre, Winnipeg
Winnipeg Gay/Lesbian Resource Centre (W.G.L.R.C.) Community Library

HOSPITALITY
Assiniboine Community College Library
Red River College Library

HUDSON'S BAY COMPANY
Manitoba Culture, Heritage & Citizenship. Hudson's Bay Company Archives, Provincial Archives of Manitoba

HUMAN ECOLOGY
University of Manitoba. Elizabeth Dafoe Library

HUMAN RIGHTS
D.P.I.'s Resource Centre
Manitoba Association for Rights & Liberties

HUMANITIES & SOCIAL SCIENCES
Brandon University. John E. Robbins Library
University of Manitoba. Elizabeth Dafoe Library
University of Winnipeg Library

HUTTERITES
Centre for Mennonite Brethren Studies

HYDROCEPHALUS
Spina Bifida & Hydrocephalus Association of Canada Resource Library

ICELANDIC STUDIES
Evergreen Regional Library
Pauline Johnson Library
University of Manitoba. Elizabeth Dafoe Library

INDIGENOUS ENVIRONMENT
Centre for Indigenous Environmental Resources (C.I.E.R.)

INDUSTRIAL HYGIENE
M.F.L. Occupational Health Centre Library

INTERIOR DESIGN
University of Manitoba. Architecture/Fine Arts Library

INTERNATIONAL DEVELOPMENT
The Marquis Project Laura Delamater Resource Centre
UNICEF Manitoba

INTERNATIONAL RELATIONS
International Institute for Sustainable Development Information Centre

JOURNALISM
Red River College Library

JUDAISM
Jewish Public Library

LABOUR LAW
Canada. Labour Canada. Central Region Resource Centre

LABOUR RELATIONS
Manitoba Labour Board Library
Manitoba Labour. Education Centre

Manitoba Labour. Research Branch

LAND USE PLANNING
Manitoba Rural Development

LAW & LEGISLATION
Aikins, Macaulay and Thorvaldson Management Services Library
Canada. Justice Canada. Library
D'Arcy & Deacon Law Library
Fillmore Riley Library
Great Library
Institut Joseph-Dubuc
Manitoba Culture, Heritage & Citizenship. Legislative Library
Manitoba Justice. Attorney General's Library
Myers, Weinberg, Kussin, Weinstein, Bryk
Pitbaldo Buchwald Asper Law Library
Taylor McCaffrey Library
Thompson Dorfman Sweatman Library
University of Manitoba. E.K. Williams Law Library
Wolch, Pinx, Tapper, Scurfield

LEARNING DISABILITIES
Society for Manitobans with Disabilities Inc. Stephen Sparling Library

LIBRARY SCIENCE
Red River College Library

LITERACY
Literacy Partners of Manitoba Resource Centre

MANAGEMENT INFORMATION SYSTEMS
Certified General Accountants Association of Manitoba

MARINE BIOLOGY
Canada. Fisheries & Oceans Canada. Freshwater Institute. The Eric Marshall Aquatic Research Library

MARKETING
Canada/Manitoba Business Service Centre
University of Manitoba. Albert D. Cohen Management Library

MEDICINE & HEALTH
The Arthritis Society (Manitoba Division) Resource Library
Brandon General Hospital Library Services
Canadian Red Cross Society
Children's Hospital Family Information Library
Concordia Hospital Library
Grace General Hospital Library
Hamiota District Health Centre Library
Manitoba Cancer Treatment and Research Education Library
The Manitoba Pharmaceutical Association Library
Misericordia Health Centre Library
Seven Oaks General Hospital Library
Society for Manitobans with Disabilities Inc. Stephen Sparling Library
Spina Bifida & Hydrocephalus Association of Canada Resource Library
University of Manitoba. Neil John MacLean Health Sciences Library
University of Manitoba. Neil John MacLean Health Sciences Library. St. Boniface General Hospital Section. Carolyn Sifton-Helene Fuld Library
Winnipeg Clinic Library

MEDIEVAL STUDIES
University of Manitoba. St. Paul's College. Father Harold Drake S.J. Library

MENNONITE HISTORY
Mennonite Heritage Village Library
South Central Regional Library
Steinbach Bible College Library

MENNONITE STUDIES
Canadian Mennonite Bible College Library
Centre for Mennonite Brethren Studies
Concord College Library

MENTAL HEALTH
Community Therapy Services Inc.
Selkirk Mental Health Centre Central Library
YM-YWCA Women's Resource Centre Library

METEOROLOGY
Environment Library/Bibliothèque de l'Environnement

MÉTIS CULTURE & HISTORY
Manitoba Métis Federation Library
The Métis Resource Centre Inc.
Societe Historique de Saint-Boniface

MICROBIOLOGY
Canada. Health Canada. Federal Laboratories Library Bibliothèque de laboratoires federaux

MILITARY HISTORY
Royal Canadian Artillery Museum Library & Archives

MILLING & BAKING
Canadian Grain Commission Library/Bibliothèque commission canadienne des grains

MINING
Manitoba Energy & Mines Library

MUNICIPAL GOVERNMENT
Institute of Urban Studies Reference Library
Manitoba Rural Development

MUSEOLOGY
Manitoba Museum of Man and Nature Library

MUSIC
Associated Manitoba Arts Festival Resource Library
Brandon University. John E. Robbins Library
Canadian Broadcasting Corporation Record Library
Canadian Mennonite Bible College Library
Concord College Library
Tiger Hills Arts Association
University of Manitoba. Eckhardt-Grammatte Music Library
Winnipeg Symphony Orchestra Music Library

NATURAL HISTORY
Sam Waller Museum

NATURAL RESOURCES
Centre for Indigenous Environmental Resources (C.I.E.R.)
David Winton Bell Memorial Library. Delta Waterfowl & Wetlands Research Station
Keewatin Community College Library
Manitoba Natural Resources Library
Manitoba Naturalists Society

NEWSPAPER LIBRARIES
The Daily Graphic Library
Winnipeg Free Press Library
Winnipeg Sun Library

NURSING
Assiniboine Community College Library
Brandon General Hospital Library Services
Brandon University. John E. Robbins Library
Grace General Hospital Library
Keewatin Community College Library
Misericordia Health Centre Library
Red River College Library
Seven Oaks General Hospital Library
University of Manitoba. Elizabeth Dafoe Library
University of Manitoba. Neil John MacLean Health Sciences Library
University of Manitoba. Neil John MacLean Health Sciences. Library. St. Boniface General Hospital Section. Carolyn Sifton-Helene Fuld Library

NUTRACEUTICALS
Manitoba Rural Development. Food Development Centre Library

OCCUPATIONAL HEALTH & SAFETY
M.F.L. Occupational Health Centre Library
Manitoba Labour. Workplace Safety & Health Library

OCCUPATIONAL THERAPY
Community Therapy Services Inc.

ORNITHOLOGY
David Winton Bell Memorial Library. Delta Waterfowl & Wetlands Research Station
Ducks Unlimited Institute for Wetland & Waterfowl Research
Fort Whyte Centre Library
Manitoba Naturalists Society

PAINTS
Guertin Brothers Coatings & Sealants Ltd. Library

PALLIATIVE CARE
Southwestern Manitoba Regional Library

PATENTS
Manitoba Industry, Tourism & Trade. Industrial Technology Centre Library and Information Services
University of Manitoba. Donald W. Craik Engineering Library

PETROLEUM RESOURCES
Manitoba Energy & Mines Library

PHARMACOLOGY
The Manitoba Pharmaceutical Association Library

PHILANTHROPY
Canadian Centre for Philanthropy

PHILOSOPHY
University of Manitoba. St. Paul's College. Father Harold Drake S.J. Library

PHOTOGRAPHIC COLLECTIONS
Manitoba Museum of Man and Nature Library
Manitoba Natural Resources. Air Photo Library
Western Canada Pictorial Index Inc.

PHYSICAL DISABILITIES
Society for Manitobans with Disabilities Inc. Stephen Sparling Library

PHYSIOTHERAPY
Community Therapy Services Inc.

PLANT SCIENCE
University of Manitoba. William R. Newman Agriculture Library

POETRY
Associated Manitoba Arts Festival Resource Library

POLITICAL STUDIES
University of Manitoba. St. John's College Library

POLITICS AND GOVERNMENT
Manitoba Culture, Heritage & Citizenship. Legislative Library

PRODUCT DESIGN & TESTING
Manitoba Industry Tourism & Trade. Industrial Technology Centre Library & Information Services

PRODUCT INFORMATION
Consumers' Association of Canada (Manitoba), Consumer Resource Library

PUBLIC AFFAIRS
Manitoba Culture, Heritage & Citizenship. Legislative Library

RECREATION & SPORTS
University of Manitoba. D.S. Woods Education Library
University of Manitoba. Elizabeth Dafoe Library

RECYCLING
Take Pride Winnipeg Inc.

REHABILITATION
Community Therapy Services Inc.
Society for Manitobans with Disabilities Inc. Stephen Sparling Library
University of Manitoba. Neil John MacLean Health Sciences Library

RELIGION & THEOLOGY
Archdiocese of Winnipeg Catholic Centre Resource Library
Canadian Mennonite Bible College Library
Centre for Mennonite Brethren Studies
Concord College Library
Conference of Manitoba & Northwestern Ontario Resource Centre
Islamic Ahmadiyya Library
Providence College & Seminary Library
St. Andrew's College Library
Steinbach Bible College Library
University of Manitoba. St. John's College Library
University of Manitoba. St. Paul's College. Father Harold Drake S.J. Library
University of Winnipeg Library
Western Christian College Library
William & Catherine Booth College Library

REPRODUCTIVE HEALTH
Sexuality Education Resource Centre, Brandon
Sexuality Education Resource Centre, Winnipeg

REPRODUCTIVE TECHNOLOGY
League for Life in Manitoba Library

RHEUMATIC DISEASES
The Arthritis Society (Manitoba Division) Resource Library

RURAL ECONOMIC DEVELOPMENT
Manitoba Rural Development

SALVATION ARMY
William & Catherine Booth College Library

SCIENCE FICTION
University of Winnipeg Library

SCIENCE & TECHNOLOGY
Brandon University. John E. Robbins Library
University of Manitoba. Sciences & Technology Library
University of Winnipeg Library

SEALANTS
Guertin Brothers Coatings & Sealants Ltd. Library

SEXUALLY TRANSMITTED INFECTIONS
Sexuality Education Resource Centre, Brandon
Sexuality Education Resource Centre, Winnipeg

SLAVIC STUDIES
University of Manitoba. Elizabeth Dafoe Library

SOCIAL WORK
University of Manitoba. Elizabeth Dafoe Library
William & Catherine Booth College Library

SOIL SCIENCE
University of Manitoba. William R. Newman Agriculture Library

SPINA BIFIDA
Spina Bifida & Hydrocephalus Association of Canada Resource

SPINAL CORD INJURIES
Tony Mann Library

STANDARS
Manitoba Industry & Trade. Industrial Technology Centre Library & Information Services
University of Manitoba. Donald W. Craik Engineering Library

SUSTAINABLE DEVELOPMENT
International Institute for Sustainable Development Information Centre

TAXATION
Canada. Revenue Canada. Winnipeg District Office Research & Library Services
Certified General Accountants Association of Manitoba
Manitoba Finance. Federal-Provincial Relations & Research Library

TELECOMMUNICATIONS
Manitoba Telecom Services. Corporate Library

TOXIC & HAZARDOUS SUBSTANCES
Manitoba Eco-Network Environmental Resource Centre

TOXICOLOGY
M.F.L. Occupational Health Centre Library
Manitoba Labour. Workplace Safety & Health Library

TRANSLATION
College universitaire de Saint-Boniface. Bibliothèque Alfred-Monnin

TRANSPORTATION
Manitoba Trucking Association

TRANSPORTATION – HISTORY
Western Canada Pictorial Index Inc.

UKRAINIAN STUDIES
St. Andrew's College Library
Ukrainian Cultural & Educational Centre Library

URBAN STUDIES
Institute of Urban Studies Reference Library

VETERINARY MEDICINE
Canada. Health Canada. Federal Laboratories Library
Bibliothèque de laboratoires federaux

VIOLENCE AGAINST WOMEN
YM-YWCA Women's Resource Centre Library

VIROLOGY
Canada. Health Canada. Federal Laboratories Library
Bibliothèque de laboratoires federaux

VOLUNTEER MANAGEMENT
Volunteer Centre of Winnipeg Library

WARFARE
Lieutenant General K.E. Lewis Memorial Library

WASTE MANAGEMENT
Manitoba Eco-Network Environmental Resource Centre
Take Pride Winnipeg Inc.
Winnipeg Water & Waste Department Resource Centre

WATER MANAGEMENT
Winnipeg Water & Waste Department Resource Centre

WATER RESOURCES
Manitoba Natural Resources Library

WEAVING
Guild of Canadian Weavers

WETLANDS BIOLOGY
David Winton Bell Memorial Library. Delta Waterfowl & Wetlands Research Station
Ducks Unlimited Institute for Wetland & Waterfowl Research
Fort Whyte Centre Library

WILDLIFE MANAGEMENT
Churchill Research Centre Library
Environment Library/Bibliothèque de l'Environnement
Manitoba Natural Resources Library

WINES
William Molloy Library

WOMEN IN RELIGION
University of Manitoba. St. Paul's College. Father Harold Drake S.J. Library

WOMEN'S ISSUES
Manitoba Women's Directorate Resource Centre

WORKPLACE SAFETY
Canada. Labour Canada. Central Region Resource Centre
Manitoba Labour. Workplace Safety & Health Library

WRITING & PUBLISHING
Canadian Authors Association Library
Manitoba Association of Playwrights
Manitoba Writers' Guild. Writers' Resource Centre
Red River College Library

YOUNG OFFENDERS
Manitoba Justice. Community & Youth Correctional Services

YOUTH SERVICES
Manitoba Justice. Community & Youth Correctional Services

ZOOLOGY
Manitoba Museum of Man and Nature Library

Index

A

Aboriginal collections, 95-99
Aboriginal Health Collection (Maclean Health Sciences), 37
Aboriginal Justice Inquiry of Manitoba (Report, 1991), 95
Adams Archibald and Alexander Morris papers, 96
Agricultural library collections, 77-80
Agriculture and Agri-Food Canada collections, 77
Albert D. Cohen Management Library, 38, 80-81
Alfred-Monin. *See* Collège universitaire de Saint-Boniface Bibliothèque Alfred-Monnin
Andrew Carnegie Foundation, 29
Angel, Dr. Michael, 86
Anhang, Abe, 113
Arborg branch (Evergreen Regional Library), 30
Archibald, A.E., 68, 84
Architecture collections, 92-94
Architecture/Fine Arts Library (University of Manitoba), 36, 92-94
  collections listed, 93-94
Archives Library (HBC), 63
Arnljotur Bjornsson Olson library, 102
Ashdown Collection of Canadiana, 40
Asian Development Bank Collection, 40
Assiniboine Community College, 41-42
Association for Teacher-Librarianship in Canada (ATLC), 44, 47
Association pour l'avancement des sciences et des techniques de la documentation (ASTED), 44, 47

B

Beattie, Judith Hudson, 62
Beaver (The) Magazine Library, 62
Beaver House Library, 63
Ben and Esther Horch Music Collection, 104
Bibliothèque de Saint-Boniface, 99
Bibliothèque St. Claude, 30
Bibliothèque Ste. Anne, 30
Bigelow, Charles and Elizabeth, 86
Board Room Library (HBC), 63
Boissevain & Morton Regional Library, 31
  Native heritage resources, 95, 97-98
Book and Periodical Council of Canada
  Library Action Committee, 16
Book talks, 54
Books and Reports collection (Legislative Library), 69
Boyne Regional Library, 30
Brandon Public Library, 30
Brandon Research Centre Library, 78
Brandon University library. *See* John E. Robbins Library
British Library Document Supply Centre, 107
Brooklands branch library (Winnipeg), 22, 23
Buchwald, Dee, 113
Buffie, Margaret, 50
Buller, A.H.R., 77
Buller collection, 77
Business sector collections, 80-82

C

Canada Institute for Scientific and Technical Information (CISTI), 57, 106, 107-8
Canada/Manitoba Business Service Centre (CMBSC), 81-82, 112
Canada-Manitoba Agreement for Environmental Harmonization, 60
Canadian Agriculture Library, 107
Canadian Association of Special Libraries and Information Services (CASLIS), 56-57
Canadian Broadcasting Corporation Collection (WCPI), 65-66
Canadian Council of Ministers of the Environment (CCME), 60
Canadian Geriatrics Research Society, 88
Canadian Grain Commission Library, 78-79
Canadian Intellectual Property Office (CIPO), 62
Canadian Library Association
  Action for Literacy Interest Group, 16
  Internet child safety, 122-23
  on library's role, 19-20
Canadian National Library. *See* National Library of Canada
Canadian National Railway Collection (WCPI), 66
Canadian School Library Association (CSLA), 44, 47
Canadian Wheat Board Library, 79
Canadiana collections, 83-86
Carnegie, Andrew, 15-16
Carnegie Foundation libraries, 15-16, 17
Carolyn Sifton-Helene Fuld Library, 37, 88
Centennial Branch. *See* Centennial Library (Winnipeg)
Centennial Library (Winnipeg), 11, 23, 82-83, 84, 106, 111-12
  Canadiana collection, 85
  user statistics, 111
Centennial Library/Arts Centre of Western Manitoba, 30
Centre for Indigenous Environmental Resources Library (CIER), 95, 96-97
Centre for Mennonite Brethren Studies, 103-4
Cereal Research Centre, 77
Chapin Collection. *See* Reverend R.T. Chapin Collection
Children's Hospital of Winnipeg Family Information Library, 89-91
Children's programming, 125-27
Church Missionary Society records, 96
CIER. *See* Centre for Indigenous Environmental Resources Library
CISTI. *See* Canada Institute for Scientific and Technical Information
City of Winnipeg, 11
Clara Lander Library, 92
Cohen, Albert D., 38
Cohen Management Library. *See* Albert D. Cohen Management Library
Collections et services en français, 99-101
College libraries. *See* Community College libraries; University libraries
Collège universitaire de Saint-Boniface Bibliothèque Alfred-Monnin, 34-35, 100
  software capabilities, 35
Commission on Canadian Studies, 83
Community College libraries, 40-42
Concept Plan (for Millennium Library Project), 112

Consumer health information collections, 87-92
Contaminated Sites Registry, 61
Cooke, Thora, 65
Cooper Rankin Architects, 21
Coopers & Lybrand, 113
Cornish Library (Winnipeg), 15
Council of Prairie and Pacific University Libraries (COPPUL), 106, 110
Craik Engineering Library. See Donald W. Craik Engineering Library
Crane, Dr. J.W., 88
Crane Memorial Library. See J.W. Crane Memorial Library of Gerontology and Geriatrics
Cultural sector, public library's role, 18

D
D.S. Woods Education Library, 36
Dafoe, Elizabeth, 37
Dafoe, John W., 37
Dafoe Library. See Elizabeth Dafoe Library
Deer Lodge Centre, 88-89
Democracy, public library's role, 18
Department of Archives and Special Collections (University of Manitoba), 84, 85-86
Department of Indian Affairs collection, 96
Desmond Smith Canadiana collection, 86
Direction des ressources éducatives françaises (DREF), 13, 67, 73-75, 100-101
  contact information, 74-75
Ditz, Lionel, 65
Dividends: The Value of Public Libraries in Canada, 16
Donald W. Craik Engineering Library, 37
Drache Collection. See Samuel J. Drache and Arthur B.C. Drache Legal Collection
Drake, Fr. Harold, S.J., 39
Drake Library. See Fr. Drake Library
Dueck, Judith, 44, 51-54
Dumont, Gabriel, 98
Dumont, Lieutenant Governor Yvon, 98

E
E.K. Williams Law Library, 38
  fee-based services, 32
Eckhardt-Gramatte Music Library, 38
Eco-Network collection, 97
Edmonton Store Executive Library (HBC), 62, 63
Electronic information sources, 11-12, 106. *See also* Internet, Manitoba libraries and
Electronic library concept, 57-59
Elizabeth Dafoe Library, 36-37
  Aboriginal collections, 95, 98
  Canadian authors' works, 86
  Canadiana, 85-86
  explorers' writings, 86
  Icelandic Collection, 101
  Slavic Collection, 102
  South Asian/Indian material, 103
Emerging technologies, public library's role, 19
Emerson library, 30
Environment Canada/Manitoba Library, 97
Environment Library/Bibliothèque de l'Environnement, 57
Environmental Assessment Harmonization, 60
Evergreen Regional Library, 30
Explorers' writings. *See* Elizabeth Dafoe Library, explorers' writings
Eyvindson, Peter, 50

F
Facility Program, A, 111
Family Information Library. *See* Children's Hospital of Winnipeg Family Information Library
Fédération des municipalités bilingues du Manitoba, 101

Fine Arts collections, 92-94
First Nations collections, 22, 95-99
  in various archives, 99
Fitchett, Bill, 27
Flin Flon Public Library, 87-88
Food Development Centre Library, 79
Fr. Drake Library, 39
Frances M. Pishker Memorial Library Fund, 126
French language resources, 12
  See also Direction des ressources éducatives françaises (DREF)
Fuld Library. See Carolyn Sifton-Helene Fuld Library
Fur Trade Libraries, 63

G
Gauvin collection. *See* Marshall Gauvin collection
Giesbrecht, Herbert, 103
Gillespie, Kay, 64
Global Supply Service (CISTI), 108
Gordon Bell High School Library, 12-13, 44, 51-55
  Aboriginal materials, 52
  information literacy program, 52
Government Publications collection, 68
Guttomur J. Guttormsson library, 102

H
Health information collections. *See* Consumer health information collections
Healthy Flin Flon, 87
Hind, E. Cora, 69, 84
Historic buildings
  used by libraries, 29-31
Historical Committee of the Canadian Mennonite Brethren Conference, 103
Home pages. *See* Internet
Horch Music Collection. *See* Ben and Esther Horch Music Collection
Hudson Bay Company, 11
Hudson's Bay Company Archives, 13
Hudson's Bay Company Archives Library, 57, 62-63
  Canada, 62
  London, 63
Hudson's Bay Record Society, 63
Hunter, Dr. R.O.A., 65

I
Icelandic Collection, 101
Industrial Technology Centre Library, 57, 61-62
Information Age, 12. *See also* Sir William Stephenson Library
Information centres. *See* Special libraries and information centres
Information, libraries and, 114
Information specialist, 116
Institute for Biodiagnostics, 13, 57
Institute of Urban Studies (University of Winnipeg) library, 40
Institute of Urban Studies Reference Library, 94
  collections listed, 94
Instructional Resources Unit (of DREF), 13
Instructional Resources Unit Library, 67, 71-73
  Multicultural Resource Collection, 95, 98-99
  services listed, 72-73
Interlibrary loan, 119
International Institute for Sustainable Development Information Centre, 57, 59-60, 97
International Organizations Documents collection, 68
Internet
  child safety guidelines, 122-23
  information evaluation resources, 123-25
  library home pages, 16
  Manitoba libraries and, 12
  navigation resources, 122

J

J.W. Crane Memorial Library of Gerontology and Geriatrics, 88-89
James A. Richardson Collection, 65
Jewish Historical Society of Western Canada, 104
John A. Toews Historical Collection, 104
John E. Robbins Library (Brandon University), 32-34
  description of holdings, 33
Johnson, Donald, 24-25, 26
Johnson, Pauline, 24-26

K

Kane, Paul, 65
Katie Peters Genealogical Collection, 104
Keewatin Community College Library, 42
Koshetz, Alexander, 105

L

Lalonde, Louise, 50
Lander Library. *See* Clara Lander Library
Larose-Kuzenko, Michelle, 44, 49-51
Legislative Library. *See* Manitoba Legislative Library
Legislative Reading Room collection, 69
Lemoine, Doris, 73
Librarian designation, 116
Libraries in Manitoba, origin, 11. *See also* Public library service, origin
Libraries in schools. *See* School libraries
Libraries, special. *See* Special libraries and information centres
Library
  functions, 114-15
  role, 114
  setting up a library, 119-22
Library assistant designation, 117-18
Library clerk designation, 117-18
Library Express Service, 106, 108
Library personnel
  classification, 115-18
  qualifications, 116
Library Services Division (Winnipeg), 113
Library technician designation, 117
Lifelong learning, public library's role, 19
Literacy, library's role, 19-20
Literacy promotion, as role of library, 16
Literacy, public library's role, 18
Lord Selkirk School Division, 28-29
Lundar, history of libraries in, 25. *See also* Pauline Johnson Library
Lundar Museum, 25

M

Macenko, Dr. Paul, 105
Maclean Health Sciences Library. *See* Neil John Maclean Health Sciences Library
Maclean, Neil John, 37
Manitoba Community and Family Histories collection, 84
Manitoba Education and Training Instructional Resources Unit. *See* Instructional Resources Unit
Manitoba Federation of Labour, 91-92
Manitoba Government Libraries Council, 67
Manitoba Government Publications Monthly Checklist, 70
Manitoba Health Libraries Association, 87
Manitoba Heritage Collections, 84
Manitoba Indian Cultural Education Centre, 95
Manitoba Legislative Library, 13, 67-70, 84-85
  holdings, 84
  Rare Book Collection, 11, 84
Manitoba library special collections, 76-105
  overview, 76
Manitoba Library Association
  web site address, 13

Manitoba Library Consortium, 106, 108-9
  electronic licensing, 108-9
  Library Express, 108
Manitoba Museum of Man and Nature, 13
  Library and Museum Archives, 57, 64
Manitoba Newspapers collection, 84
Manitoba Public Libraries Information Network (MAPLIN), 106, 109-10
Manitoba Research Centres, 77
Manitoba's 100th birthday
  libraries and, 11
Marshall Gauvin collection, 86
Mayer, Jeni, 50
McClung, Nellie, 69, 84
McDonald Heritage Centre. *See* W.J. (Joe) McDonald North American Native Heritage Resource Centre
McDonald, Joe, 98
McPhillips branch library (Winnipeg), 22
Mennonite resources. *See* Centre for Mennonite Brethren Studies
Métis Resource Centre, 97
MFL Occupational Health Centre Library, 91-92
Milbury, Peter, 51
Millennium Library Project, 13, 23, 106, 111-13
Millennium Library Square, 112
Miller, A.J., 65
Milton, Turid, 26, 27
Mol, Leo, 21
Morden Research Centre Library, 77
Morris area library development. *See* Valley Regional Library
Multicultural collections, 101-5
Multicultural Education Resource Collection (IRU), 95, 98-99
Multicultural issues
  in school libraries, 52, 54
Multilingual collection, 22

N

National Library of Canada
  interlibrary loan/location service, 107
National Research Council, 107
National Research Council Information Centre (Winnipeg), 13, 57-59
National Science Library, 107
Native studies collections, 95-99
Sir William Stephenson branch, 22
Neil John Maclean Health Sciences Library, 37, 88
  fee-based services, 32
Newman, Dr. William R., 36
Newman Library. *See* William R. Newman Agriculture Library
Newspapers collection, 68-69
NRC Information Centre.
  See National Research Council Information Centre (Winnipeg)

O

Oblate Fathers' Collection (WCPI), 65
Olson library. *See* Arnljotur Bjornsson Olson library
Online catalogues, 12
Online public access catalogue (OPAC), 16

P

Panaschuk, Heather, 51
Pauline Johnson Library (Lundar), 12, 24-26
Pelly, Sir John Henry, 63
People's Library and Resource Centre
  (Manitoba Indian Cultural and Education Centre), 95
Peters Genealogical Collection. *See* Katie Peters Genealogical Collection
Pierce, Lorne, 83
Planning Parameters, 111

Poland, P.R., 63
Potoroka Memorial Library, 91. See William Potoroka Memorial Library
Preliminary Patent and Trademark Searching Service, 62
Pritchard, Joanne, 54
Provencher, Msgr, 34
Provincial Archives of Manitoba, 68
Public libraries
 financial situation, 17
 information and, 17-18
 local economy and, 17, 18
 origin, 11
 roles, 16
 rural Manitoba, 16-17, 24-31
 students and, 18-19
 value of, 17-19
Public Libraries Act, 120
Public Library Services Branch, 12, 13, 67, 68, 70-71
 establishment of rural libraries, 16-17, 29-31
 holdings, 71
Public Registry, 61

Q
Quality and Innovation Centre (QUIRC) collection, 69

R
Ralph Estey library, 86
Rare Book collection (of Legislative Library), 69
Red River College Library, 40-41
Red River Library, 11
 surviving rare books, 69, 84
Red River Regional Library Fund, 29
Redahl, Gretta, 87
Rees, A.M., 87, 90
Resource sharing issues, 106
Resource-based learning, 53-54
Reverend R.T. Chapin Collection, 66
Richardson Collection. See James A. Richardson Collection
Riddell, Ronald, 65
Robbins Library. See John E. Robbins Library
Robertson, J.P., 68, 84
Ross, Flora Margaret, 37
Royal Commission on Aboriginal Peoples (Final Report, 1996), 95
Roznick, Marie, 54
RPG Partnership, 111-12
Rural Manitoba library services, 16-17, 24-31
Russell, John S., 83
Rutherford Collection on British History, 40

S
S.J. McKee Archives (Brandon University), 33
Samuel J. Drache and Arthur B.C. Drache Legal Collection, 40
Saul, John Ralston, 76
Schmidt, Claudia, 26, 27
School libraries, 43-55
 Internet and, 43, 48
 National Symposium views, 47-50
 new directions, 44
 teacher-librarian role, 46
Schreyer, Rt. Hon. Edward, 112
Science and Technology Information Centre (China), 108
Science and Technology Library (University of Manitoba), 39
Selkirk and St. Andrews Regional Library, 29
Selkirk Carnegie Library, 15, 29
Selkirk Community Library, 28-29
Selkirk settlers
 and Red River Library, 11
Sera, Hart, 52, 55
Shastri Indo-Canadian Institute (SICI), 103
Shastri, Lal Bahadur, 103

Shelter Canadian Properties Inc., 21
Shewchuk, Barbara, 26
Sir William Stephenson Library, 12, 20-23
 and Information Age, 16
 and Internet access, 22
 popularity, 23
Slavic Collection, 102
South Interlake Regional Library, 30
Special collections. See Manitoba library special collections
Special libraries and information centres, 56-66
Special Libraries Association, 56
St. Boniface Library, 12, 16, 23-24
St. John's Library (Winnipeg), 15, 38
St. Paul's College Library, 39
Staff Technical Library (HBC), 63
Stephan G. Stephansson library, 102
Stephenson, Sir William, 20
Storytelling, 54
Stubbs, Judge Roy St. George, 86
Sullivan, Francis Conroy, 30
Sun Valley School Library Program, 12-13, 44, 49-51
 new technologies, 51
Swan River branch (North-West Regional Library), 30
Symons, Thomas, 83-84
Symposium on Information, Literacy and the School Library in Canada, 44, 47-49

T
Teacher-librarian, 117
Technical Library, 63
The Pas Public Library, 31
Toews Historical Collection. See John A. Toews Historical Collection
Treaty and Aboriginal Rights Research Centre of Manitoba (T.A.R.R.), 95-96

U
Ukrainian Cultural and Education Centre Library, 105
United Church Archives, 40
University libraries, 32-40. See also College libraries
University of Manitoba Libraries, 35-39
 combined holdings, 35
University of Winnipeg Library, 39-40
 holdings, 39
 software, 40
Urban Studies collections, 94

V
Valley Library Foundation, 26-27
Valley Regional Library (Morris), 26-28
Virtual library. See Winnipeg Public Library Millennium Library Project; Virtual Western Canada University Library
Virtual Western Canada University Library, 106, 110-11

W
W.J. (Joe) McDonald North American Native Heritage Resource Centre, 97
Wanka Collection on Sudeten Germans, 40
Wells, Eric, 65
Western Canada Pictorial Index, 13, 57, 65
William Potoroka Memorial Library, 91
William R. Newman Agriculture Library, 79-80
Williams Avenue Carnegie Library (Winnipeg), 15, 16
Williams Law Library. See E.K. Williams Law Library
Winnipeg Art Gallery Archives, 92
Winnipeg Free Press Collection, 66
Winnipeg Library Foundation, 82, 106, 112-13
Winnipeg Public Library, 106
 Centennial Branch. See Centennial Library
 children's programs, 125-27
 Millennium Project. See Millennium Project

Winnipeg Public Library Board, 112
Winnipeg Public Library Plan, 1996-2000, 112
Winnipeg Research Centre Library, 77
Winnipeg Tribune Collection, 66, 86
Winnipeg. *See* City of Winnipeg
Woods Education Library. *See* D.S. Woods Education Library
Woodsworth, J.S., 69, 84

Donna G. Strike is a writer and editor who holds an MLS degree from Dalhousie University and teaching degrees from the Collège universitaire de Saint-Boniface and the University of Winnipeg. She has lectured at Red River College and the University of Manitoba.